THE STILL MOMENT
EUDORA WELTY
PORTRAIT OF A WRITER

THE STILL MOMENT

EUDORA WELTY

PORTRAIT OF A WRITER

PAUL BINDING

Published by VIRAGO PRESS Limited 1994
42–43 Gloucester Crescent, London NW1 7PD

Copyright © Paul Binding 1994

The right of Paul Binding to be identified as the author of this work has been asserted
by him in accordance with the Copyright, Designs and Patents Act 1988

A CIP catalogue record for this book is available from the British Library

Typeset by Florencetype Ltd, Kewstoke, Avon
Printed in Great Britain by Mackays of Chatham plc, Chatham, Kent

CONTENTS

ACKNOWLEDGEMENTS

My first debt must be to Eudora Welty herself.

I must also thank here all those who made my time as Eudora Welty Visiting Professor of Southern Studies at Millsaps College, Jackson, Mississippi, so rewarding: Dean Robert King; Bob Padgett; Paul Hardin; Ellen Douglas (Jo Haxton); Austin and Chrissy Wilson; Rick Mallette; Carol and Fletcher Cox; Hunter Cole; Suzanne Marrs; Patti Carr Black; Jane Reid Petty. This is the place too to mention with gratitude the friendship of Reynolds Price.

I would also like to express my gratitude to Patchey Wheatley who made the Omnibus film on Eudora Welty screened on BBC Television in 1987, the video of which she kindly provided me while I was writing this book.

I must thank Anne Tyler and Richard Ford for their answers to my queries. Ingrid Hudson and Alex Ramsey (both professional photographers) were most helpful in relation to the pages on Eudora's photographs.

Personal assistance during my work on the book has come from Mark Todd; Claire and Francesco Morresi; Johnny de Falbe.

At Virago I have met with such consistent help and friendliness over the years that it is hard to express my feelings adequately. Carmen Callil, commissioning me in 1980, after many lively and sympathetic meetings, to write introductions to two novels by Ellen Glasgow set in train a relationship with the publishing house that has been one of the greatest joys of my mature life. In Lynn Knight, I have had an editor unsurpassable for enthusiasm, interest and patience.

LIST OF ABBREVIATIONS FOR FOOTNOTES

C.E.W	*Conversations with Eudora Welty* (ed.) Peggy Whitman Prenshaw
C.S.	*Collected Stories*
D.W.	*Delta Wedding*
Eye	*The Eye of the Story*
G.A.	*The Golden Apples*
L.B.	*Losing Battles*
O.D.	*The Optimist's Daughter*
O.W.B.	*One Writer's Beginnings*
P.H.	*The Ponder Heart*
Photographs	*Eudora Welty: Photographs*
R.B.	*The Robber Bridegroom*

Collected Stories: Penguin edition (Harmondsworth, 1983).
All other works in Virago editions, except *One Writer's Beginnings*: Harvard University Press edition (Cambridge, MA, 1984).

For Claire and Francesco (and also Lara)

PART ONE

ONE WRITER'S
PROGRESS

1

'OF A TRUE AND HUMAN WORLD'

I

I N JACKSON, Mississippi, on 15 June 1963, after months of worsening tension and violence, the black civil rights leader Medgar Evers was shot from behind outside his home. The murder outraged both the black community and a significant section of the white, and triggered off riots all over the Southern States. Before long Bob Dylan, still very young, was plangently delivering the name Medgar Evers to the listening world. In Jackson itself the response of its most famous citizen, Eudora Welty, was immediate, passionate and profound:

> I was writing a novel at the time, and when Medgar Evers was assassinated here – that night, it just pushed up to what I was doing. I thought to myself, 'I've lived here all my life. I know the kind of mind that did this.' This was before anyone was caught. So I wrote a story in the first person as the murderer, because I thought, 'I am in a position where I know. I know what this man must feel like. I have lived with this kind of thing.'[1]

This story's will to surface demanded that it should be written at a sitting; 'Where is the Voice Coming From?' was therefore completed on the very day of Medgar Evers's death, and then dispatched to

---

1. C.E.W. p. 100.

William Maxwell at the *New Yorker*, who decided to publish it in the next issue. Editing had to be done over the telephone, by which time, however, an arrest had been made. Such had been Eudora Welty's mediumistic rapport with the life of Jackson that the facts of the case, as they now emerged, corroborated the circumstantial details of her story, which had to be altered forthwith for fear of being prejudicial to the arrested man. The route taken, the hour, the how and why of the crime – Eudora Welty had divined them all. 'I done what I done for my own pure-D satisfaction,' boasts her unrepentant and as yet unapprehended killer whose voice she assumes, and his satisfaction terrifyingly informs his entire narrative.

He tells how, exasperated by the ubiquity in the media of local black activist Roland Summers, he decided to take justice quite literally into his own hands. Towards four o'clock in the morning, with the sign outside the Branch Bank registering the night's temperature at 92 degrees, he set off in his brother-in-law's truck to Summers's home. On arrival he found the garage empty, but it was no problem to park the truck and wait behind a selected tree for his return. There would be no mistaking him:

> Never seen him before, never seen him since, never seen anything of his black face but his picture, never seen his face alive, any time at all, or anywheres, and didn't want to, need to, never hope to see that face and never will.[2]

Killing him turned out to be uncannily easy:

> . . . it wasn't till the minute before, that the mocking-bird had quit singing. He'd been singing up my sassafras tree. Either he was up early, or he hadn't never gone to bed, he was like me. And the mocker he'd stayed right with me, filling the air till come the crack, till I turned loose of my load. I was like him. I was on top of the world myself. For once.[3]

His pride and contentment persist. His wife – who shares his views,

---

2. C.S. p. 604.
3. ibid.

with a fund of racist jokes of her own – is supportive, reminding him:

> 'Well, they been asking that – why somebody didn't trouble to load a rifle and get some of these agitators out. . . . Didn't the fella keep drumming it in, what a good idea? The one that writes a column ever' day?'[4]

His identity thus acquires new lustre in his eyes. Hasn't he acted true to his own and his community's convictions, and, unlike some others, found the ability to carry his action through? His secret fame (for he is a talked-of man) causes him only delight, particularly when he reads in the papers that 'the shooting was done by an expert (I hope to tell you it was!)', and it sustains him when he makes himself face up to the possibility of arrest – and even of the electric chair. Yet he feels compelled to confess:

> Once, I run away from my home. And there was a ad for me, come to be printed in our county weekly. My mother paid for it. It was from her. It says: 'SON: You are not being hunted for any-thing but to find you.' That time I come on back home.
> But people are dead now.
> And it's so hot. Without it even being August yet.
> Anyways, I seen him fall. I was evermore the one.
> So I reach me down my old guitar off the nail in the wall. 'Cause I've got my guitar, what I've held on to from way back when, and I never dropped that, never lost or forgot it, never hocked it but to get it again, never give it away, and I set it in my chair, with nobody home but me, and I start to play, and sing a-down. And sing-a-down, down, down, down. Sing a-down, down, down, down. Down.[5]

What can we think of such a man? How can we bring home to him the wrongness of an act which causes him only to exult? How can we persuade him to pity when he has long since let hatred – inherited and gladly accepted – stifle any promptings of it? If there is pathos in him

---

4. C.S. p. 605.
5. C.S. p. 607.

– with his fellow-feeling for a mocking-bird, his still living memories of a turbulent youth, and his almost devotional attachment to his old guitar – it is a pathos of which he himself is entirely unconscious, and which he would be unable ever to see or understand. Rather, he feels he has triumphantly vindicated that dark romanticism in which he and his fellows have moved their whole lives long – the totems of which are the gun and the guitar, to which he has been so loyal. Thanks to its power, he can find no place for humdrum regrets, or even for fears for his life.

Only once before (on her own admission) had Eudora Welty written a story at one sitting, in that same possessed state of mind – over twenty years before, after hearing Fats Waller play at a concert and dance in Jackson. On her return home she tried to abandon herself to the music still present within her, and let it dictate the flow, the form, of her story, 'Powerhouse' (in *A Curtain of Green*, 1941), named for the black musician at its centre. The name truly seems the only one possible, so irresistible is the energy he gives out – to the supporting instrumentalists and dancegoers and beyond, to the writer herself and her readers. Powerhouse is presented in the present tense – and how could he not be? His vitality makes him eternally present.

> This is a white dance. Powerhouse is not a show-off like the Harlem boys, not drunk, not crazy – he's in a trance; he's a person of joy, a fanatic. He listens as much as he performs, a look of hideous, powerful rapture on his face. When he plays he beats down piano and seat and wears them away. He is in motion every moment – what could be more obscene? There he is with his great head, fat stomach and little round piston legs, and long yellow-sectioned strong big fingers, at rest about the size of bananas. Of course you know how he sounds – you've heard him on records – but still you need to see him. He's going all the time, like skating around the skating rink or rowing a boat. It makes everybody crowd around, here in this shadowless steel-trussed hall with the rose-like posters of Nelson Eddy and the testimonial for the mind-reading horse in handwriting magnified

five hundred times. Then all quietly he lays his finger on a key with the promise and serenity of a sibyl touching the book.

Powerhouse is so monstrous he sends everybody into oblivion.[6]

Monstrous too is his private behaviour; of this there are disquieting glimpses, as he talks to fellow-musicians above the instruments during the performance and later in the intermission. Claiming to have had a telegram saying that his wife has died, he proceeds to make jocular, grotesque speculations as to how this could have come about:

'. . . it's the night-time. She say, What do I hear? Footsteps walking up the hall? That him? Footsteps go on off. It's not me. I'm in Alligator, Mississippi, she's crazy. Shaking all over. Listens till her ears and all grow out like old music-box horns but still she can't hear a thing. She says, all right! I'll jump out the window then. Got on a night-gown. I know that night-gown, and her thinking there. Says, Ho hum, all right, and jumps out the window. Is she mad at me! Is she crazy! She don't leave *nothing* behind her!'[7]

But maybe his wife is *not* dead; indeed, maybe he's never received a telegram (for the reader never sees it). When he returns to the piano, he displays anew 'outrageous force' – and anyway – '. . . who could ever remember any of the things he says? They are just inspired remarks that roll out of his mouth like smoke.'[8]

One could, with good grounds, judge Powerhouse and find him wanting – for his mendacity, his sexism, his arrogant self-absorption, his brutal humour. Such condemnation, however, would be quite irrelevant to any estimation that acknowledges Powerhouse as Powerhouse. The standards by which the condemnation would be made would not be standards that interest him; he would dismiss them. Again – as with the killer of 'Where is the Voice Coming From?' – we could find a pathos in him (for he belongs to an excluded race; the wife and kin of this stupendous artist would not be allowed into

---

6. C.S. p. 131.
7. C.S. p. 137.
8. C.S. p. 141.

the dancehall; after all, this is a *white* dance!). Pathos, however, is the last quality Powerhouse would discern in himself – nor does Eudora Welty traffic in it, portraying here not a black misfortunate but a black genius. 'A person of joy, a fanatic', 'rapture' (though it is at once, in a telling oxymoron, both 'hideous' and 'powerful'), 'sibyl' – these are the important words here. Our trite summings-up of things are surely sent 'into oblivion' by him and his like. He may not be admitted into respectable society, but that is society's loss. Eudora Welty is recording here a human instrument expressive of deep, unbrookable forces, one which can no more cease expressing them than could – in his terrible way – that sorry white assassin whose voice she captured a quarter of a century later.

The year following 'Where is the Voice Coming From?' was perhaps the most terrible in Mississippi history – the year we have come to call that of 'Mississippi burning'. And two years after that, when Southern unrest was both compounded and echoed by unrest in the nation as a whole, centring on intensifying US involvement in Vietnam, Eudora Welty wrote another story, 'The Demonstrators' (1966), named for the most emblematic persons of the mid 1960s ('We must march, my darlings'). This story is set, for the greater part, during a single night in a small Mississippi town, Holden: 'Just one house and one church farther, the Delta began, and the cotton-fields ran into the scattered paleness of a dimmed-out Milky Way.'[9]

After an evening of bridge at his club and a visit to the town's old invalid schoolmistress, the spartan Miss Marcia Pope, white Dr Strickland is accosted by a small black girl wanting his help. 'We got to hurry,' she tells him. She leads him to her home where, attended by a veritable crowd, her older sister lies dying: 'a young, very black-skinned woman . . . in a white dress with her shoes on. A maid?' She is dying from a wound she received just below her breast, dealt, he correctly diagnoses, by an ice-pick.

'Who did this to her? . . . Where? Where did it happen? How did she get here?'

---

9. C.S. p. 615.

He had an odd feeling that somewhere in the room somebody was sending out beckoning smiles in his direction. He lifted, half turned his head. The elevated coal that glowed at regular intervals was the pipe of an old woman in a boiled white apron standing near the door.

He persisted. 'Has she coughed up anything yet?'

'Don't you know her?' they cried, as if he never was going to hit on the right question.

He let go the girl's arm, and her hand started its way back again to her wound. Sending one glowing look at him, she covered it again. As if she had spoken, he recognized her.

'Why, it's Ruby,' he said.

Ruby Gaddy *was* the maid. Five days a week she cleaned up on the second floor of the bank building where he kept his office and consulting rooms.[10]

As maid she has been virtually invisible to him (like G.K. Chesterton's postman in his Father Brown story). Similarly he fails at first to identify both Lucille, the woman whose lamp is somewhat too harshly illuminating the deathbed ('"I was washing for your mother when you was born,"' she is obliged to tell him) and 'the old woman in the boiled apron' with the pipe, another who had appeared to him simply as a figure on some background frieze: 'In the days when he travelled East to medical school, she used to be the sole factotum at the Holden depot when the passenger train came through sometime between two and three in the morning.'[11]

By temperament Dr Strickland is not an unobservant or unimaginative man, but the culture that has nurtured him has encouraged a near-blindness, a near-deafness, to the black people around him, and only *in extremis* can he rise above it. Ironically, it is only when they are nearing death that they really come alive for him. That same night he confronts another dying black, young Dove Collins, who (one assumes) ice-picked Ruby and was ice-picked by her in return.

---

10. C.S. pp. 610–11.
11. C.S. p. 614.

Dr Strickland stopped the car short and got out. His footsteps made the only sound in town. The man raised up on his hands and looked at him like a seal. Blood laced his head like a net through which he had broken. His wide tongue hung down out of his mouth. But the doctor knew the face.

'So you're alive, Dove, you're still alive?'

Slowly, hardly moving his tongue, Dove said, 'Hide me.' Then he haemorrhaged through the mouth.[12]

'The Demonstrators' abounds in images of light and darkness – of light both confusing and confused, light diffused, fractured, and darkness that deceives and, paradoxically, illuminates. The lamp brought to bear on dying Ruby's bed is, in literal truth, unbearable for both doctor and patient, as it swings and jumps; preferable is the live coal in the old black woman's pipe (the glow from what is to be found deep in the earth) – and that eventually goes out. The moon, which should shine down tranquillity on Dr Strickland, his doomed visit of mercy at an end, suddenly seems indissoluble – indeed, indistinguishable – from humdrum terrestrial existence and all its complications: 'From the road, he saw the moon itself. It was above the tree with the chickens in it; it might have been one of the chickens flown loose.' There is to be no swift, all-conquering descent of light.

The doctor is by no means an unsympathetic man – in the double sense of that adjective. He has his own private close-hugged tragedies: the death of his little girl, the malformed Sylvia; the defection of his wife, who has preferred to join the young with their protest demonstrations for causes that only bemuse him. Will anything, can anything, ever really change him? Even the birds he likes so much he really notices only 'in the fall of the year'. Yet he has a good heart, and a mentality greatly superior, for example, to that exhibited by the local paper, whose windy, dishonest pharisaisms Eudora Welty gives us in the form of its account of the deaths of Ruby and Dove:

[An ice-pick] is believed to have served as the instrument in the

12. C.S. p. 619.

twin slayings, the victims thus virtually succeeding in killing each other.

'Well, I'm surprised didn't more of them get hurt,' said Rev. Alonzo Duckett, pastor of the Holden First Baptist Church. 'And yet they expect to be seated in our churches.' County sheriff Vince Lasseter, reached fishing at Lake Bourne, said, 'That's one they can't pin the blame on us for. That how they treat their own kind. Please take note our conscience is clear.'[13]

All three stories powerfully render the ineluctable in human beings. Pity and a desirable moral solution have no dramatic part to play in them, yet clearly their creator believes in compassion and has a strong moral vision. Otherwise we, too, would feel that it was a good thing to kill Roland Summers, or best to tread cautiously and avoid confrontation in a perilously divided community. As it is, we feel the contrary, while we are persuaded of the unassailable reality of these beliefs.

The stories testify above all else to their author's principles as writer: to see her subjects clearly, including their own self-view; and also to see them in perspective, as part of some greater whole. The first principle demands that there is no evasion, disguising, fudging or fakery; the second that the subject is scrutinized until it gives forth manifestations of the larger life of which it is a component – so that stubborn racist, megalomaniacal musician and conventional small-town citizen reveal an elaborate complex of forces behind them.

The revelation of these forces – which, of their very nature, escape precise definition – comes through the concentrated artistry of the stories: in the selection of significant detail; in the shaping of the demanding, invariably defiant material into a form that is in itself meaningful; in the creation of similes and metaphors which relate that material to other areas of existence.

Consider even the titles; each, as usual with Eudora Welty, is inextricable from the work to which it belongs. Here her art resembles – and not for the only time – a poet's. (How could 'Sailing to Byzantium' or 'The Second Coming' have any titles but those Yeats chose?) 'Where is the Voice Coming From?' can refer to the author's own mysterious

---

13. C.S. p. 621.

apprehension of the black activist's killer, for where did she find her own knowledge of person and events? It can suggest, too, some deep malignity in the community, born of history and geography (hence the insistence on the heat), of which the confessor is the uncomprehending listener-victim. But don't the words 'Where is the Voice Coming From?' also hint at some deep-feared and unacknowledged voice whispering somewhere in the back of the possessed killer's own mind, telling him of a universal law profounder still than the one he believes he is serving, a law that enjoins all of us to do as we would be done by?

The title 'Powerhouse' is surely meant to apply beyond the eponymous musician. Every black person, not only this musical genius – and every white person too, for that matter – should be thought of as a 'powerhouse', as a store of potentially transforming energy that can both destroy and create. As for 'The Demonstrators', its title is, I think, the most thought-provoking and interesting of the three. For who *are* the demonstrators? In the normal use of the term demonstrators appear off-stage only, in thoughts and in photographs; and certainly, neither they nor the causes behind them elicit much sympathy from Dr Strickland, or from anyone else in the story. They provide, however, a telling point of reference, not least in placing events in their time; and act as indicators of the perpetual human qualities of hope and desire for renewal. So deep are these qualities that we can see all people, even in the isolation of private life, as demonstrators, and certainly in this story each character, each happening, is making a plea, and so constitutes a demonstration – a plea to be valued, to be respected and even loved: dying Ruby, dying Dove, the white *bien-pensants*. After all, what are public demonstrations but dramatic, physical statements that individuals have to be respected for what they are, not for what others think they should be? Even the birds at the story's end, the cock who spreads 'one wing, showy as a zebra's hide, and with a turn of his head show[s] his red seal' and the hen who receives his display, can be seen as demonstrators of the mysteries of needing and being needed.

By attending to the intimacies of the story, all of which are inseparable from the whole, new insights can be gained into the relation between microcosm and macrocosm, both within and outside the terms of the narrative. The society in which these stories were written and set was riven, unjust, violent, often intolerably cruel. The stories themselves do not pretend otherwise, but the very intensity of their art is in itself an act of transcendence: it makes us aware of different, opposing, redemptive human qualities, which point to other possibilities for action, other modes of living. Furthermore, each story concentrates on a moment – the moment of death-dealing in 'Where is the Voice Coming From?'; the moment of release from both facts and fantasy through music in 'Powerhouse'; the moment of witnessing death in 'The Demonstrators'. Each of these moments is irreversible, yet also multilayered, containing other truths with other outcomes than the dominant one. To forget that every moment is so structured is to live superficially – always disastrous for both the individual self and, ultimately, for society. But to remember it, and to act on that remembrance, this is a task of appalling difficulty. This task, however, has been Eudora Welty's all her life.

It has been the more demanding for the prevalent climate of her own society, the American South, which – to the outside world, anyway – appeared determined, for the greater part of her lifetime, to resist progression or progress, to hold the moment back. This study has opened with three short works which were prompted by the writer's intimate knowledge of and identification with real events which encapsulated the Southern problem: the inherited inequality and tension between the white and black races.

All three are fine representatives of Eudora Welty's art, yet without contradicting that statement one must also say that neither in subject nor in their creation are they characteristic. In her introduction to her *Collected Stories* (1980) Eudora Welty says:

> In general, my stories as they've come along have reflected their own present time, beginning with the Depression in which I began; they came out of my response to it. These two [above] written in the changing sixties reflect the unease, the ambiguities, the sickness and desperation of those days in Mississippi. If they have any special virtue in this respect, it would lie in the fact that they, like the others, are stories written from within. They come from living here – they were part of living here, of my long familiarity with the thoughts and feelings of those around me, in their many shadings and variations and contradictions.[14]

---

14. C.S., Introduction, p. x.

The key word is 'within'; Eudora Welty's art is fed by a profound knowledge that can come only from long and sustained intimacy with people and place. On the whole it has not been necessary for her to seize the day, and serve it – but it is obvious from the early tribute to both 'Powerhouse' and the two 1960s stories that when she wants to do so, she succeeds superbly.

It seems entirely appropriate that Eudora Welty still lives and works in the house in Jackson, Mississippi, which has been her home since she was sixteen. So the piece that Katherine Anne Porter wrote as an introduction to her first book, *A Curtain of Green* – about the work of 'a quiet, tranquil-looking modest girl' of thirty-two, unknown to the American book-buying public – still holds good today of the internationally acclaimed and honoured writer in her mid eighties. This in itself offers one explanation of the depths of understanding that Eudora Welty's work reveals. She still associates with people she has known from her early years, and is still a member of the community into which she was born; so that her novels and stories draw from great stores of sympathy and knowledge.

II

'Miss Welty', Katherine Anne Porter tells us, 'was born and brought up in Jackson, Mississippi,' and after a college education away from the South, she still lives:

> among her life-long friends and acquaintances, quite simply and amiably. . . . She loves music, grows flowers very successfully, and remarks that she is 'underfoot locally', meaning that she has a normal amount of social life.
>
> She spends an immense amount of time at writing. 'I haven't a literary life at all,' she wrote once, 'not much of a confession, maybe. But I do feel that the people and things I love are of a true and human world, and there is no clutter about them . . .'[15]

Eudora Welty was born on 13 April 1909 in a house on North Congress Street, Jackson. Her early family life was full of the greatest,

15. Katherine Anne Porter, Introduction to *A Curtain of Green*, Penguin edition (1947) p. 8.

warmest love and affection. In 1925 her family moved to her present Jackson home on Pinehurst Street. Her father, President of the Lamar Life Insurance Company in Jackson, took the keenest interest in the building of the house, using the architect who had been responsible for the Lamar Life Building itself.

Christian Webb Welty was to die six years after the move, in 1931; her mother – with whom Eudora Welty made her home – died in 1966. She had two brothers – Edward, three years younger; and Walter, three years younger again, both of whom married and spent their lives in Jackson. The Belhaven house, in which Eudora Welty still works in her upstairs bedroom, therefore contains by far the greater part of her familial life, and almost all of her internal development as a writer.

Katherine Anne Porter goes on to praise her subject's determination to derive 'nourishment from the source natural to her', as well as her essential tranquillity of mien and nature. She sees these as – paradoxically – giving her the strength to face up to and deal with the turbulence and cruelties of the wider world. The stories which do not take place in Mississippi can be counted on one hand: 'Flowers for Marjorie' (in *A Curtain of Green*) and 'Music from Spain' (in *The Golden Apples*), which respectively re-create New York and San Francisco, feature Mississippians, and owe their power to the author's understanding of these Mississippi men's bewildered minds.

Katherine Anne Porter speaks too of Eudora Welty's deep, extensive and thoughtful reading. She was, she says, 'just the right age to find first W.B. Yeats and Virginia Woolf in the air around her'; she also mentions her particular interest in folklore and myth, and their oral preservation.

The artistry of even the earliest stories immediately makes it clear that Eudora Welty has thought deeply about the nature of story and literature, and has looked to other writers not for anything as straightforward as instruction, but to have her ever-curious mind sharpened, stimulated. This attentiveness has also made her an excellent and (for all that she addresses herself principally to writers she admires) a formidable critic, although she is too modest about her attainments in this field, preferring to see herself as a reviewer (which, of course, she also is). She has written persuasive essays on – among others – Chekhov, Willa Cather, Faulkner and Henry Green, and each essay reveals her wide and considered literary knowledge. Her interest in myth, and in the mythic element in literature, is apparent everywhere; perhaps its most complex expression is the story sequence *The Golden Apples* (1949). Myth was, of course, a dominating concern of Modernists such as Yeats, Rilke, Eliot, Stravinsky, Picasso, Lorca and Faulkner. (Katherine Anne Porter was right – and presciently so – to note the importance of Yeats for Eudora Welty, something which bore overt creative fruit in *The Golden Apples* with its second story, 'June Recital'. But his influence is pervasive throughout.) Eudora Welty's lively interest in the life of her State, with the rich folklore of both its black and white communities, would anyway have brought the mythic into the course of her work.

But for all her sensitivity to the art of others, Katherine Anne Porter finds specially commendable:

> Miss Welty's instinctive knowledge that writing cannot be taught, but only learned, and learned by the individual in his own way, at his own pace and in his own time, for the process of mastering the medium is part of a cellular growth in a most complex organism; it is a way of life and a mode of being which cannot be divided from the kind of human creature you were the day you were born.[16]

She then goes on to say (though I suspect that she is doing some self-projection here, bearing in mind her own long years of labour on what became *Ship of Fools*): 'But there is a trap lying just ahead, and all short-story writers know what it is – The Novel. . . . It is quite possible she can never write a novel, and there is no reason why she should.'[17]

Not only has Eudora Welty proved able to write novels, she has written novels for which the overworked adjective 'great' is, for once, entirely appropriate, and has been used by serious critics. But in fact every one of them, examined more closely, is an obvious product of the short-story-writer's art, and Eudora Welty herself has drawn attention to this. That art is, of its very nature, a more visionary matter

16. Katherine Anne Porter, Introduction, p. 9.
17. Katherine Anne Porter, Introduction, p. 10.

than the conventional novelist's; it embodies and centres around a moment of perception. Even (or especially) the long, ramified – if masterfully structured – *Losing Battles* (1970) is redolent of the short story – indeed, on Eudora Welty's own admission, it started out as one.

This gives Eudora Welty's fiction a very special quality. Whatever their length, her works are intensely illuminating artefacts, crystallizations of experiences and apprehensions. 'First Love', 'A Still Moment' and *Losing Battles* have more in common with – to take examples from attainments dear to their author – Cézanne's studies of apples or Rilke's sonnets to Orpheus than with such 'novelistic' novels as, say, Saul Bellow's *The Adventures of Augie March* or Angus Wilson's *The Middle Age of Mrs Eliot*.

So in this Katherine Anne Porter has been proved literally wrong yet spiritually right. Her next statement, however, though one can see why she made it, requires amendment. Referring to Eudora Welty's comparatively sequestered lifestyle, she says: 'She escaped . . . a militant social consciousness, in the current radical-intellectual sense, and she has not expressed, except implicitly, any attitude at all on the state of politics or the condition of society.'[18] Certainly her active awareness of social injustice never seems to have led her to doctrinaire Marxism; she seems to have held aloof from the fellow-travelling of her fellow-intellectuals of the 1930s. That is presumably what Katherine Anne Porter is getting at here; if it is not, the pronouncement is, for once, misleading. There is always, of course, a sense, in literature, in which the implicit works more powerfully and persuasively than the explicit, than the ideologically dogmatic with its totalitarian demands on fiction-writers and their material. In the very next sentence Katherine Anne Porter speaks eloquently of the 'unanswerable, indispensable moral law, on which she is grounded firmly'. But in fact even the stories in *A Curtain of Green* itself – and certainly Eudora Welty's fiction as a whole – exhibit the most profound concern with the condition of society, and add up to what can be seen as a political testimony (though it is much else besides).

As our century has progressed from its virtual midpoint, when Eudora Welty's first book appeared, all Western societies have become

---

18. Katherine Anne Porter, Introduction, p. 9.

more politicized, including those sections of America and Britain which incline to resistance against this, with their near-obsessional belief in the supremacy of the private life. True, Eudora Welty is one of private life's great celebrants. What E.M. Forster called the 'outer life of telegrams and anger' has little appeal for her, yet her sensitivity is such that she cannot altogether ignore it, and she certainly has no intention of ignoring its fruits. She takes the keenest, most vigilant interest in what is going on, in her own country and elsewhere, and for a time she was involved with politics in the most literal and practical way (working for Adlai Stevenson [1900–65], that humane intellectual who was the Democrat candidate for the presidency in 1952 and 1956). However private – indeed, intimate – their particular domains, her writings reflect with total clarity her deep sense of public responsibility, and offer the most complete challenge to the callousness of (still prevalent) Reaganomics and Thatcherism, just as they once did – and do – to the cruelty of racial segregation. Eudora Welty herself wrote: 'we are all agreed upon the most important point: that morality as shown through human relationships is the whole heart of fiction, and the serious writer has never lived who dealt with anything else.'[19]

Visionary, responsible humanist, apologist for privacy, complex Modernist-influenced artist – all these persons are present in the Eudora Welty whom Katherine Anne Porter introduced in 1941, as they are triumphantly present now. A whole *œuvre* was to be created in that quiet house in Belhaven, Jackson: *A Curtain of Green* (short stories), 1941; *The Robber Bridegroom* (novella), 1942; *The Wide Net* (short stories), 1943; *Delta Wedding* (novel), 1946; *The Golden Apples* (sequence of short stories), 1949; *The Ponder Heart* (novella), 1954; *The Bride of the Innisfallen* (short stories), 1955; *Losing Battles* (novel), 1970; *One Time, One Place: Mississippi in the Depression* (photograph album with introduction), 1971; *The Optimist's Daughter* (novel), 1972; *The Eye of the Story* (essays), 1978; *One Writer's Beginnings* (memoir), 1984 – to which must be added *The Collected Stories* (1980) and *Eudora Welty: Photographs* (1989).

When I first visited that Pinehurst Street house, all these books had been published except the last three, though *The Eye of the Story* was

---

19. Eye p. 148.

new on the shelves, and was just being reviewed in the national press. Southern literature itself had moved on since Katherine Anne Porter's introduction of a promising neophyte. Flannery O'Connor, Elizabeth Spencer, Walker Percy, Peter Taylor, Madison Jones, William Styron, Ernest Gaines, Reynolds Price, Anne Tyler – these writers had found Eudora Welty part of their own inheritance, had been moved and stimulated by her work.

I first met Eudora Welty in summer 1978, in the course of the exploration of Southern literature which was to become my book *Separate Country* (1979). The meeting was an epiphany for me, and not just an epiphany but a beginning – of something that has come to a climax in the writing of this book. My appreciation of the greatness of Eudora Welty's achievement had come – appropriately – through appreciation of the power and universality of Southern literature, my conviction of its greatness, which had led me to make a journey through the South, interviewing *in situ* those of its writers who still lived and worked there. The South was not to be separated from their fiction; all these writers saw themselves as Southern: the South had nurtured them, the South held the life they turned to when they wanted to make their artistic correlatives. They were emphatically not regional writers; they addressed the whole world in their novels, feeling Southern experience relevant to – indeed, illuminative of – it. To what should one attribute this confidence, this sophistication of art and attitude? Help towards a resolution of this question came to me from an essay ('Dodo, Phoenix or Tough Old Cock') by Reynolds Price (born 1933):

> The South can come honorably out of a cool examination of its fiction in the past forty years. In fact its record as a country can stand with the simultaneous record of any country – with France, Britain, Germany, the rest of America. . . . And whatever new subjects, new forms of life the New South is offering . . . the Old South will go on offering its life as subject for another fifty years at least – the working life of those who are children in it now. Not offering but imposing.[20]

The South should be considered as a country, then – as an entity, with

20. Reynolds Price, *A Common Room: Essays 1954–1987*, Atheneum (1989) p. 166.

history, lore, mores, demands, outlook, inherited images, tensions and expectations all its own, and demanding a response from its children. And then one remembers the obvious truth that, as the Confederate States of America, it *had* been a separate country – if only for those four years of bloody war 1861–1865.

III

William Faulkner declares in his novel *Intruder in the Dust* (1949):

> For the Southern boy fourteen years old, not once but whenever he wants it, there is the instant when it's still not two o'clock on that July afternoon in 1863, the brigades are in position behind the rail fence, the guns are laid and ready in the woods and the furled flags are already loosened to break out . . . and it's all in the balance, it hasn't happened yet, it hasn't even begun yet, it not only hasn't begun yet but there is still time for it not to begin.[21]

The 'it' of Faulkner's prose elegy is the Battle of Gettysburg, the turning point of the Civil War. Although there were to be some further victories for the Confederacy, it in effect lost the war it waged with such passion and brilliance on those first three days of July 1863 to which Faulkner refers. Officially the War ended almost two years later, with Robert E. Lee's surrender to Ulysses S. Grant on 9 April 1865.

The losses the South sustained in the four years of war, from the opening shots at Fort Sumter (12 April 1861) to its close at Appomattox, were of terrible proportions: it has been estimated that if the United States had suffered commensurately in World War II, it would have lost 6,000,000 men instead of just over 300,000. In addition to these appalling casualties and the general ignominy this martial-minded would-be-nation experienced in defeat, there was all the punitive harshness of the Reconstruction period, the reorganization judged necessary within each of the former Confederate States before they could be readmitted to the Union. Reconstruction ended with the 1876 presidential election, but the bitterness it incurred lived on: the

---

21. William Faulkner, *Intruder in the Dust*, Chatto Standard Edition, (1949), p. 194.

bitterness at the unscrupulousness of the Northern 'carpetbaggers' who had descended on the South; and also the bitterness of the black people encouraged by the 'Federals' to register themselves for voting. Although a principal aim of the Reconstruction was to ensure civil rights for the South's substantial black population, the methods used were too often counterproductive. By the last decade of the nineteenth century, the Southern States had drawn up constitutions which ensured control for their white citizens. The constitution of the Confederacy had protected slavery, the Southern States' 'peculiar institution'. In the reconstructed South black Southerners found themselves denied any real equality by the iniquitous 'Jim Crow' laws, and the implementations of poll taxes.

Obviously white Southerners had to find visions of the past that they could live with, if only to excuse or explain the tormented present. While the Fugitives, the 1920s movement originating in Nashville, Tennessee, with their offshoot the Agrarians, gave the idea intellectual definition and cohesion, it was quite widely accepted that the fundamentally agricultural antebellum South was an organic society which should have been allowed to evolve in its own way, but which instead had had alien systems and codes forced on it. Many of the contemporary South's problems could therefore be attributed to these impositions. The old order – so bravely fought for, but accorded no respect by its opponents – was seen as more likely to have conferred happiness on both white and black Southerners than the industrial, commercial and progressive orders of the Yankees' world.

The South's literary tradition before, during and immediately after the War-between-the-States is not remarkable. But emergence from a long period of hardship and humiliation into a far from certain present and future galvanized the Southern mind; it could view what had happened as a bloody, fierce and unequal conflict between a society committed to tradition, preservation and conservation, and a new society wedded to ideals of material prosperity and unswerving advancement. This situation satisfactorily lent itself to Darwinist interpretations, and it is no accident that the first great writer of the South, Ellen Glasgow (1874–1945), had, by the time she was twenty, renounced orthodox religion in favour of a stark but courageous

– and deeply pondered – Darwinist determinism. Throughout her long writing life she sought to present the history and the present condition of the South in novels that would do for it what Balzac's *comédie humaine* had done for post-Revolutionary French society, or – a more immediate influence on the novels themselves – Thomas Hardy's for Wessex. (She knew Hardy, and can perhaps be accounted his most considerable follower.) Her own family, who came from the Upper South, Virginia, had suffered dreadfully during the Civil War and the Reconstruction, and her earlier novels deal with these periods as they affected her Virginia, treating all sections of society and showing history working itself out in the lives of individuals – some conscious of its processes, others stubbornly not so. She shows how those with their hands on the tiller of the future are bound to win, however morally dubious, however superficial they are, while those committed to superseded or threatened ways of life, however strong and noble in themselves, have to go under.

After a shattering nervous breakdown during the year of America's entry into World War I, Ellen Glasgow's tragic vision intensified, enabling her to create works in which life in the South in (roughly) her own times – particularly among descendants of the Scottish-Irish in rural Virginia – takes on a universal metaphoric significance. In my view her deeply moving novel *Barren Ground* (1925), set among the 'good people' of her region and showing how Dorinda prevails against appalling manifestations of the blind brute force of Nature, while herself remaining virtuous and sensitive, is the first Southern novel which deserves the adjective 'great', which indubitably enters world literature. Exactly sixty years after Lee's surrender at Appomattox, the South artistically came of age.

In *Barren Ground*, *The Sheltered Life* (1932) and *Vein of Iron* (1932) the position and nature of women are of crucial importance; either educated to be beautiful ornaments (upper-class girls such as the eponymous heroine of *Virginia* [1913]) or poorer Scottish-Irish girls, cast in working roles completely taken for granted by society, Ellen Glasgow's women have to develop inner strengths and wisdom if they are to have any dignified meaning for themselves, let alone for others. Their sensibility – often tough as the male's never can be – is also viewed as a counterblast to the kind of values attributed to the antebellum South, and apostrophized after its defeat. A sane present, a desirable future, lie in women's power only.

The 1920s, the decade of *Barren Ground* and *The Romantic Comedians* (1926), saw what has been commonly called the Southern Renaissance. Its principal and most seminal theatre was Vanderbilt University, Nashville where intellectuals – in particular some remarkably gifted young men – assembled round the poet and critic John Crowe Ransom (1888–1974). His preoccupations can perhaps best be seen in one of his finest lyrics, 'Antique Harvesters':

> Tawny are the leaves turned but they still hold.
> And it is harvest; what shall this land produce?
> A meager hill of kernels, a runnel of juice;
> Declension looks from our land, it is old.
> Therefore let us assemble, dry, grey, spare
> And mild as yellow air.[22]

The land that should be harvested is the post-Reconstruction South, venerable and ransacked and stubborn; the 'we' who must assemble are the poet and his friends, who feel that they have had their noble, non-commercialist culture routed by the 'carpetbaggers' and people like them. The young men who want to live vigorously are the new generation who are tempted to leave the South.

> We pluck the spindling ears and gather the corn.
> One spot has special yield? 'On this spot stood
> Heroes and drenched it with their only blood.'
> And talk meets talk, as echoes from the horn
> Of the hunter – echoes are the old man's arts,
> Here come the hunters, keepers of a rite;
> The horn, the hounds, the lank mares coursing by
> Straddled with archetypes of chivalry;
> And the fox, lovely ritualist in flight
> Offering his unearthly ghost to quarry;
> And the fields, themselves to harry.
> Resume, harvesters. The treasure is full bronze

---

22. John Crowe Ransom, *Poems*, Alfred A. Knopf (1963).

Which you will garner for your Lady, and the moon
Could tinge it no yellower than does this moon;
But gray will quench it shortly – the field, men, stones,
Pluck fast, dreamers; prove as you amble slowly
Not less than men, not wholly.[23]

Thankless though the work may seem, the new generation, mindful of the civilizing antiquity of the society to which they are heirs, must continue to work it in the old way, the Lady – borrowed from troubadour poetry, which fuses the Virgin Mary and the chatelaine – standing for the spirit of the South, not in its first youth but wise with experience and tested virtue.

Of the young men who assembled around Crowe Ransom to form the Fugitives ('a Fugitive was quite simply a Poet; ... the man who carries the secret wisdom around the world') the two most spectacularly brilliant (and later productive) were Allen Tate (1899–1978) and Robert Penn Warren (1905–91). Men of great influence as critics and editors (particularly in relation to the distinguished *Southern Review*, which was to publish her early work) and eminent creative writers themselves, both were to become friends of Eudora Welty and admirers of her writing. While the life and traditions of the South always interested them, at first they were probably more concerned with general ideas of culture; their departure from the South and the extraordinary heat generated nationwide by the Scopes or 'Monkey' trial in Dayton, Tennessee, in 1925 galvanized them into a reappreciation of their Southernness.

Scopes was a young teacher who insisted on teaching Darwinist evolution (in the light of Southern history, the whole issue has a curiously ironical symbolic resonance) even though the state of Tennessee had banned this; he was prosecuted in Dayton, found guilty and fined, though the fine was never imposed. When the rest of the United States, with H.L. Mencken as a witty spokesman, derided the South for its lack of enlightenment, its own intellectuals – including John Crowe Ransom, Allen Tate, Robert Penn Warren – rose to its defence, finding order and spiritual beauty in its conservative inheritance. A result of this collective return was the anthology

---

23. ibid.

of essays by 'twelve Southerners' guided by the fine poet Donald Davidson, *I'll Take My Stand* (1930), subtitled 'The South and its Agrarian Tradition'. The title, of course, comes from the South's one-time 'national anthem', that stirring march 'Dixie':

I wish I was in Dixie, hooray, hooray!
In Dixieland I'll take my stand
To live and die in Dixie
Away, away, away down South in Dixie!

In the introduction, the twelve voices speak as one:

The authors contributing to this book are Southerners. . . . All the articles bear in the same sense upon the book's title-subject: all tend to support a Southern way of life against what may be called the American or prevailing way; and all as much as agree that the best terms in which to represent the distinction are contained in the phrase, Agrarian versus Industrial.

Nobody now proposes for the South, or for any other community in this country, an independent political destiny. That idea is thought to have been finished in 1865. But how far shall the South surrender its moral, social and economic autonomy to the victorious principle of Union? That question remains open. The South is a minority section that has hitherto been jealous of its minority right to live its own kind of life. The South scarcely hopes to determine the other sections, but it does propose to determine itself, within the utmost limits of legal action.[24]

So far so good, though the dangers inherent in the Agrarian position are evident in the last sentence. Self-determination as an article of faith exonerates the South from any need to reform its racially discriminatory code. Moreover, an illogicality is revealed: how can the South claim its 'minority right' – a claim with which, in principle, one could be tempted to sympathize – while it shows itself so wilfully blind to that of its own, very considerable minority, the black people?

For the British reader the aspects of Southern culture extolled here

---

24. 'Twelve Southerners', *I'll Take My Stand* (1977) Louisiana University Press, (1977), ed. Donald Davidson, p. 1.

are highly reminiscent of those championed by the British contemporary of Allen Tate and his circle, F.R. Leavis (1899–1978), with their insistence on the moral importance of an organic community, whose values should be expressed in the arts and crafts it produces. Significantly, Leavis was to be associated with perhaps the Fugitive/Agrarians' most important intellectual legacy, the New Criticism movement. By attaching paramount importance to the words of a literary text, it originally lent itself for use as part of a profoundly conservative war against Freudianism and Marxism, denying the relevance or value of personal or societal factors in the consideration of literature. But in the hands of its most generous practitioners – Tate, Warren, Cleanth Brooks, Leavis himself – it became itself an index for measuring a society and its moral health. It is hard not to see the rigour it imposed on its adherents as entirely salutary.

Nevertheless, in the whole Vanderbilt-cradled Fugitive/Agrarian movement there is a profound weakness, perhaps not unconnected to its exclusively male provenance. It is far too easily satisfied with theory, speculation, Platonic levels of apprehension, so that it can – and does – overlook the human realities of situations; often, indeed, it would appear not to consider empirical experience particularly relevant to any debate. When John Crowe Ransom, an entirely humane and honourable man, tells us in his essay in *I'll Take My Stand* that the old slave-holding South was 'a kindly society, yet a realistic one . . . people were for the most part in the right places', one has the uncomfortable feeling that he really does not know what he is talking about; that he has never bothered to consider either the hard facts or the obstinate human feelings of the case at all, but has let it all dissolve in persuasive, if high-minded, theorizing. Nor is he alone here; all of them worked too easily and too extensively on a level of paradoxical romantic notions of classicism, and spared too little thought for real people and their real problems. In practice Allen Tate and Robert Penn Warren modified their ideas; in 1938 Allen Tate, known primarily as a poet, brought out his only novel, *The Fathers*, a first-person presentation of the cultural and psychic tensions of the Civil War that is a major achievement by any standards, wholly redeemed from thesis-making by its psychological insights; Robert Penn Warren, perhaps best-known for large-scale and ambitious novels – *Night*

Rider (1939), *All the King's Men* (1946) and *World Enough and Time* (1950) – produced poems and short stories (for example, 'Blackberry Winter') which richly distil the essence of Southern rural life.

It must be said, however, that the international attainments of all the Fugitives pale into comparative insignificance compared with those of a Southern novelist who was their contemporary and who held aloof from them and, indeed, all literary groups, Eudora Welty's fellow-Mississippian William Faulkner (1897–1962), one of the greatest novelists in the English language, the peer of Balzac, Dickens and Dostoyevsky and, in his own time, of James Joyce and D.H. Lawrence. William Faulkner's deployment of the South and its history has been called mythic by Allen Tate:

> . . . it was every Southerner's myth from 1865 to about 1940, or up to World War II. Had Faulkner invented the myth, it would not have been as good for his purposes; nor would the myth of Oedipus, had Sophocles invented it. For the Southern legend is a true myth which informed the sensibility and thought, at varying conscious levels, of the defeated South. By myth I mean a dramatic projection of heroic action, or of the tragic failure of heroic action, upon the reality of the common life of a society, so that myth *is* reality. [25]

This myth sees the Old South as cursed with the evil of slavery, for which no one can be held responsible, as mankind has been with Original Sin, and therefore obliged to perform acts of contrition by way of expiation. It sees defeat in the Civil War as a tragic hubris, but is sufficiently in accord with the ideas of the Fugitives and their fellows to dissociate from any Yankee idea of the War's necessity – even virtue. It grants to the upholders of the Old South – as, indeed, to the Negroes themselves – great dignity and often beauty of motive; it sees the South equally likely to fall from within as from without, by the evolution of its own 'scalawag' class, represented by Faulkner's destructive – if galvanic – Snopes clan, whose members are everything his nobler Compsons are not and who, in his major trilogy *The Hamlet* (1940), *The Town* (1957) and *The Mansion* (1960), have taken

---

25. Allen Tate, *Memoirs and Opinions*, Carcanet, 1976, p. 151.

over just about everything. Therefore Faulkner's vision approaches that of the Greek tragedians, yet involves an essentially Christian sense of human moral responsibility.

For admirers of his novels, Faulkner's Southern myth is, of course, second in significance to what he does with it; nevertheless, it gives a framework to his tragic and original vision of human behaviour that he can psychically endorse: without his sense of the Old South's high culture, from which they have fallen, his magnificent portraiture of the Compsons would be the weaker. And who could subtract the South's intimate association of Fundamentalist notions of damnation and unease about colour from his presentation of Joe Christmas in *Light in August*?

But if his mythic power is what readers primarily revere in Faulkner's work, that power is also unimaginable without the extent and depth of his knowledge of the South – in his case, as in Eudora Welty's, of Mississippi: its geography, its history from pre-Columbian times onwards, its wildlife, its network of families, their habits, their traditions. In this respect, while it is appropriate to use the adjective Dostoyevskyan for *Absalom, Absalom* or *Light in August*, the novelist Faulkner is nearest to is Balzac, whom he (like Ellen Glasgow) admired so greatly and whose complex interrelationships between novels he adopted. In the range and richness of his territory, as in emotional power, he is vastly the superior of Glasgow or any of the Fugitives, for all their excellent qualities.

The shape of Faulkner's career is a fascinating subject for scrutiny, but it is too well-known for more than an outline here. He had the greatest difficulty in getting the novel he called *Flags in the Dust* published; it was chiselled by his editor and friend Ben Wasson into the form of *Sartoris* and appeared in 1929. Meanwhile, Faulkner had written a novel he thought would interest nobody; it was published later in the same year. *The Sound and the Fury*, in style, form and subject, is one of the key works of this century.

Its creation unleashed prodigious and extraordinary energies in Faulkner, who proceeded to follow it with novels no less remarkable: *As I Lay Dying* (1930), *Sanctuary* (1931), *Light in August* (1932) – for me, his masterpiece, original, dense, passionate – and *Absalom, Absalom*, perhaps his fullest and most demanding working of the

Southern myth, which appeared in 1936. This was an important year in the annals of Southern literature: it saw the publication of Eudora Welty's first story in the magazine *Manuscript*, and of the century's most spectacular and influential bestseller: the Civil War romance *Gone With the Wind*, by Margaret Mitchell.

So Eudora Welty was beginning her career in a society which, though far away from metropolitan activity, was in fact in the vanguard of literary activity. By the time *A Curtain of Green*, her first collection of short stories, appeared in 1941, the career of Thomas Wolfe (1900–40) had run its tempestuous course; W.J. Cash had produced his thought-provoking and seminal *Mind of the South* (1941); Katherine Anne Porter had published some of the most impressive of her sophisticated, powerful stories, – 'Noon Wine', 'Pale Horse, Pale Rider' and 'Old Mortality' – and with *The Heart is a Lonely Hunter* (1940) Carson McCullers had started her series of fictions which for many years were to be more widely admired outside the South than any other Southerner's. Reaction against her once great reputation seems to have set in (one Southern academic told me that no one who knew the South could admire her work), and I have to confess that I go along with this. Often her work seems full of poeticisms rather than poetic. But *The Heart is a Lonely Hunter* remains an extraordinary first novel, with fine things in it (the portrait of the two lonely deaf-mutes) despite overschematization, and among other things it is important because it contributed so largely to Patrick White's *Riders in the Chariot* (1962). *The Member of the Wedding* (1946) has proved, if anything, more durable. Surely it is not an exaggeration to say that the literary achievements of the American South in this period were unsurpassed in any other part of the world.

As I travelled round the South during the course of my work, it became increasingly clear to me that Southern writers did see themselves as products of a common country with shared memories, challenges and duties. The South lacks a pivotal centre. Nashville, despite the intellectual movements that grew around Vanderbilt University, is not such a centre, nor is New Orleans, so cosmopolitan, so original, so very much itself. Atlanta is the South's most considerable city – an enterprising and stimulating place, its vigour epitomized by its dazzlingly bold downtown architecture and its huge-scale airport, yet weighed down by appalling social problems. It cannot be thought of as a Southern capital either, however; it is too much of the New South, too tenuously related to the older culture without.

But as I journeyed from one end of the Southern States to another, it seemed to me that this very lack of centre served only to bind the Southern writers closer together; they had this in common with each other as well.

In this culturally outstanding context, the writings of Eudora Welty were from the very first recognized as being of quite extraordinary quality. Perhaps something of both the complexity and the clarity of what she was offering can be attributed to the fact that although she is indeed a Southerner, a Mississippian, by birth and by life, she is not by parentage. Her father, who was of Swiss extraction, came from the Ohio countryside, and a wholly different tradition from the Southern (he was a Republican, for example); her mother (though she may have considered herself a 'Southerner of the deepest water') came from the state of West Virginia, which had broken away from Virginia proper at the time of Secession. The young Chestina Andrews Welty's mountain life – so free and independent, so different from rural Mississippi – was to exert a powerful spell on her daughter. So although Eudora Welty wrote as an insider, her vision had been educated, sharpened, by the influence of outsiders.

The extent to which she was appreciated by already eminent Southerners is shown by the fact that Katherine Anne Porter, whose own reputation in the late 1930s and early 1940s was extremely high, wrote that introduction to her first book while William Faulkner expressed his admiration for her second, the novella *The Robber Bridegroom*. Her long and rewarding friendship with Katherine Anne Porter had begun as a result of the letters the older writer had written to Eudora on reading her early stories for *The Southern Review*. She was living in Baton Rouge at the time, and invited Eudora Welty to go and see her, but it took the younger woman the best part of a year to pluck up the courage to do so. She has described Katherine Anne Porter as 'wonderfully generous'; the two stayed at the writers' community at Yaddo together, though they spent a lot of their time going to the races at nearby Saratoga. Eudora Welty's marvellous photographs of her friend, showing her wide, sensual, mysterious face, suggest her essentially wild nature; she was married four times and had many lovers (Allen Tate always used to say: who knew – she might have dropped another husband somewhere along the line). During the 1940s, after spending the previous decade in both Berlin and Paris, she lived in Hollywood and Washington DC. Her collected stories, *The Leaning Tower* (1944), make use of her cosmopolitan experiences to express the decay and tensions of European society and the complexity of Texas and the South.

Eudora Welty has often been questioned about Faulkner. In the years before he was awarded the Nobel Prize in 1949, his books were not kept in print; she had to hunt around second-hand bookstores for copies of the work she admired so enormously. She knew him 'slightly, and over a long period of time, but not well':

> I liked him ever so much. We met at a dinner-party in Oxford, just old friends of his and old friends of mine, which was the right way for it to happen, and it was just grand. We sang hymns, and we sang some old ballads – and the next day he invited me to go sailing. If we ever met in New York, we just talked about being in Oxford. He didn't bring up writing, and if he didn't, you know, I wasn't going to bring it up! But when he was working in Hollywood, he once wrote me a two-line letter – this was long before we met – and told me he liked a little book of mine called *The Robber Bridegroom*, and said would I let him know if he could ever do anything for me. It was on a little piece of notebook paper, written in that fine, neat sort of unreadable hand, in pencil – and I've lost it.[26]

It is hard to deduce from this, as from Eudora Welty's other accounts of Faulkner, the driven alcoholic of so many portraits, the Hollywood lecher, the closed, neurotic recluse who opened his mouth on social occasions only to snub or to offer offensively maverick remarks. Faulkner's genius recognized Eudora Welty's; a man whose imagination was so powerful and penetrating that it must have been an encumbrance as well as a blessing, he was – and not nearly as infrequently as certain biographies have chosen to make out – capable of generous and

---

26. C.E.W. p. 79.

good actions. It is a pleasure to note that the Mississippian nearest to him in gifts brought out only the best in him.

The 1940s were to be a less remarkably productive decade for Faulkner than the 1930s, although it opened with *The Hamlet*, the first volume of his great comprehensive trilogy. Perhaps his best work of the decade was *Intruder in the Dust* (1948) – warmer in tone and easier, freer in style than its predecessors, the story of the exculpation of Lucas Beauchamp, an old black farmer wrongly accused of murder, by the offices of a young white boy, Charles Mallinson, and his black buddy, Alex Sander. Eudora Welty reviewed this book, reading it in the context of Southern pain, as

> defining a hope, prayer, that we should one day reach the point where it will be *Thou shalt not kill at all*, where Lucas Beauchamp's life will be secure not despite the fact that he is Lucas Beauchamp but because he is.[27]

The South and its concerns are inextricable from Eudora Welty's work, though, as with William Faulkner, it is what she has done with her subject and how she has brought her own personality to its treatment that gives her *œuvre* its universal significance.

The writers of the South were not alone among their fellow-citizens in their ability to command the attention of the world, in tapping the resources of their culture. The South had copiously bestowed its genius on the world – and, roughly concurrently, with the productions of its writers – through the music it gave birth to and developed. The white South, above all in Appalachia (eastern Tennessee, Virginia), both preserved and developed the traditional music (for both dance and song) brought over by settlers from Britain. The black community – and here Louisiana and Mississippi are the key States – evolved from its African heritage its passionate forms of jazz and blues. Both, especially when they met and fused, revolutionized the world. Scarcely a popular musical genre that our century has embraced did not originate in the South: ragtime, jugband, bluegrass, Cajun, zydeco. And rock'n'roll; my own generation saw a whole musical and social revolution of indisputably Southern genesis. Elvis Presley himself was

27. Eye p. 208.

a Mississippian, whose break came because he, a white boy, was judged to be able to sing like a black one. It is a moving irony that at the time when white Southerners were most viciously resisting their black fellows, musically they were giving out to the world a loving fusion of the two races, the honours of the performance of which were equally shared – creating the most potent and widely adopted amorous/erotic vocabulary in the entire history of human culture.

The vitality of the 'country' that had produced all this was something I was continually made to appreciate during my long travels in 1978 – so was something else. If the best-known, the most internationally revered, of literary Southerners was still William Faulkner, whom I had admired intensely ever since my teens, then the one whom fellow-writers looked up to the most, had found consistently the most inspiring and creatively helpful, was, I discovered, Eudora Welty. Reynolds Price wrote again:

> . . . understanding came not from Faulkner but from Eudora, whom I read and admired long before I ever got to Faulkner. I read Eudora Welty's early stories as a high-school student and knew immediately that I had grown up hearing stories exactly of this sort, knowing people who expressed themselves in exactly these same comic idioms, metaphors, similes, and my natural conclusion was – my own experience constitutes the potential building blocks for works of fiction, works of art![28]

While Anne Tyler (born 1941), perhaps the most dazzlingly gifted and successful Southern writer of her generation, has said:

> Eudora Welty has been an enormous influence on me since I read *The Wide Net*, at age fourteen. . . . It wasn't so much an influence on the style of my writing as on the fact that I write at all; I had thought, till that moment, that you had to have epic heroes if you were going to write, not just the kind of people I met daily in the North Carolina tobacco fields.[29]

---

28. *Reynolds Price in Conversation with William Ray* (1976) Memphis State University Press.
29. Letter to the author.

Increasingly such tributes did not surprise me, since the more closely I read her, the more I appreciated Eudora Welty's greatness. Obviously there was no need to enter into a Faulkner versus Welty debate – something that would be inimical to the spirit of both writers, and would contribute to an understanding of neither. On the other hand, one could not ignore judgements made in Eudora Welty's favour by writers and readers; it had to tell one something important about her art and its relation to the South. Moreover, the twelve years that separated her from Faulkner, together with the comparatively late date of her two masterpieces, *Losing Battles* and *The Optimist's Daughter*, and the comparatively early date of his sequence of great novels (1929–1936) had, I saw, enabled Eudora Welty to speak for a later age than Faulkner (to speak for our own, even though *Losing Battles* is set in the 1930s, and *The Optimist's Daughter* makes excursions to life at the turn of the century).

I have not only maintained the estimation of Eudora Welty that I reached in 1978; repeated familiarity with her works has only intensified my regard for them. She seems to me now – with her equally successful and equally generous command of so many different modes: historical, *à la page* contemporary, fairytale, tragedy, comedy – to possess a truly Shakespearian quality, which I have also found among great artists of this century, in the Spaniard Federico García Lorca and the Swede Ingmar Bergman.

My first meeting with Eudora Welty is an indelible memory – not only because it was the logical culmination of all my investigative journeys round the South, but also because quite simply, my life has never been the same since.

IV

It was in sweltering heat (fiercer by at least ten degrees than on that night of murder in 'Where is the Voice Coming From?') that in Memphis, Tennessee, I boarded a bus for Jackson, Mississippi.

Memphis, a huge, sprawling city that grew up on the bluffs of the Mississippi River, is the principal gateway from the north into the state of Mississippi. The bus station jukebox – which had played the same record too many times over – seemed to be confirming a thought of mine which would not quite go away: that Mississippi – the Deep South, only a matter of miles off now – would deliver the South as a country in its quintessential, most uncompromising form. Johnny Cash's bass voice boomed out:

'There ain't no good in an evil-hearted woman,
And I ain't cut out to be no Jesse James,
And you don't go writin' hot cheques
Down in Mississippi,
And there ain't no good chain gang.'

And did not this song, with its pounding accompaniment and insistent melody, belong to the terrifying world of the 'voice' in Eudora Welty's story, who would surely have known it? Did it not make violence sweet, with its simple but somehow infectious gun-and-guitar romanticism? And had not I, times beyond counting, been seduced by that romanticism – into vicarious activity?

'Down in Mississippi' – the 'Magnolia' State, whose official flower and tree is indeed the magnolia, just as the mocking-bird is its official bird. 'Thank Heavens for Mississippi' (I'd been told countless times) was an Arkansas saying because were it not for Mississippi, that State would come lowest (or highest) in all condemnatory surveys – *per capita* income or illegitimacy rate, for instance. 'What has four i's and cannot see?' went the old punning pejorative joke. None of the Southern states had an uglier record for racial violence. Yet from Mississippi had come the two greatest writers the South had produced: William Faulkner from Oxford in its northern part, Eudora Welty from Jackson in its centre.

I had not been on the bus, had not crossed into Mississippi for so very long, before the flat, featureless, steamy country on either side of the highway (with the Delta lying away to my right) established its own kind of sovereignty. Temporarily, even the possibilities of other landscapes receded. I might have known Mississippi all my life, yet how utterly foreign it was! At once fertile and stubborn, it offered, as it stretched to invisibility under its vast sky, no views, no prospects for change, no respite from itself – from its huge expanses of cotton-fields, its slow channels of water, its interpolations of swampy woods.

This was a land without towns of any consequence; its villages were small, drab, poor, their shabby-porched houses often seeming ready to sink back down into the loamy earth. Theirs was a predominantly black population, something which at once distinguished this State from neighbouring Tennessee, where most rural communities are basically white. Tennessee – especially, I think, that lovely area between Nashville and Memphis bisected by the wide Tennessee River – gives a British person a sense of kinship with its woods and farms. Other very different kinships were suggested by this country, now stretching indomitably southwards; indeed, it came as no surprise later to realize that Mississippi lies on the same latitude as that other great cotton-growing region of the world, the lower Nile in Egypt.

Even in the bus's atomized interior (with its pungent, unnaturally sweet smell) you were aware of the heat outside (106, said the public barometers now), and perpetually ahead on the roadway was a shimmering, into which we always seemed to be moving. But when you stepped out for a break, for refreshment, you immediately felt the heat pressing down, rolling on you like some immense, damp-backed, sun-soaking, smothering reptile. Heat – as 'Where is the Voice Coming From?' makes plain – is a major player in the drama of the South. Its inexorability on that long southbound journey was surely what caused me to feel something like awe, even fear, at the subject I was pursuing, at the whole dark complexity of Southern culture.

I told myself: it's 1978, and we're only halfway through the presidency of Jimmy Carter – liberal, not to say progressive, Democrat, Southerner from Georgia, key State of the New South. The Old South is over now; this very bus proves it. If I think back to the time of 'Where is the Voice Coming From?', fifteen years ago, the interior would have been divided according to race, and there would have been no possibility at all of a black bus-driver. Now, on the contrary, black and white were mixed up; I was sitting next to a rather talkative black woman in her late twenties – the topic she returned to again and again, however, was the difficulty of being a black woman even in today's South. Her stories seemed uncomfortably to become part of the humid countryside; both, perhaps assisted by the unrelenting heat, seemed to make demands on me which I felt afraid to meet.

It was not morally permissible to sustain a tourist's role; one had a duty to reach out and enter, yet land and people proclaimed the difficulty of doing this; proclaimed, too, the carapace of convention behind which one preferred to live and move.

One wanted – *I* wanted – so much to believe in instant progress, in the immediate efficacy of enlightened (or comparatively enlightened) legislation, banishing any uncomfortable need for retrospective remorse or responsibility – let alone long, slow, painful knowledge. The talk of the black woman at my side suggested the callowness of such wishes. One should (as the stories of William Faulkner and Eudora Welty bade one do) consider life in society with all the layers of its past, and layers of the future too, discernible behind the present – comprising hopes, fears, resentments, and the inevitable consequences of actions.

Take even 'Where is the Voice Coming From?' By the time of my journey, obviously, some of the speaker's references belonged to time gone by: the anti-Kennedy joke, the sneer at James Meredith (Mississippi's first black student at a hitherto all-white university). But the story was still a living one; the killer's voice convinced. Besides, confessor and victim's family could still be said to exist, with all their feelings and demands – the activist's wife, for example, whose love of gardening the killer had noted: 'It was mighty green where I skint over the yard getting back. That nigger wife of his, she wanted nice grass! I bet my wife would hate to pay her water bill.'[30] So lives and the communities in which they are led – including those through which I was passing – should be seen not only through the eyes of liberal hope but through eyes that could appreciate them as the sums of complex, intertwining histories that could yet beget futures, and futures that could well confound that liberal hope. Such eyes as those of the writer I was travelling to see.

A mutual friend had given me Eudora Welty's telephone number; she certainly had not sounded intimidating when I spoke to her, only insistent that she meet me at the bus station. It would be so easy for her, she said, and so much nicer for me than arriving by myself in this

---

30. C.S. p. 605.

hot weather in a strange town. How could I not have assented? Arrival at Greyhound or Trailways terminuses is always so depressingly like departure anyway – the people waiting, the self-service and rest rooms, the information desk and jukebox, all permeated by a sense of impermanence – one might as well be where one started out from.

At last Jackson was creeping up on us. The State capital it may be (and by a long way this predominantly rural State's biggest city) but it is no Nashville, no Memphis; it is of no great size, and does not have the aspect of an important centre. The bus station came into view; would I, even though I had seen photographs of her distinctive, almost craggy face, on the covers of books, recognize Eudora Welty?

Of course I did – at once! Anyway she was on the look-out for me, sitting in her car by the passenger exit, smiling, welcoming, somewhat curious (I now realize) but not in any way disconcertingly so, about the English visitor she was greeting, who had made so long a bus journey to get to Jackson. This friendly curiosity only enhanced the warmth of her welcome, for it suggested a woman who was not interested, despite her seniority and fame, in being on her dignity, in being a distinguished interviewee, but one who habitually responded to anyone she met. From the first moments it was clear that she was anxious to find bases of common interest and concern. Her voice and her soft eyes complemented one another attractively. Her voice was low, quiet, noticeably Southern, not least in its warmness; it was at once animated and composed, calm and calming. Her eyes – large, observant, lit from within – suggested these qualities too. (During conversation with her I was later to think that the phrase 'speaking eyes' had an all but literal truth where she was concerned, just as the tones of her gentle voice often seemed to be holding one, searching one with interest.)

As I got into the car beside Eudora Welty her preoccupation was with my possible tiredness (which was already beginning to recede). When she was working for the WPA (Works Progress Administration), she said, she used to make many bus journeys all over Mississippi; she knew the road from Memphis to Jackson well.

She would have liked to put me up at her house, she then went on to say; normally she would have done so. She would have been happy to have me as her guest. But, as I would soon see for myself, she had the decorators in; the place was upside-down at the moment.

She really did apologize. She had booked me a room in a hotel nearby, and suggested that she should take me to her house for a drink before driving me there. Later she would be very pleased if I would be her guest for dinner. 'I want to hear where-all you've been,' she said, 'and about all the people you've been talking to.' She had set aside the following morning to answer my questions.

The house – dating from the 1920s, and built for her father in the then admired mock-Tudor style – is set in a piney part of the town, and stands well back from the road, facing Belhaven College. As I write now, I feel again the sensation of leaving the car that evening, still bowing down under the day's heat (the light was dimming now, with the onset of that thick kind of darkness Mississippi shares with other subtropical regions) and following Eudora Welty into the house that had been her home since her youth. The sitting-room was cool, well-ordered, cheerful, yet it exuded quiet taste (or rather, that taste which finds quietness a positive, not a negative, thing). It was an expression of personality, too, and of a way of living, with its pictures (some watercolours), among them a portrait of Eudora Welty herself as a young woman; photographs, its many books on shelves and on tables, along with current reviews; its carpets, its flowers. Among the books I could see titles by E.M. Forster, Elizabeth Bowen, Elizabeth Taylor, V.S. Pritchett. Theirs was a world I knew, whose perceptions and values had shaped my own . . . I had arrived at a place of refreshment and, as such, the sitting-room, and the house itself, became, virtually at once, a metaphor for the nature of Eudora Welty's art – for Eudora Welty's writing, whether she is dealing with the cruelties of racial hatred or with the pleasures and confusions of a 'hot' dance, is distinguished by a refinement that imposes order on the intractable or the inchoate, and springs from deep inner certainties. She gave me a Bourbon with chunks of ice – its colour made me think, as always, of rich earth liquefied into another element entirely – and then showed me work by the Mississippi nature-mystic artist Walter Inglis Anderson, and told me of an encounter she and Elizabeth Bowen had had which could be explained in terms of the supernatural.

I knew then, as I believe now, that Eudora Welty was to play a part in my life long after this visit to Jackson, and so it has turned out.

She was very helpful over *Separate Country*, though she made no attempt to influence its opinions or judgements. When I returned from America I became involved with the timely republication of her work in Britain. Then, in 1984, I was invited back to Jackson to give an address at Millsaps College's celebrations for Eudora Welty's seventy-fifth birthday, an occasion that brought together critics and writers from all over America and beyond, and enabled me to appreciate Eudora Welty's continuing meaning for generations of Americans. For the academic year 1985–6 I was appointed Eudora Welty Visiting Professor of Southern Studies at the College, and examined her work with students who were themselves Southerners, albeit children of the New South. During this period I lived literally just round the corner from that house I had first visited on that hot summer evening in 1978. I was then – if for a limited time – a member of the community of which Eudora Welty is so firmly a part. We have also met during her visits to England.

In interviews she has been firm in her view that it is the work of any artist that is the important thing, showing a healthy suspicion of literary biographies – a suspicion I share, especially when the subject is still alive. Here I intend to give a portrait of a creative spirit – principally as revealed in Eudora Welty's writings, but also drawing on my experiences of her and of those who have known her for many years.

2

OF ONE TIME, ONE PLACE?

I

I F THE consummate artistry of many of Eudora Welty's earlier stories (still among her most famous and successful productions) suggests transcendence of their time and place, then it is also true that this consummate artistry is itself a result of the young writer's intense response to the harsh, demanding life of the South during the Great Depression.

Eudora Welty has said: 'The Depression, in fact, was not a noticeable phenomenon in the poorest state in the Union'[1] – half of the population lived on unproductive tenant-farms, and poverty was commonplace. Nevertheless, the Depression became a fact of American life, a state of being, informing and transforming personal lives throughout the country. Economic distress brought out in the American psyche – forged, after all, through the experiences of emigrants and pioneers – a surge of energy, a determination not to go under, but to build up and outwards. In his thoughtful study of the literary relationship between America and Britain, *Love–Hate Relations*, Stephen Spender says:

> Strangely it was in America's time of economic disaster that the gigantism of the continent first seemed to cast a huge shadow across the world. Everything was worse than everywhere else just

---

1. Eye p. 350.

as everything had been better. There were none of those irrelevancies like that of the British royal family having their Jubilee before a delighted public in the midst of economic crisis, which act like soft cushions or sound-proofing in England and which are socially valuable just because they are irrelevant. They make people look somewhere else. John Dos Passos, in inventing a paragraph in which from sentence to sentence events hundreds of miles apart were seen collapsed within the same moment, imitated exactly the lack of such cushions and buffers in American life. The public world of crisis invades everyone's privacy and the most private utterance has public resonance.[2]

American writing during the Depression is characterized by an adventurousness, a determination that, by unflinchingly grappling with the cruel problems of the day, the nation would win through. It has a demotic vitality that is hard to parallel. Interestingly, this kind of literary activity predates F.D. Roosevelt's first electoral victory, acting as an index of change in the American people. In 1930, for example, the first volume of Dos Passos's *U.S.A. (The 42nd Parallel)*, Faulkner's novel of poor (desperately poor) whites, *As I Lay Dying*, and Katherine Anne Porter's collection of stories *Flowering Judas*, with its cast of Mexican peasants and revolutionaries and poor Texan countryfolk, were published; while in 1932 came the first book of James T. Farrell's magnificent *Studs Lonigan* trilogy (*Young Lonigan*). All these writers carried on from the achievements of the great modernists, building on the battles hard won by *Ulysses* and *À la recherche du temps perdu*; at the same time, it is hard not to say that their work democratizes these attainments, thanks to the pressure from without.

The work of Dos Passos, Faulkner and Farrell matches the ambition of the politico-social targets of the decade. Eudora Welty is of these writers' number; she is thus a double literary citizen: of the South, and of the United States as a whole.

When Roosevelt won his landslide victory against Herbert Hoover in November 1932, and promised the 'New Deal' – the very term defining an ideal and helping to combat national maladies – he told the

---

2. Stephen Spender, *Love–Hate Relations: A Study of Anglo-American Sensibilities*, Hamish Hamilton (1974), p. 217.

American people: 'The country needs, the country demands bold, persistent experimentation.' Experimentation meant the huge incomparable programme of public works and public rescue that did indeed galvanize citizens, some thirteen million of whom were without jobs; and galvanized them the more so as operations were presented as part of a vast, virtuous, quasi-religious movement: 'The money-changers have fled from their high seats in the temple of our civilization. We may now restore that temple to the ancient truths.'[3]

The end of Roosevelt's first hundred days saw the NRA (the National Industry Recovery Act), allocated three billion dollars to stimulate the economy through public works. One million jobs came out of the TVA alone (the Tennessee Valley Authority, established in summer 1933); 1.7 million jobs were created by the American Federation of Labor in September of that year. And in January 1935, the Works Progress Administration came into being.

It was the WPA that gave Eudora Welty (appropriately, it now seems) her first full-time paid job. She became publicity agent, junior grade (because she was a woman) in the WPA's State office in Jackson, and she was sent out all over Mississippi, visiting every one of its eighty-two counties.

After taking her BA at the University of Wisconsin, she had decided that she would prefer a career in business to one in teaching (she dreaded getting stuck, trapped, in her mother's old profession); she then attended the Columbia University School of Business in New York, where she studied – and practised – advertising. After her year there she tried to find work in New York, but the economic situation made this impossible, so she went home to Jackson. In New York the Depression meant spectacular queues and groups of the unemployed which Eudora Welty was to evoke a few years (and many short return visits) later in her story 'Flowers for Marjorie'. Here the dejected out-of-work protagonist is sitting on a park bench:

A row of feet rested beside his own where he looked down. Beyond was the inscribed base of the drinking fountain which

---

3. Hugh Brogan, *History of the United States*, Longman's (1985).

stemmed with a troubled sound up into the glare of the day. The feet were in Vs, all still. Then down at the end of the bench, one softly began to pat. It made an innuendo at a dainty pink chewing-gum wrapper blowing by. . . . Somebody spoke. 'You goin' to join the demonstration at two o'clock?'[4]

In Mississippi ('poorest of the poor') the predicament was more one of intensification of how things had been since the end of the Civil War. Even there, however, the socioeconomic experiments of the 'New Deal' required a change of mentality in significant quarters.

Not long after her return to Jackson, Eudora's father died of leukaemia, then a virtually unknown fatal disease that took only weeks to progress. His wife tried to save him by giving her own blood in a transfusion. It did not work; she was at his side when he died in hospital. Chestina Welty, who never recovered emotionally from this tragic shock, was left with two sons still in high school to support. There was no question of Eudora herself not taking employment, though her mother (to a much greater extent than her father) sympathized with – indeed, encouraged – her already indomitable ambition to become a writer.

Thus while Eudora Welty still speaks of her WPA journeys as the daring ventures of someone from a sheltered home, when we read the early work we must always bear in mind that its creator shared the troubles of her time, its anxieties and the courage needed to bear them. The travels that provided material for the photographs and fill the stories of these years – of small-scale salesmen, itinerant workers, men and women (both white and black) looking for jobs; of workless hobos – are analogues of her own journeys, and the difficulties they involved must have been compounded by the sadness at home, however stoically borne. Perhaps this gives the grit, the sense of endurance, that exists in both their visual and verbal translations.

As well as being a terrible loss in personal terms, Christian Webb Welty's death also had a disturbing symbolic resonance. A Republican, he had believed strongly in progress, business, technology, and had been proud to proclaim, on its grand opening in 1925, that for

4. C.S. p. 98.

the erection of the Lamar Life Building, 'Jackson's first skyscraper', 'not a dollar was borrowed nor a security sold'. It was through such enterprises that he hoped the South might be delivered from its economic backwardness. Now the end to such hopes was proclaimed everywhere. Now, ironically, Southerners were grateful for the chance to be paid by the Federal authority for recording their folk heritage (Alan Lomax's seminal *American Ballads and Folksongs* came out in 1934) or for painting murals on public buildings.

Poignantly, Eudora Welty's very first job, a part-time one, was in the Lamar Life Building, with the radio station that her father, with his strong belief in improved and innovative communications, had founded. Among her duties was writing the schedule for the radio programmes which the *Jackson Daily News* would not carry because it considered radio treasonous competition. A general atmosphere of amateurism prevailed, about which Eudora Welty can still be very funny, as in this interview with her friend Jane Reid Petty:

> We worked up there in the clock tower. It was our office and about as big as a chicken coop. There was just enough room for Mr Wiley Harris, who ran the station, and one other person – that was me. Mr Harris was the announcer and the manager and everything. He'd go in the clock tower and start cleaning out the canary bird's cage, and somebody would yell: 'Mr Harris! Mr Harris!' . . . at first he wouldn't notice because he was cleaning out the bird cage. Finally they'd get his attention, and he'd go in there and say, 'This is Station . . . uh, this is. . . . This is Station . . . ' We'd finally hold it up to him – WJDX – and then he'd say it.[5]

After this came other freelance writing and copywriting commissions – including a Sunday column about Jackson social life for the Memphis-based *Commercial Appeal* – and then the position with the WPA.

Her office was in the Tower Building in Jackson, under a professional newsman, Louis Johnson. She was sent to every part of the State, putting up booths in country fairs, following a Bookmobile route,

5. C.E.W. p. 203.

conducting interviews – with a judge for a new juvenile court, with those carrying out a Braille project, with beneficiaries of one or another of the WPA's schemes. Communications in Mississippi were extremely poor. The WPA constructed 'farm-to-market' roads with tarred or gravelled surfaces to assist its farmers or farmworkers who otherwise would not have been able to travel at all in rainy weather; it made landing fields for aeroplanes all over the state.

Eudora Welty journeyed for the most part by bus, as her mother needed the family car back in Jackson. Distance could mean that she spent the night away, and then she would avail herself of the kind of cheap hotel she describes in 'The Hitch-Hikers':

> In his room, Harris lay down on the bed without undressing or turning out the light. He was too tired to sleep. Half blinded by the unshaded bulb he stared at the bare plaster walls and the equally white surface of the mirror above the empty dresser. Presently he got up and turned on the ceiling fan, to create some motion and sound in the room. It was a defective fan which clicked with each revolution, on and on. He lay perfectly still beneath it, with his clothes on, unconsciously breathing in a rhythm related to the beat of the fan.[6]

(There was *always* a defective fan, she now observes.)

Before very long Eudora Welty was taking a camera on her assignments. Although her work sometimes required her to take photographs, the majority of the many hundred that she took during the 1930s were taken on her own account, if in WPA time. Later she was to write about them in the introduction to her first collection of photos, *One Time, One Place*:

> A better and less ignorant photographer would certainly have come up with better pictures, but not these pictures, for he could hardly have been as well positioned as I was, moving through the scene openly and yet invisibly because I was part of it, born into it, taken for granted.[7]

---

6. C.S. p. 71.
7. Eye p. 351.

The high proportion of black people among rural Mississippians is reflected by the high proportion of them among the subjects of her photographs. She goes on:

> They explained that this would be the first picture taken of them in their lives. So I was able to give them something back, and though it might be that the picture would be to these poverty-marked men and women and children a sad souvenir, I am almost sure that it wasn't all sad to them, wasn't necessarily sad at all. . . . In taking all these pictures I was attended, I now know, by an angel – a presence of trust. In particular, the photographs of black persons by a white person may not testify soon again to such intimacy. It is trust that dates the pictures now, more than the vanished years.[8]

Sympathy encountered sympathy, a young and ardent life confronted other lives – almost always ardent on some level, if not always young. Her photographs and stories began as tributes to an obstinate spirit that animated and redeemed a multitude of Mississippi lives of a difficulty she had hitherto scarcely suspected. Her Mississippi stories have a concern for people the equal of, say, Farrell's for his Chicago Southsiders, and a warmth and width that his didactic purpose could not quite attain.

Specific things that Eudora Welty saw or heard in her WPA travels over Mississippi set her creative imagination in motion. The hotel – one of the controlling places of 'The Hitch-Hikers' – was re-created, emotionally as well as physically, for that story. On one assignment she started talking to a man building a booth at a fair, who told her of 'a little Negro man' at a carnival, forced to eat live chickens. 'That's the only actual story I've used . . . it was too horrible to make up,'[9] says Eudora Welty of 'Keela, the Outcast Indian Maiden'. 'Death of a Traveling Salesman' grew not only from her trips to the hill country of north-east Mississippi but also from something told her by a family friend, who travelled for the Mississippi Highway Department, buying up property for right of way: 'he quoted this man

---

8. Eye p. 352.
9. C.E.W. p. 5.

saying that they didn't have any fire and he had to go to Mr Somebody's house and "borry some fire". Well, those words just hit me. They were electrical. You could just see a whole situation from that.'[10] As for 'A Worn Path', Eudora Welty describes its genesis with great clarity in her essay on this story:

> One day I saw a solitary old woman like Phoenix. She was walk-ing; I saw her at middle distance, in a winter country landscape, and watched her slowly make her way across my line of vision. That sight of her made me write the story. I invented an errand for her, but that only seemed a living part of the figure she was herself: what errand other than for someone else could be making her go? And her going was the first thing, her persisting in the landscape was the real thing, and the first and the real were what I wanted and worked to keep. I brought her up close enough, by imagination, to describe her face, make her present to the eyes, but the full-length figure moving across the winter fields was the indelible one and the image to keep, and the perspective extending into the vanishing distance the true one to hold in mind.[11]

This passage brings home, of course, the intimate relationship between photography and the writing of stories in Eudora Welty's life at the time.

II

Eudora Welty's father, with his belief in and love of the progressive, the technical, had himself been an accomplished photographer: 'he had a nice Eastman camera with a bellows that pulled a good long way'. Long after his death his daughter found negatives of scenes from his early married life (before her birth). Her parents had developed these, printing them by night and thus anticipating their daughter's activities when, after a day 'on the road', she would set up a darkroom in the kitchen and work there by night with 'the enlarger clamped on the kitchen table'. Of her father's pictures she comments now, with

10. C.E.W. p. 319.
11. Eye p. 161.

a simple gratitude: 'They charm me.' His later photos were familial scenes (they have survived; some were included in the album *Eudora*, brought out by the Mississippi Department of Archives and History for her seventy-fifth birthday). Christian Webb Welty was also concerned with the establishment of the Standard Photo Company in Jackson, which was to develop Eudora's own films, and give her advice for many years.

Eudora Welty herself started with a small Eastman Kodak, went on to use first a Recomar, then a larger and more costly Eastman Kodak (which 'proved unhandy'), and then a Rolleiflex – with a single lens plus a portrait attachment which she did not use particularly often because of her wish to include as much of her subjects' background as she could: 'I wanted to set people in their context.'

She took photographs of Mississippians of all kinds – black and white, old and young, at work and at play. More often than not – and certainly by far the greater part of the individual portraits – her pictures are interesting hybrids between the informal (the spontaneous) and the formal (posed). She took her photos with their subjects' consent, with the subject often 'addressing' the camera, a tribute to the trust she inspired. They are thus the fruits of an understanding, something which surely explains their quite unusual warmth, the sense they so often convey of a gift being offered. On the other hand – since almost without exception they came about through her travels, through encounters on WPA assignments, in which Eudora Welty could not have known who she was going to meet – they are utterly unlike conventional studies, either of the studio kind or of the journalistic; indeed, there is sometimes a – by no means always detrimental – roughness to their art. Experience taught her how best to watch and wait:

> I learned quickly enough when to click the shutter, but what I was becoming aware of more slowly was a story-writer's truth: the thing to wait on, to reach there in time for, is the moment in which people reveal themselves. You have to be ready, in yourself; you have to know the moment, when you see it. The human face and the human body are eloquent in themselves, and a snapshot is a moment's glimpse (as a story may be a long look,

a growing contemplation) into what never stops moving, never ceases to express for itself something of our common feeling. Every feeling waits upon its gesture.[12]

So the progress of Eudora Welty the photographer led to the emergence of Eudora Welty the short-story-writer. (Since her early years she had wanted to be a writer, and had indeed written things.) Her pictures – either in the Mississippi Archives, to which she bequeathed them, or in the albums *One Time, One Place* (1971) and *Eudora Welty: Photographs* (1989) – do proceed from the same imaginative response to life as the stories in *A Curtain of Green* (though these above all) and all her fiction, including even so aural a story as 'Where is the Voice Coming From?'. They are at once intimate and evidence of individuals belonging to something larger than themselves, geographical, economic, societal, ethnic, ecological – for beyond the people, place asserts itself in all its stubborn strength.

Take the wonderful photo of the woman in a buttoned sweater, baldly entitled 'A Woman of the 'Thirties/Hinds County/1935' (*Photographs*, p. 1). In her poise, in the expression on her face (she is both aware of the camera and gravely preoccupied), she is above all her single unrepeatable self, with a world of experiences and emotions which are not, and can never be, ours. But she is also representative of a whole people, a way of life; years of a society's hardship and determination to survive show in her eyes, in the firm, downturned line of her mouth. And the beaten grass on which she stands, and the wooden shack a little blurred at her back, tell us of the conditions of her country, whose predicament she echoes. All Eudora Welty's best photographs go through and beyond their truthful particularity to the universal. The young black woman waiting on her porch for her date, and resting the upper half of her strong graceful body on a portion of wall, certainly suggests the 'Saturday Off' of its title (p. 15); Mississippi at leisure seems to be embodied in her. But she is also confronting us – smiling, pleased – on behalf of young women everywhere and at any time who feel – however briefly, however illogically – a contentment with life, a contentment with themselves.

---

12. Eye p. 134.

For despite the frequent grimness of the context – the transparently severe poverty, the ugliness, the almost total lack of harmonizing aesthetic in the rural communities – and despite, too, Eudora Welty's refusal to flinch from all this, these photographs of Depression Mississippi are characterized by a ubiquitous joy – the subjects', the photographer's – in the obstinate fact of being alive.

> Whatever you might think of those lives as symbols of a bad time, the human beings who were living them thought a good deal more of them than that. If I took picture after picture out of simple high spirits and the joy of being alive, the way I began, I can add that in my subjects I met often with the same high spirits, the same joy. Trouble, even to the point of disaster, has its pale, and these defiant things of the spirit repeatedly go beyond it, joy the same as courage.[13]

It is only fitting, then, that many of the photographs which live most vividly in the mind should portray happiness: the jubilant relaxation of 'Tomato-packers' Recess/Copiah County/1936' (p. 30), the simple infectious delight of the children in 'Pet Pig'/'Jackson/1930s' (p. 47) and the gently erotic pleasure of 'Making a Date/Grenada/1935' (p. 71). The photograph which delighted me above all the others when Eudora Welty presented me with *One Time, One Place* remains my favourite: the one of the three small boys at a fair ('Sideshow, State Fair/Jackson/1939') (p. 139) looking at something which we cannot see, but is obviously of mesmeric interest. Eudora Welty told me it was a particular favourite of hers too: 'I love the differences in expression between the three of them, don't you? Admiration, incredulity, and then, in the youngest, sheer wonderment.' This picture also brings home to me, more even than its fellows, both the strength – the eternity, if you prefer – of a moment and its helplessness in the inexorable forward march of Time. Those boys will be in late middle age now; will they even so much as remember that moment of joy and unity?

Photography, with its determination to absorb technology into art and to democratize art forms, played a strong part in the literary culture of the 1930s. In Britain there was Mass Observation, whose

---

13. Eye p. 352.

apologists and exponents were often also writers (Tom Harrison, Charles Madge, Kathleen Raine) and whose photographic productions have points of contact with Eudora Welty's. But the movement (founded in early 1937) was at once declaredly far more sociological and anthropological, and more closely related to such anti-Establishment (anti-capitalist) artistic movements as Surrealism (Humphrey Spender, Humphrey Jennings). When Kathleen Raine writes of Charles Madge: 'the expression of the unconscious collective life of England, literally, in writings on the walls, telling him of the hidden thoughts and dreams of the inarticulate masses',[14] she could be writing of Eudora Welty, with her many pictures of revealing signs and notices, such as the 'Blue Heaven Lunch Stand':

AT 4.30 AM
WE OPEN OUR DOORS
WE HAVE NO CERTAIN
   TIME TO CLOSE
The COOK WILL BE
GLAD to SERVE U
WITH A 5 and 10 c
         STEW.[15]

But Eudora Welty would never have felt obliged to justify her interest in popular culture, as Kathleen Raine apparently did. She was far closer to her material, and while she was aware that her origins were distant from those of her subjects, she assumed no such position of conscious (albeit well-intentioned) superiority. Likewise, her deep-seated humanism made the detachment as well as the distortion of Surrealism impossible to her.

The most famous practitioner of the camera-lens approach to fiction in British literature was Eudora Welty's older contemporary, Christopher Isherwood (1905–86), friend or associate of many of the Mass Observationists. The famous opening of *Goodbye to Berlin* (1939) sums up his approach:

---

14. Quoted in Valentine Cunningham, *British Writers of the Thirties*, Oxford University Press (1988), ch. 10.
15. Eye p. 350.

I am a camera with its shutter open, quite passive, recording, not thinking. Recording the man shaving at the window opposite and the woman in the kimono washing her hair. Some day, all this will have to be developed, carefully printed, fixed.[16]

Eudora Welty could not have written this. She was never the voyeur, as Isherwood was among Berlin's working class; with her there was no question of suspension of moral reaction. She surely came near the truth about herself as artist-recorder when she spoke of her camera as a 'shy person's protection'; it was a means of communicating on mutually cordial and respectful terms with people who seemed very unlike herself, but people with whom she found – and through whom she celebrated – a common humanity.

In the United States in the 1930s the power of photography was saluted as a weapon against social injustice. This was the decade of Dorothea Lange and Walker Evans, the latter inextricable from the South in the public mind. Under the auspices of *Fortune* magazine (1936) Walker Evans, a professional photographer of some distinction, accompanied the young writer James Agee to Alabama to investigate the lives of poverty-stricken cotton-growing sharecroppers. The result, after a publishing hiatus, was *Let Us Now Praise Famous Men* (1941). Eudora Welty felt – and still feels for that matter – that for all the skill of Walker Evans's photographs and the sincerity of James Agee's mission, there was something reductive about the whole business: people became exempla, if not specimens – fodder for the young men's radical intentions. Told that some of Walker Evans's original subjects had recently been tracked down in Alabama and rephotographed, she said: 'It would seem to me that that was exploiting them. For a second time.'

Early on Eudora Welty had the satisfaction of an exhibition in the gallery of a New York camera shop. She had gone into Lugene's on Madison Avenue just to buy supplies, and found that it showed work by amateurs. The owner of the shop liked hers, and gave her sound advice (which she took). Eudora Welty printed up what she considered to be her best pictures. She was a little amused to find

---

16. *Penguin New Writing*, No. 1, Penguin (December 1940) , p. 31 ('A Berlin Diary' by Christopher Isherwood).

the exhibition billed as that of a 'primitive', but anything and anybody from Mississippi easily qualified for this term. In New York there was a lot of prejudgement to combat concerning the South in general, and maybe Mississippi in particular.

This surely explains the lack of interest in *Black Saturday*, a book Eudora Welty made of photographs and short stories:

> I got a combination ring book and pasted little contact prints in what I fitted up as a sequence to make a kind of story in itself. I used the subject of Saturday because it allowed the most variety possible to show a day among black and white people, what they would be doing, the work and the visit to town, and the home and so on. I submitted along with the pictures a set of stories I had written, unrelated specifically to the photos, except that all were the South, and tried to interest book publishers in the combination.[17]

The juxtaposition sounds irresistible, but resist it book publishers did, calling the idea 'amateurish'. In fact all the stories were eventually published – first in magazines, then in *A Curtain of Green* and *A Wide Net*; and the photographs made up a substantial part of that first album, *One Time, One Place*. Nevertheless, it seems a pity that this attractive and original idea was never realized, and one can appreciate the young woman's disappointment at the ill-considered rejections:

> Back in the '30s, you could go from Jackson to New York and stay three weeks on a hundred dollars. The train (it was later called the Pelican) would take you to Washington, where you could get that special round trip fare to New York for three dollars and fifty cents. When I got there, I'd stand in Penn Station and sell my ticket back to Washington. All you had to do was wave the ticket in the air and somebody would snatch it up. They were as poor as I was, and with my deal, they got a ticket cheap and I made a little profit.
>
> I stayed at this place called the Barbizon, a hotel for women. It was $9 a week. Very strict: no men allowed above the mezzanine.

---

17. Photographs p. xvii.

That was when I was trying to peddle a book of my short stories. I'd go in and leave the manuscript on some publisher's desk, and I'd fully expect him to have a yes or no by the next day. . . . But it never worked like that, and I'd have to stay on a few days longer so I could take my manuscript to another publisher.[18]

I think it is very important that Eudora Welty wanted her photographs and her stories to be placed, and therefore received, in relation to each other. We who were denied that book can nevertheless find many connections between her work in the two genres – and by this I do not mean only in individual scenes or portraits. Look at a picture like the poignant 'Day's End/Jackson/1930s' (*Photographs*, p. 9) with its poor, obstinate, dignified black subject, remember that account (quoted above) of the genesis of 'A Worn Path', and then consider its opening:

It was December – a bright, frozen day in the early morning. Far out in the country there was an old Negro woman with her head in a red rag, coming along a path through the pinewoods. Her name was Phoenix Jackson. She was very old and small and she walked slowly in the dark pine shadows, moving a little from side to side in her steps, with the balanced heaviness and lightness of a pendulum in a grandfather clock. She carried a thin, small cane made from an umbrella, and with this she kept tapping the frozen earth in front of her.[19]

Do not the same questions arise from both the photo and the prose: who is this old woman, and what is she engaged on? What sort of journey is she undertaking, and for what purpose? What feelings is she bringing with her on her slow, determined trudge? The story can, obviously, try to answer them, whereas the photograph can only propose them – hence Eudora Welty's surely inevitable decision to concentrate on the story form. But how close to the photograph is Eudora Welty's method of presentation in that opening: the central figure arises and confronts the reader, just as her real-life sister did the young Eudora. She is seen very precisely, and in context; the story moving from the weather, to place, to physical appearance, stature,

18. C.E.W. p. 145–6.
19. C.S. p. 142.

dress, accoutrements. Her movement is caught, as in a series of stills, and emphasized by an inwardly illuminating comparison. Yet as in any successful photograph, detail is subsumed into a whole, and it must never detract from that. A photograph *is* a whole; the photographer's art is, above all, one of significant and harmonizing concentration – Eudora Welty was to practise that concentration throughout her entire *œuvre*.

But what of the photographer's own sensibility, state of mind, reactions, not to say personality? The very choice of subject made, the angle adopted, the moment decided on – all must say something about the person behind the camera. Isherwood's statement 'I am a camera' is one of intention only; it can never be true, and his very individual fiction is a proof of this. Eudora Welty tackles the problem of the personal nature of the 'eye' head-on in two early stories, 'A Memory' and 'The Key'. 'A Memory' is her most overt fictional statement of the conflicts that are inevitably present in artists as they make pictures of the life around them, and when she returned to the subject directly in *One Writer's Beginnings*, she singled out for special mention this particular story, in which the child, being remembered by the woman she became, is trying to act like a painter, in the belief that painters can see into the heart of things:

> I do not know even now what it was I was waiting to see: but in those days I was convinced that I almost saw it at every turn. To watch everything about me I regarded grimly and possessively as a *need*. All through this summer I had lain on the sand beside the small lake, with my hands squared over my eyes, finger-tips touching, looking out by this device to see everything: which appeared as a kind of projection. It did not matter to me what I looked at; from any observation I would conclude that a secret of life had been nearly revealed to me – for I was obsessed with notions about concealment, and from the smallest gesture of a stranger I would wrest what was to me a communication or a presentiment.[20]

---

20. C.S. pp. 75–6.

Written in a discursive manner that marks it out from other stories, 'A Memory' presents an eye who is centrally, preoccupyingly 'I' – introspective, fastidious (if not at times censorious), demanding that the life of others answers queries, and satisfies expectations and ideals, of her own. Her passion for imposing order on the heterogeneous muddle of the world by framing it with her fingers is intimately connected to her desire for life to be as she feels it ought to be: intense, attractive, personally interesting, directly addressed to the depths of her own being. It should surely be perpetually like that 'state of exultation' she knows when she is near the boy at school whom she loves (but to whom she has never spoken). Everything she has observed him doing – even swinging his foot as he sits at his desk, 'softly, barely not touching the floor' – can be translated into the static terms of a picture that she can take out later, like a snapshot in an album, to look at, use as a touchstone – more, a measuring-rod – for the rest of existence. Occasionally, of course, the boy, moving obliviously across her rapt loving line of vision, involuntarily imposes on her his own intransigent reality – in a Latin lesson, for instance:

> [he] bent suddenly over and brought his handkerchief to his face. I saw red – vermilion – blood flow over the handkerchief and his square-shaped hand; his nose had begun to bleed. I remember the very moment; several of the older girls laughed at the confusion and distraction; the boy rushed from the room; the teacher spoke sharply in warning.[21]

(How telling is that interpolation of the poetic word 'vermilion' to assist the narrator in bearing, or disguising, the – to her – crude unpleasantness of the boy's nosebleed!) She admits: 'Through some intensity I had come almost into a dual life, as observer and dreamer.' Lying on the beach of a small lake in her neighbourhood park, she tries to live this dual life; her fingers nicely frame – and therefore break up – the view of the park, while her inner eye can dwell on pictures of the boy who is her love. But her complacency is to be shattered; her vision is filled with very different and all-too-human objects: a family (or so one supposes them to be) in ribald jokey mood:

---

21. C.S. p. 76.

There were a man, two women, two young boys. They were brown and roughened, but not foreigners; when I was a child such people were called 'common'. They wore old and faded bathing-suits which did not hide either the energy or the fatigue of their bodies, but showed it exactly.[22]

(Surely these last words suggest that man and boys are from time to time tumescent in their excitement, as they stuff sand down the older woman's breasts? A refined, protected, young girl such as this 'I' would certainly have been shocked by this.)

'I still would not care to say which was the more real – the dream I could make blossom at will, or the sight of the bathers. I am presenting them, you see, as simultaneous.'[23] But the beauty of the dream causes the girl to be filled with real hatred for those she perforce observes, and – courageously – Eudora Welty does not mince her words. ('I wished they were all dead.') The observed themselves are completely unaware of what they have engendered in the observer; the man pouring sand inside the fat woman's bathing-suit takes in the watching girl as he looks round, but no more. His being proceeds literally regardless of her, and her reaction has no power whatsoever to change it. That is the first truth the artist as observer must recognize. The *wish* to change is another matter; the two must not be confused, otherwise a sense of reality is impaired.

But are not the girl's reactions real too? 'Sensation is sensation,' as Samuel Johnson said. And truly not to meet, recognize and record these would be another form of evasion. That is why the surrogate Eudora Welty insists on this presentation 'as simultaneous'. In the same way her passion for the boy she has never spoken to is a reality; just because it does not spring from demonstrable interaction, it is not to be dismissed. What 'A Memory' is saying is that the internal and the external have their own laws of being, deserving respect, though neither is beyond moral analysis. The danger comes when the line between the two is blurred. There are uncomfortable truths behind this story; the girl's contempt for the bathers, the bathers' crass insensitivity – neither is attractive.

---

22. ibid.
23. ibid.

If 'A Memory' is something of a warning to the photographer-writer's 'eye', then 'The Key' points to how things could be. In its assemblage of people in the waiting-room of a remote little station at night, 'The Key' brings Eudora Welty's actual photographic studies to mind. Physical situations impose on and translate people, even while they reveal important aspects of them. Two rows of people sit in discomfort and silence. Our attention – which has also been directed to the quiet, disturbed only by insects, 'their embroidering movements' outside, their thuddings inside – focuses first on a couple in early middle age (Ellie and Albert Morgan, who have brought with them a badly strapped suitcase that hangs open 'like a stupid pair of lips', and who have nothing to say to one another) and then on a solitary individual:

Among the others in the station was a strong-looking young man, alone, hatless, red-haired, who was standing by the wall while the rest sat on benches. He had a small key in his hand and was turning it over and over in his fingers, nervously passing it from one hand to the other, tossing it gently into the air and catching it again.

He stood and stared in distraction at the other people; so intent and so wide was his gaze that anyone who glanced after him seemed rocked like a small boat in the wake of a large one. There was an excess of energy about him that separated him from everyone else, but in the motion of his hands there was, instead of the craving for communication, something of reticence, even of secrecy, as the key rose and fell. You guessed that he was a stranger in town; he might have been a criminal or a gambler, but his eyes were widened with gentleness. His look, which travelled without stopping for long anywhere, was a hurried focusing of very tender and explicit regard.[24]

One of the dispossessed, disconnected young men whom the Depression produced and who stalk the pages of the literature of the times, he is both observer and observed. He possesses a quality that others note, and which should be imparted, yet he is not concerned with anything so obvious, so rational, as 'communication'.

---

24. C.S. p. 30.

The young man drops his key (a key unlocks; it is thus in itself a means of entry or release, rather than communication as such) and everyone turns round except Ellie and Albert Morgan. Watching them, seeing how Albert notices the key that has fallen at his feet, and then 'talks' to his wife with his fingers, we realize that they are deaf and dumb. Just as photographers cannot reproduce sounds, just as the most attentive novelists cannot know what is said between people when they are not there, so the young man – and with him the others in the waiting-room, and we too – is in the presence of a way of living that cannot be directly understood, let alone set down, *only apprehended*. This is the perfect metaphor for Eudora Welty's kind of art, whether photography or fiction. And while a key can have important consequences, as it does here, there is much that it cannot do. The young man, having lost that key to Albert Morgan, takes a second key from his pocket, and gives it (loses it) to Albert's wife:

> He did not wait to see any more, but went out abruptly into the night. He stood still for a moment, and reached out for a cigarette. As he held the match close he gazed straight ahead, and in his eyes, all at once wild and searching, there was certainly, besides the simple compassion in his regard, a look both restless and weary, very much used to the comic. You could see that he despised and saw the uselessness of the thing he had done.[25]

But if the gift was useless, maybe ultimately pointless – as a bestowal of himself, as a reception of essential emotions and preoccupations in the couple – the young man's action was profoundly successful. After all, readers already know that:

> He looked very strong and active; but there was a startling quality, a willingness to be for ever distracted, even disturbed, in the very reassurance of his body, some alertness which made his strength fluid and dissipated instead of withheld and greedily beautiful. His mouth by now did not seem an important thing about him; it was a medium for his activity, no doubt, but as he stood there frowning and smoking you felt some apprehension

---

25. C.S. p. 37.

that he would never express what might be the desire of his life in being young and strong, in standing apart in compassion, in making any intuitive present or sacrifice, or in any way of action at all – not because there was too much in the world demanding his strength, but because he was too deeply aware.

You felt a shock in glancing up at him, and when you looked away from the whole yellow room and closed your eyes, his intensity, as well as that of the room, seemed to have impressed the imagination with a shadow of itself, a blackness together with the light, the negative beside the positive. You felt as though some exact, skilful contact had been made between the surfaces of your hearts to make you aware, in some pattern, of his joy and his despair. You could feel the fullness and the emptiness of this stranger's life.[26]

The truly humane and artistic recorder is not necessarily the one most equipped with the capacity for decisive action, nor is action the only or the most desirable course. Eudora Welty – like the young man in this fine, seminal passage, where the comparison with photography is at last perfectly explicit – approaches her subject and takes the likenesses with her heart. One can say that the girl in 'A Memory' and the stranger in 'The Key' represent opposite directions for the imaginative observer, and that Eudora Welty chose the second way.

Both the young man and the ideas he contains recur throughout her work. His direct successor, for instance, appears in her first novel proper, *Delta Wedding*, in the character of George Fairchild. 'Everyone', we read in 'The Key', 'stared at [Albert's] impassioned little speech as it came from his fingers.' And different ways of apprehending others, especially when conventional communication is impossible, form a major motif in Eudora Welty's work. Another deaf and dumb protagonist features in 'First Love' (in *The Wide Net*); in *Delta Wedding* the strange child, Maureen, cannot talk properly. Loch Morrison, the sick boy in 'June Recital' (in *The Golden Apples*) is obliged to witness events in the next house through a telescope and upside-down (hanging from the tree outside his bedroom window). In 'Music from Spain' a

---

26. C.S. p. 33.

language barrier prevents Eugene from understanding or talking to the Spanish musician whom he follows all over San Francisco; in *The Optimist's Daughter* the judge's eyes are gravely impaired. This preoccupation surely started with trying to hold the Mississippians of the Depression within a camera lens.

The relationship between observer and observed is a dominant preoccupation of the stories in *A Curtain of Green*, and mutual recognition of another's 'thereness' – a recognition which, unlike the child's in 'A Memory', should be accompanied by studied practised kindness – is their overriding concern.

III

In 'Death of a Traveling Salesman' the salesman himself, R.J. Bowman – who travels through Mississippi for a shoe company and, in its red-clay hill country, learns truths more substantial and profound than any he has cared to learn before – is a clear analogue for the writer herself. Eudora Welty has confessed that it was in hilly Tishomingo County that she realized she was, above everything else, a writer, although she is anxious to stress: 'I didn't have a blinding moment of revelation.' (This was the territory she was to revisit fictionally for her longest, most ambitious work, *Losing Battles*, with its interesting echoes of this her very first story.)

Bowman, seasoned traveller though he is, has got lost on a 'rutted dirt path' such as those that the WPA was trying to replace in the mid 1930s. His aim is to reach Beulah by nightfall, but this seems increasingly unlikely. The name Beula(h) is to be found all over Mississippi, and often a town's main hotel is the Beula(h) (compare *The Ponder Heart*). The original founders of Mississippi, soaked as they were in the Protestant tradition, had in mind not only the land of Beula(h) in the Bible (Isaiah 62: 4) but also that in Bunyan's *Pilgrim's Progress*, which lies beyond the Valley of the Shadow of Death and the powers of Giant Despair, and within sight and sound of the Heavenly City. Here the name can be read as a pointer to Bowman's nearness to death. The irony of the story lies in his utterly secular nature, his unpreparedness – even though he has been seriously ill with influenza – for the momentous event that has to occur sooner or later.

Bowman is on his 'first day back on the road' in his Ford car, and not only has his fever returned, but his mind is bothered by unaccountable thoughts of his long-dead grandmother. He does not understand why; already, however, readers can. As in 'A Memory' we are simultaneously aware of what is without and what is within, the country through which Bowman is travelling and the images he entertains: 'The cloud floated there to one side like the bolster on his grandmother's bed. It went over a cabin on the edge of a hill, where two bare chinaberry trees clutched at the sky.'[27]

Bowman has a car accident; he has to get out of his Ford and see it roll over the edge of a ravine, into 'a tangle of immense grape vines'. The 'death' of the car both portends and symbolizes Bowman's own death; the Ford has been a part of his identity as a salesman. (And what more representative figure of twentieth-century America could be found – the Ford brand name proclaimed the hugest democracy in history, founded on ownership and consumerism? It is important that the title contains the generic.) Stripped of his vehicle, the traveller must travel unassisted, just as the individual goes alone into death. Yet the car also provides an ironic contrast to Bowman's fate. It will be rescued, set back on the road and 'turned to go back where she came from'. No such resurrection and second chance await Bowman himself.

As he walks to the nearest house, a smallholding, he suffers a minor heart attack, described in visual terms, as if it is an external experience, something that can be witnessed like the 'death' of the car. No early example of the parallelism between internal and external in Eudora Welty's work is more remarkable than this, a kind of X-ray picture of the event:

Then all of a sudden his heart began to behave strangely. Like a rocket set off, it began to leap and expand into uneven patterns of beats which showered into his brain, and he could not think. But in scattering and falling it made no noise. It shot up with great power, almost elation, and fell gently, like acrobats into nets. It began to pound profoundly, then waited irresponsibly, hitting in

---

27. C.S. p. 120.

some sort of inward mockery first at his ribs, then against his eyes, then under his shoulder blades, and against the roof of his mouth when he tried to say, 'Good afternoon, madam.'[28]

The heart attack Bowman has sustained, together with his continuing fever, account for his confused state of mind for the rest of the story. He takes some time to understand that the couple on whose hospitality he throws himself are husband and wife, and even to appreciate the woman's age (she is young enough to be pregnant). Yet his difficulty, on this his last day, is also what the entrant into life experiences. So, in following the dying Bowman's confusions, readers make a kind of baptismal journey into unknown territory; everything, everybody, takes some discerning, and possesses multiple aspects, multiple identities, leading to a single truth: that the complexity of life is beyond our making or knowing, and becomes bearable only when this truth is accepted.

To come to this, Bowman has to unlearn much: to unlearn what society has imposed on him, screening him from deeper reality. "'I have a nice line in women's low-priced shoes . . .'" he says, reeling from the heart attack, to the bewildered young woman. And later, only minutes from death, watching the hard-earned fire also die – they have had to borrow fire ('borry some fire') to warm their unexpected guest – he finds himself 'repeating quietly: "There will be special reduced prices on all footwear during the month of January."'

The couple on whom he has stumbled take on the properties of woman and man *tout court*, from the Edenic couple onwards. Thus they have the salesman's needs of a lifetime focused on them:

> . . . he wanted to leap up, to say to her, I have been sick and I found out then, only then, how lonely I am. Is it too late? My heart puts up a struggle inside me, and you may have heard it, protesting against emptiness . . . It should be full, he would rush on to tell her, thinking of his heart now as a deep lake, it should be holding love like other hearts. It should be flooded with love. There would be a warm spring day. . . . Come and stand in my heart, whoever you are, and a whole river would cover

28. C.S. p. 121.

your feet and rise higher and take your knees in whirlpools, and draw you down to itself, your whole body, your heart too.[29]

The observers have a life of their own – the child they are soon to have is a source of great joy to them, dour though they seem – one which the plight of their visitor cannot touch. But while the couple do not provide all that Bowman's ailing heart is now craving, they are his (mostly unconscious) conductors to the elements of life – to fire (after all, the story began as a result of Eudora Welty's hearing about a man who had to 'borry some fire'), to that water of life, whisky, to water itself.

The discovery of water is most imaginatively done. Bowman becomes aware of a significant sound. '"You might hear the stream,"' the woman admits grudgingly, when he asks. Then, in the night, he hears the sound again, prompting him to perhaps the most extraordinary and consequential thoughts of his life. He wishes that the child the woman is carrying were his (wanting continuity in life), and that he could 'get back to where he had been before'. But where is that? Not where he set out from, surely. We have no awareness of any cherished places in Bowman's past. No, it must be the placeless, timeless realm outside this life that he is thinking of, to which dying could return him.

One of the story's most mysterious passages, prophetic of the later writer, occurs after Sonny has left his house to get Bowman's car out of the ravine:

> In a few minutes Sonny passed under the window with a rope, and there was a brown mule with quivering, shining, purple-looking ears. The mule actually looked in the window. Under its eyelashes it turned target-like eyes into his. Bowman averted his head and saw the woman looking serenely back at the mule, with only satisfaction in her face.[30]

To try to explain the mule in mythological terms, as some commentators have done, is, I believe, to be reductive, just as it is to liken the fire-borrowing Sonny to fire-stealing Prometheus. Rather, Eudora

---

29. C.S. p. 125.
30. C.S. p. 124.

Welty has selected components of such depth that they can call forth mythopoeic dimensions. The operative word in the passage just quoted is surely 'target-like', for what can the mind of a mule 'target'? We cannot know, yet the reality of the animal's glance *is*; furthermore, because it is, it elicits response. The possibilities for some level of dialogues in life between observer and observed are frighteningly and wonderfully limitless.

In 'A Piece of News' a young wife, Ruby Fisher, reads an old newspaper story that seems to be about herself: 'Mrs Ruby Fisher had the misfortune to be shot in the leg by her husband this week.' Of course it is a different Ruby Fisher (anyway, it is a Tennessee newspaper), but her sense of identity has been jolted. Taking place against marvellously evoked rainfall, the story dramatizes the limitations and complexity of our knowledge – of ourselves and others; and a significant comment on Ruby can extend to almost all artists' human subjects: 'When she was still, there was a passivity about her, or a deception of passivity, that was not really passive at all. There was something in her that never stopped.'[31]

'Flowers for Marjorie' is one of Eudora Welty's few stories that are set outside the South – in Depression-hit New York – but the South is ever-present in it, for Howard, the young man at its centre, is a Mississippian who has come north in vain to look for work. Mississippian too is Marjorie, his young, soft-mannered, pregnant wife, whom he kills. 'It was hard to remember, in this city of dark, nervous, loud-spoken women, that in Victory, Mississippi, all girls were like Marjorie – and that Marjorie was in turn like his home.'[32]

The very opening sentence of the story is grimly ironic: 'He was one of the modest, the shy, the sandy-haired – one of those who would always have preferred waiting to one side . . .'[33] – a natural passive subject for a passing photographer. But, the times are against him, are galvanizing even the most reluctant into a bitter intensity of response.

---

31. C.S. p. 13.
32. C.S. p. 99.
33. C.S. p. 98.

'Work?' he said sternly, backing away from her, speaking loudly from the middle of the room, almost as if he copied his pose and his voice somehow from the agitators in the park. 'When did I ever work? A year ago . . . six months . . . back in Mississippi . . . I've forgotten! Time isn't as easy to count up as you think! I wouldn't know what to do now if they give me work. I've forgotten! It's all past now. . . . And I don't believe it any more – they won't give me work now. They never will – '

'Why, Howard, you don't even hope you'll find work any more,' she whispered.

'Just because you're bound to have a baby, just because that's a thing that's bound to happen, just because you can't go around for ever with a baby inside your belly, and it will really happen that the baby is born – that doesn't mean everything else is going to happen and change!' He shouted across at her desperately, leaning across the wall. 'That doesn't mean that I will find work! It doesn't mean we aren't starving to death!'[34]

The Depression is one of the characters in this story, and certainly the most powerful one. Such is its power that Howard – unhappy, exhausted, out of his normal wits – murders his wife almost without understanding what he is doing; his hatred of his situation, and of Marjorie's part in it, takes him over:

Howard walked unsteadily about and came to the stove. He picked up a small clean bent saucepan, and put it down again. They had taken it with them wherever they had moved, from room to room. His hand went to the objects on the shelf as if he were blind. He got hold of the butcher knife. Holding it gently, he turned toward Marjorie.

'Howard, what are you going to do?' she murmured in a patient, lullaby-like voice, as she had asked him so many times.

They were both now far away, remote from each other, detached. Like a flash of lightning he changed his hold on the knife and thrust it under her breast.[35]

---

34. C.S. pp. 100–01.
35. C.S. p. 101.

The surprise of his action to him is further expressed in the near-hallucinatory but somehow guiltless state in which he walks about New York, witnessing Depression scenes that could indeed have been recorded by an urban Walker Evans or a Mass Observationist a year or two earlier, but filtered through psychic stress, through a mind brought by suffering out onto the far side of reason – and morality. Howard's encounters following the murder constitute a veritable paradigm of New York life: Sixth Avenue, the doughnut machine, the bric-a-brac shops, the purposeless crowds, the subway with its graffiti, the beggars, the bar with the nickelodeon, the WPA office, the arcade into which he passes, only to be greeted with:

> 'You are the ten millionth person to enter Radio City, and you will broadcast over a nationwide red-and-blue network tonight at six o'clock. What is your name, address, and phone number? Are you married? Accept these roses and the key to the city.'[36]

Here the writing is very close (both in richness of language and in feeling) to Federico García Lorca's tumultuous *El poeta en Nueva York* (*Poet in New York*), a poem cycle also born of the Depression (indeed, for a while Eudora Welty and Lorca were in New York City at the same time):

> Los primeros que salen comprenden con sus huesos
> que no habrá paraíso ni amores deshojados:
> saben que van al cieno de numeros y leyes,
> a los juegos sin arte, a sudores sin fruto.

> La luz es sepultada por cadenas y ruidos
> en impúdico reto de ciencia sin raíces.
> Por los barrios hay gentes que vacilan insomnes
> como recíen salidas de un naufragio de sangre.

> (Those who go out early know in their bones
> there will be no paradise or loves that bloom or die:
> they know they will be mired in numbers and laws,
> in mindless games, in fruitless labors.

---

36. C.S. p. 104.

The light is buried under chains and noises
in an impudent challenge to rootless science.
And crowds stagger sleeplessly through the boroughs
as if they had just escaped a shipwreck of blood.)[37]

'Naufragio de sangre', 'shipwreck of blood', is as good a phrase as any
to describe Howard's terrible condition at the story's end. Indelibly
Eudora Welty's, this story, with its overt violence, is unlike any later
one – though its legacy can, I think, be found in the stories in *The
Golden Apples* about the MacLain twins: 'The Whole World Knows'
and 'Music from Spain'. And the concept of the power of a moment –
which is to be so vital throughout her work – is particularly boldly
treated here. After killing his young wife Howard throws his clock out
of the window; time can be said to stop as it crashes to the ground far
below; in a sense, of course, that moment has made time stop anyway
for Howard, and for murdered Marjorie, as is made quite explicit
towards the end.

'Lily Daw and the Three Ladies' is a slighter, more cheerful tale
about a young girl whom her community thinks is best placed in the
Ellisville Institute for the Feeble Minded in Mississippi, but who
takes the question of her future into her own hands – by deciding
to get married. In its juxtaposition of the single, isolated person with
the choric, it anticipates patterns of later work – again, most notably,
the stories that make up *The Golden Apples*.

'Old Mr Marblehall' takes us to Natchez to meet one of that elegant
historic Mississippi town's respectable older citizens:

> There has been an old Mr Marblehall in Natchez ever since the
> first one arrived back in 1818 – with a theatrical presentation
> of Otway's *Venice*, ending with *A Laughable Combat between
> Two Blind Fiddlers* – an actor![38]

(This, perhaps, is the first instance of Eudora Welty's growing awareness of the historical/cultural background to her characters' lives: she
became an ardent historicist.) This present-day Mr Marblehall is very

---

37. 'La aurora', from Federico García Lorca, *El poeta en Nueva York* (Poet in New York),
transl. Greg Simon and Steven F. White, Viking (1989).
38. C.S. p. 93.

probably a bigamist with a second family, yet such is the enervated quality of life in Natchez, that he may well get away with it. Perhaps the humorous tone here is a little too insistent. And perhaps Mr Marblehall, who dreams that 'he is a great blazing butterfly stitching up a net', is not wholly appropriate for this sustained tone. 'The Whistle', on the other hand, presents the poverty-stricken lives of a middle-aged married couple with a tragic contained poetry; the dreams the wife Sara has of their past, when they were less poor, less cold, when tomato-growing led to the exuberant festivities of the tomato-shipping season, are keenly felt. (Sara's memories take us to Eudora Welty's photograph 'Tomato-packers' Recess/Copiah County, 1936'.)

'A Curtain of Green' is the first of Eudora Welty's stories to feature a black person, and it provides an extremely interesting variant on her theme of the significant moment. After her husband's death Mrs Larkin – after whose father-in-law her little town had been named – devotes herself to (somewhat ill-informed) gardening:

> The daily summer rains could only increase her vigilance and her already excessive energy. And yet Mrs Larkin rarely cut, separated, tied back . . . To a certain extent she seemed not to seek for order, but to allow an over-flowering, as if she consciously ventured for ever a little farther, a little deeper, into her life in the garden.[39]

Her helper in the garden is Jamey, a little black boy. The fear that has stalked her ever since her husband's fatal accident, caused by a falling tree, gets the better of her, and is released in the form of a rush of irritation at Jamey, even for his docility, his passivity. She suddenly appreciates – armed as she is with a hoe – how she could hurt him:

> When she was directly behind him, she stood quite still for a moment, in the queer sheathed manner she had before beginning her gardening in the morning. Then she raised the hoe above her head; the clumsy sleeves both fell back, exposing the thin, unsunburned whiteness of her arms, the shocking fact of their youth.

---

39. C.S. p. 108.

She gripped the handle tightly, tightly, as though convinced that the wood of the handle could feel, and that all her strength could indent its surface with pain. The head of Jamey, bent there below her, seemed witless, terrifying, wonderful, almost inaccessible to her, and yet in its explicit nearness meant surely for destruction, with its clustered hot woolly hair, its intricate, glistening ears, its small brown branching streams of sweat, the bowed head holding so obviously and so deftly its ridiculous dream.[40]

The contrasts between the two – the murderous woman and the unaware innocent – are potent: old versus young, educated versus uneducated, female versus male, white versus black. In the malignity of the moment countless scores are being entertained for the paying off; no matter that the recipient of the blow is an inadequate representative of all those ills. In fact, the rain comes down abruptly (the title clearly contains the suggestion of a theatre curtain) and it is Mrs Larkin who has an attack, requiring help from Jamey, who turns out to have been not so utterly unaware of the situation after all: 'He remembered how something had filled him with stillness when he felt her standing there behind him looking down at him, and he would not have turned around at that moment for anything in the world.'[41] The story then describes a dance, a sequence of exploiter and exploited, in which, however, the roles can suddenly be reversed. There is impressive compactness and tautness here.

'Petrified Man' has enjoyed popularity and fame; Katherine Anne Porter draws attention to it in her introduction – it offers: 'a fine clinical study of vulgarity – vulgarity absolute, chemically pure, exposed mercilessly to its final subhuman depths'.[42] But perhaps that description is too austere; vulgarity must be reckoned – and surely is reckoned here – a failure in sensibility, regrettable rather than morally reprehensible. (Readers must not commit the 'crime' of the girl in 'A Memory'.) Here the backbiting gossip of the women in the beauty parlour serves as the vehicle for the presentation of Mr Petrie, a rapist (wanted on four charges) who hides from the law in a travelling freak

40. C.S. p. 110.
41. C.S. p. 112.
42. Introduction to first edition ofr *A Curtain of Green*, p. 11.

show. Maybe, however, the gossip is somewhat too prolix (as the author seems now to think), is given somewhat too much attention in its own right, so that Mr Petrie's story (which points up the ethical confusions of the fairground world) is slightly submerged.

Another travelling salesman – this one deals in office supplies, and is only thirty years old – is the central figure in 'The Hitch-Hikers', published three years after 'Death of a Traveling Salesman' and, I consider, Eudora Welty's first truly major achievement. Many years later Reynolds Price told her that she had written no story better than 'Death of a Traveling Salesman' (and he is second to none in his admiration for her work), but while it is an astonishing production for so young and untried a writer, Eudora Welty's genius was to lie in finding the revelatory, the numinous, in the humdrum or the arcane (and often both); whereas her choice of subject matter in her first story had been in favour of the portentous.

Just how rich 'The Hitch-Hikers' is was revealed to me when I taught it at Millsaps College. One student would praise its feeling and still valid representation of the Delta Country; another saw in the doomed musician a reworking of – a complex variant on – the story of Orpheus. Its theme, the moral fruit of Eudora Welty's long travels across Mississippi, is that even people encountered in a wholly casual spirit, whom we choose to register only superficially, have an irreducible life of their own that can erupt and spill over us, threatening our equilibrium – even our very existence.

The photographic/cinematic nature of its beginning is noteworthy, since its surface calm is – much to its protagonist's surprise – to be cruelly broken on account of inner components that should have been apparent to the deeply observant:

> Towards evening, somewhere in the middle of the Delta, he slowed down to pick up two hitch-hikers. One of them stood still by the side of the pavement, with his foot stuck out like an old root, but the other was playing a yellow guitar which caught the late sun as it came in a long straight bar across the fields.
>
> Harris would get sleepy driving. On the road he did some things rather out of a dream. And the recurring sight of hitch-

hikers waiting against the sky gave him the flash of a sensation he had known as a child: standing still, with nothing to touch him, feeling tall and having the world come all at once into its round shape underfoot and rush and turn through space and make his stand very precarious and lonely. He opened the car door.[43]

The two paragraphs contrast: the first is objective, and gives the general geographic context 'somewhere in the middle of the Delta' and the particular temporal moment, the physical moment of encounter itself (the moment of the clicking of the shutter): the sun-shaft striking the yellow guitar. The second paragraph is subjective, of a subjectivity at once imposed on and stimulated by the externals of the first: Harris's private boyhood apprehension of the turning world. This memory has perhaps surfaced because of some intuitive knowledge he has of the consequences of stopping for these two men, even if he cannot know the exact sorry little tragedy which will ensue (and demonstrate that the world *does* indeed turn, that lives *do* come to an end – and for all that, the world goes on turning).

Tom Harris's meeting with the two men brings into juxtaposition representatives of 1930s maleness – the salesman with the car (who is past his first youth) and the two hobos, one of whom is a guitar-player – and will therefore involve the humours, dreams, romanticisms that go with this condition, all ultimately unsatisfying, and as redolent of restlessness, and loneliness as the road at sunset itself. This is the world of which Woody Guthrie was laureate. As he drives through the Delta towards Memphis, Harris is 'thinking he would like to do something that night', and when he comes to the little town of Dulcie, it is clear that he has an understanding with a woman there, Ruth, and is a popular figure at its parties – easy come, easy go. Country music is the language all the men know; Tom Harris listens to it on his radio; the guitar-player, familiar with it from his own early years, plays it:

They rode without talking while the sun went down in red clouds and the radio programme changed a few times. Harris switched on his lights. Once the man with the guitar started to sing 'The One Rose That's Left in My Heart' which came over the air,

---

43. C.S. p. 62.

played by the Aloha Boys. Then in shyness he stopped, but made a streak on the radio dial with his blackly calloused fingertip.

'I 'ppreciate them big 'lectric gittars some have,' he said.[44]

But playing the guitar has not enabled the speaker to earn any kind of living for himself, and from the first Harris realizes this, even while he asks him: '"Couldn't you stop somewhere along here and make money playing this?"'[45] His feeling for the guitar is part of the strong, if unacknowledged, bond uniting him, an apparently respectable man in employment, with the vagrants; they are really from the same human stable, always on the move, always seeking, even though Harris can be described as 'sent by heaven' by an enthusiastic young woman, while the tramps repel all – the guitar-player with his calloused fingertips, his silent companion with his sullen manner and his belches. Perhaps this bond is first brought home when all three light up – three men with cigarettes heading north, sitting side by side, as they might in a photograph by Eudora Welty herself.

The line of causality in this story can be perceived only with hindsight, so thorough is the author's empathy with Harris, with his casual approach to events. It is her triumph that on rereadings one can partake of the seeming inconsequentiality of Tom Harris's experiences, and yet find the dark logical line running through them.

Before Harris reaches Dulcie he stops at a hamburger joint, and buys three hamburgers and three bottles of beer. At Dulcie he checks into the Dulcie Hotel, where he is a familiar guest. While Harris is asking Mr Gene, the proprietor, if the tramps can sleep on the back porch (for it goes without saying that they would not be welcome in the hotel itself), violent action erupts but – appropriately, for this most subtle treatment of the observer/observed theme – Tom Harris does not witness it; therefore the reader does not either. It happens beyond the lens of the story, outside the frame, yet it is a result of what went on within and will further affect that frame.

---

44. C.S. pp. 62–3.
45. C.S. p. 64.

A boy bursts into the hotel with the news:

'I knew that was your car, Mr Harris,' said the boy. He was nervously trying to tuck a Bing Crosby cretonne shirt into his pants like a real shirt. Then he looked up and said, 'They was tryin' to take your car, and down the street one of 'em like to bust the other one's head wide op'n with a bottle. Looks like you would 'a' heard the commotion. Everybody's out there. I said, "That's Mr Tom Harris's car, look at the out-of-town licence and look at all the stuff he all the time carries around with him, all bloody."'[46]

It is the man with the guitar who has been struck – with a beer bottle by his silent, sulky companion. Harris takes the injured man to the local hospital, while the other man is arrested and, as there is no room in the gaol for him ('got a nigger [there] already') is, with tragicomic irony, locked up in a room next to Tom Harris's own in the Dulcie Hotel itself. Harris proceeds to contact Ruth; it transpires that she is having a party, and has got a date for him. The incident with the hitch-hikers makes Harris something of a celebrity in the eyes of her guests, especially in those of his date, Carol Thames. Harris – tired, his mind full of the assault – extricates himself from the party and goes back to the hotel, but Carol follows him and rouses him into going to the All-Nite for a Coke. She tells him that though he hadn't recognized her, they had known one another before, down on the Gulf, when she had been crazy about him. The next morning Harris finds out that during this time the guitar-player has died.

These bare happenings form a whole which constitutes a metaphoric statement about transitoriness, contingency, marginality, our perpetual vulnerability to the unpredictable emotions of others. Densely worked, 'The Hitch-Hikers' yields treasures of both interior and exterior observation with each reading; here I can hope to indicate only some of its more significant features.

As they pull out of the hamburger joint, the man with the guitar sings out the words 'Aw river!'. The other lifts his empty beer bottle and looks 'beseechingly' at his mate, who realizes what he wants.

46. C.S. p. 66.

'"Drive back, mister,"' he tells Harris, '"Sobby forgot to give her" (the girl at the joint) "back her bottle."' But Harris feels that to do so would be to acknowledge some authority in the hobo which he – a man with a job – is reluctant to accord him. Pleasant-natured though he is, Harris is asserting both his social and his psychological superiority when he refuses this request. Had he complied, of course, the silent man would have had no weapon with which to kill his friend, and who knows? – maybe in that 'beseeching' look he was giving an unconscious intimation of what he knew he was capable of. So the action of the story turns on a decision so small that no one – including the reader, on first reading – realizes that it was made at all. All Harris says is a casual (if firm) '"Too late!"'. Certainly the request does not seem to stick in his own mind, for when he tells the story to his admiring friends at Ruth's party, he omits it, whereas he includes what the guitar-player sang out as they left the joint. And that, in turn, makes an impression on Carol: '"Aw river"' said the girl in the white dress. "Isn't that what the little man said?"[47] (And the word 'river' is one of great metaphoric resonance – the Mississippi itself, which created the Delta Country, the river of life, and the river of death, which will soon bear the guitar-player away.)

The Dulcie Hotel contributes richly to the development of the story's themes. It has 'been about a month to the day' since Harris stayed there last, but within a month much can happen (as it can in a night, as this story shows); Time moves inexorably on, and we should take nothing for granted. The hotel has an old dog, who becomes a medium for communicating this truth – and more (Eudora Welty has progressed here from the mule in 'Death of a Traveling Salesman'): he is a sentient being with emotional importance for other beings (notably his owner, the hotel proprietor Mr Gene, and Harris himself:

'Mike's sick. Come here, Mike, it's just old Harris passin' through.'
    Mike was an ancient collie dog. He rose from a quilt near the door and moved over the square brown rug, stiffly, like a table walking, and shoved himself between the men, swinging his long

---

47. C.S. p. 71.

head from Mr Gene's hand to Harris's and bearing down motion-
less with his jaw in Harris's palm.

'You sick, Mike?' asked Harris.

'Dyin' of old age, that's what he's doin'!' blurted the proprietor
as if in anger.

Harris began to stroke the dog, but the familiarity in his hands
changed to slowness and hesitancy. Mike looked up out of his eyes.

'His spirit's gone. You see?' said Mr Gene pleadingly.[48]

This moving passage (how imaginative is the choice of the word
'pleadingly'!) shows Eudora Welty herself fulfilling one of the
story's demands: that we should not limit our powers of compassion-
ate empathy, but extend them as far as we can. And we can extend them
to the dog's owner himself, who – with his attachment to Mike, his
drinking, his need for affection and conversation – maybe suggests
what Harris, still dashing and sexy at thirty, could become: it is implied
that he too has – or has had – a drink problem.

The treatment of the young woman, his date at Ruth's party, further
endorses the idea that lives which manifest themselves only in the
background must be taken – to say the least – with full seriousness.
We are never quite sure that Carol *did* know Harris down on the coast;
it is possible that she is confusing him, as he suggests, with someone
else. Yet the point remains. As in 'A Memory', with the narrator's love
for the boy with the nosebleed, Harris (or pseudo-Harris) has a valid
reality of his own in the young woman's mind, one which must be
respected – as indeed he does respect it. '"I appreciate it. . . .' he tells
her, "You're sweet."'

Harris is marvellously drawn; in no way a remarkable person –
indeed, possibly (to outward eyes, anyway) rather commonplace – he
is seen as unfailingly – and, perhaps, unknowingly – exercising
his heart. He is, almost unconsciously, a good man: he does his best for
the hobos, both before and after the violent incident; he is forgiving,
not least to them; he behaves with kindness and respect to those he
encounters, accepting Carol's tears and tributes as he accepts
the disconcerting news that the man with the guitar, the hobo he

---

48. C.S. pp. 65–6.

had preferred, had been the one to think of running off with his car.

Yet he moves through life – analogous here both to the photographer and to all artists exercising their gifts – unattached. He deserves the name 'Hitch-Hiker' as much as the hobos do. He too is getting rides from one place to another, from one set of people to another, refusing binding commitment. His unsatisfactory itinerant life is, in interesting ironic ways, a respectable and more lucrative version of the tramps'. And in all this, does he not also stand for the male in contemporary society (American above all) – expected to be on the go, to be at the ready, to be 'cool', not encouraged to dig down, to go deep? No passage in Eudora Welty's earlier work is more affecting than the one in which the truth behind his life breaks over Harris like a wave over a bather:

> he shut his eyes suddenly. When they were closed, in the red darkness he felt all patience leave him. It was like the beginning of desire . . . he could forgive nothing in this evening. But it was too like other evenings, this town too like other towns, for him to move out of this lying still clothed on the bed, even into comfort or despair. Even the rain – there was often rain, there was often a party, and there had been other violence not of his doing – other fights, not quite so pointless, but fights in his car; fights, unheralded confessions, sudden love-making – none of any of this his, not his to keep, but belonging to the people of these towns he passed through, coming out of their rooted pasts and their mock rambles, coming out of their time. He himself had no time. He was free; helpless.[49]

And with these thoughts we are back at the opening of the story, with Harris's boyhood fantasy of the precariousness and loneliness of standing upon the turning earth.

The story ends with Harris handing 'the po' kilt man's gittar' to the 'little coloured boy' who wanted it. Music being the great unifying bond between black and white, in the South above all places, the gift has a restorative quality, makes the story end on an upturn (just as

49. C.S. pp. 71–2.

Harris, 'fresh from the barber-shop', will go on his way and recover his spirits). Those who know *El poeta en Nueva York* will recall the Spanish poet's vision of a black child heralding America's regeneration –

Quiero que . . .
. . . un niño negro anuncie a los blancos del oro
la llegada del reino de la espiga.

I want . . .
. . . a black child to announce to the moneyed whites the arrival
of the kingdom of corn.[50]

– and perhaps see an avatar of him here, the sheer pressure of the writer's understanding endowing symbolic proportions on a child who comes as naturally into the story as he arose from the street of the Delta town.

A black boy features unforgettably in 'Keela, the Outcast Indian Maiden'. '"The way it started was," said Steve, [the young white man whom the horror of the situation has never left] "the show was just travellin' along in ole trucks through the country, and just seen this little deformed nigger man sittin' on a fence, and just took it. It couldn't help it."'[51] What deep and intolerable truths lie in that dehumanizing 'it' – used, indeed, throughout the vernacular parts of the narrative. Little Lee Roy, the crippled 'nigger man', is dressed up as an Indian girl and made to bite off the heads of live chickens. '"They had to whup it some to make it eat all the chickens."'
Eudora Welty says:

'Someone told me about something like "Keela . . ." which I'd never heard of. . . . Nothing in this world would have induced me to go and look at the show. It's a psychological story. . . . I was interested in what sort of points of view people could have toward such an atrocious thing, including that of the victim himself.'[52]

---

50. 'Oda a Walt Whitman', from Federico García Lorca, *El poeta en Nueva York*, trans. Paul Binding.
51. C.S. p. 43.
52. C.E.W. p. 179.

It is a psychological story with general relevance, for Eudora Welty is concerned with the workings of conscience, the dignity of her subjects – the possible attitudes to adopt when one is confronted by pain and evil not of one's own making. It marks a further extension of her powers of compassion.

Little Lee Roy survives – though surely at a price. In order to do so he has to translate his hideous sufferings into something they were not; he copes with the pain of his past by at first feigning and then acting out a pride in what he was made to do. Consequently he is able to boast to his children of '"de ole times when I use to be wid the circus"'. Indeed, it is questionable whether he has not survived better than the guilt-ridden Steve (another casualty of worklessness, another virtual itinerant) who had sold tickets for the revolting exhibition and even advertised it through a pasteboard megaphone, and who has long been disturbed by his memories. '"You know,"' says Steve, telling his companion of the arrival of the white man who is to be the black boy's deliverer:

> 'when that man laid out his open hand on the boards, why . . . it didn't know what to do. Then it drug itself to where the fella was standin' an' leaned down an' grabbed holt on to that white man's hand as tight as it could an' cried like a baby. . . . It wanted him to help it. So the man said, "Do you wanta get out of this place, whoever you are?" An' it never answered – none of us knowed it could talk – but it just wouldn't let that man's hand a-loose. It hung on, cryin' like a baby . . .'[53]

Even across the gulf of years, I find this almost unbearably distressing.

The intense artistry of 'The Hitch-Hikers' must have given Eudora Welty new confidence in her powers, for not only is 'Keela, the Outcast Indian Maiden' a fine story, but its successors are among her most brilliant productions: 'A Worn Path', 'Why I Live at the P.O.', 'Powerhouse' and 'The Key'. 'Why I Live at the P.O.' has an aural nature, for it is a monologue that reveals much of the speaker and her life, far more than she realizes. This inspired and justly celebrated story will be considered with *The Ponder Heart*, its next of kin. Here I will

---

53. C.E.W. pp. 42–3.

content myself with saying that the importance of voice in it does not affect its relationship with the photography; the speaker sits herself down in front of the camera (that is to say, in front of the reader), and fills the entire lens, so determined is she to be taken notice of!

'A Worn Path' began when Eudora Welty saw an old black woman move across her line of vision and disappear into the woods. In conversation with the distinguished Mississippi folklorist Bill Ferris, she amplifies this; they have been discussing folk-knowledge – part-intuitive, part gained through close attention to natural detail – and Bill has told her how a mule trader, Ray Lum, could always tell if a dog was heading for home or not by the way he walked. Eudora Welty says:

And it's like your friend, Mr Lum said – I knew [the old black woman] was going somewhere. I knew that she was bent on an errand, even at that distance. It was not anything casual. It was a purposeful, measured journey that she was making. And what I felt was . . . that you wouldn't go on an errand like that, so purposefully, unless it were for someone else, you know. Unless it were like an emergency. And so I made it into a story by making it the one you'd be most likely to go for – a child. And so I wrote that. But another time, on this same road, and in similar circumstances, an old woman came down the road – I don't know whether she was the same one or not. But she stopped and talked to us, and she used the words to me, 'I was too old at the Surrender.' Which was about something else – maybe it was learning to read and write. I don't know. But that was indelible in my mind. '. . . too old at the Surrender.' And so I put that into my story because it belonged in it.[54]

Phoenix Jackson moves into our vision as she moved into the author's; we come closer to her and marvel at the obstinate beauties of her aged appearance – for if, as she says later, echoing that real old woman, she was 'too old at the Surrender' (of the South on 9 April 1865), she must be getting on for ninety. This is photography at its most tender and most attentive:

---

54. C.E.W. pp. 167–8.

Her eyes were blue with age. Her skin had a pattern all its own of numberless branching wrinkles and as though a whole little tree stood in the middle of her forehead, but a golden colour ran underneath, and the two knobs of her cheeks were illuminated by a yellow burning under the dark.[55]

Instead of letting her disappear into the woods, Eudora Welty follows her through them and out the other side – on her way where? – and becomes privy to her encounters, her thoughts, her rhetorical outbursts – for she talks to herself, and addresses the plants and animals as she goes – and also to her fantasies, for her mind is confused; she even sees a little boy bringing her a slice of marble-cake, which, of course, vanishes as she tries to take it. Not until the end, however, do we become aware of the purpose of this journey. Throughout its length she seems to be propelled, often with difficulty, by instinct, by an extra sense, but she is never in doubt of the route: '"Up through pines," she said at length. "Now down through oaks."' And again:

> In a ravine she went where a spring was silently flowing through a hollow log. Old Phoenix bent and drank. 'Sweet-gum makes the water sweet,' she said, and drank more. 'Nobody knows who made this well, for it was here when I was born.'[56]

Even as Natchez shines ahead, all lit up for Christmas, and its bells ring out, we are still ignorant of the purpose of her journey. Even at the hospital, her destination, we have to wait for the nurse to say why Phoenix is there, for Phoenix herself seems abstracted, tired after her journey. She has come, as she does, 'just as regular as clockwork', for her grandson's medicine. He is a 'charity case'.

> 'Is his throat any better?' asked the nurse. 'Aunt Phoenix, don't you hear me? Is your grandson's throat any better since the last time you came for the medicine?'
> With her hands on her knees, the old woman waited, silent, erect and motionless, just as if she were in armour.
> 'You mustn't take up our time this way, Aunt Phoenix,' the

---

55. C.S. p. 142.
56. C.S. p. 144.

nurse said. 'Tell us quickly about your grandson, and get it over. He isn't dead, is he?'

At last there came a flicker and then a flame of comprehension across her face, and she spoke.

'My grandson. It was my memory had left me. There I sat and forgot why I made my long trip.'

'Forgot?' The nurse frowned. 'After you came so far?'

Then Phoenix was like an old woman begging a dignified forgiveness for waking up frightened in the night. 'I never did go to school, I was too old at the Surrender,' she said in a soft voice. 'I'm an old woman without an education. It was my memory fail me. My little grandson he is just the same, and I forgot it in the coming.'[57]

In the fifty years that have passed since the publication of this story Eudora Welty has been besieged with letters arising from this quietly moving interchange, asking whether that little grandson were really alive or dead. Eudora deals with the very interesting questions about the *art* of the short story that this demand for information raises in her essay 'Is Phoenix Jackson's Grandson Really Dead?':

> . . . you work all your life to find your way, through all the obstructions and the false appearances and the upsets you may have brought on yourself, to reach a meaning – using inventions of your imagination, perhaps helped out by your dreams and bits of good luck . . . you have to assume that what you are working in aid of is life, not death.
>
> But you would make the trip anyway – wouldn't you? – just on hope.[58]

However, the knowledge of whether he is dead or not is quite irrelevant to the story itself; Phoenix's mind is old, as worn as the path of the title, and thus errant, unable to make the keen distinction between memory and actuality, fact and fantasy, as younger minds do. Has she not already spoken to a boy who isn't there, and taken a scarecrow for a dancing man? Our inability to be sure whether her grandson is alive

---

57. C.S. pp. 147–8.
58. Eye p. 162.

or not corresponds with the state of affairs in Phoenix's own mind; no certainty is possible. When she leaves the hospital, he has become alive again, thanks to the dialogue quoted above – alive enough for her to want to buy him (in a beautiful passage) a little Christmas windmill: '"He going to find it hard to believe there such a thing in the world."' And that is an end to it.

Perhaps the most remarkable part of the story, however, comes earlier, almost exactly at its halfway point. It has provoked rather less discussion than the matter of the grandson's actual existence, but is equally important to the overall meaning. On her journey, Phoenix comes across a young white man, a hunter with a dog; he lifts her up from where she has fallen and is, according to his rather arrogant lights, helpful and friendly enough. As a result of his ministrations a nickel falls out of his pocket. Phoenix sees it, diverts his attention (cunningly and effectively), and then:

> Her fingers slid down and along the ground under the piece of money with the grace and care they would have in lifting an egg from under a sitting hen. Then she slowly straightened up, she stood erect, and the nickel was in her apron pocket. A bird flew by. Her lips moved. 'God watching me the whole time. I come to stealing.'[59]

No moral judgement is passed here; how could it be? The curious, the remarkable thing about this episode is that it in no way impairs our perception of Phoenix as a virtuous, praiseworthy woman. Obviously, in part, our refusal to condemn rests on our apprehension of the injustices meted out to Phoenix and her kin throughout their lives – but it is not quite as simple as that, otherwise Phoenix would not rebuke herself as she does. Surely it is that were we to imagine a God watching her, we know He would find her misdeed insignificant compared with the loveliness of the greater part of her life and being. The white man, albeit in a somewhat innocent way, is crass, coarse-fibred and dismissive: '"Now you go on home, Granny, he says."' Compare Phoenix's own participation with the creature world, on terms of amiable equality, with the young hunter's callousness (he has with him 'one of the

---

59. C.S. p. 146.

bob-whites, with its beak hooked bitterly to show it was dead'). Phoenix would never have stolen from a nice-natured person such as the white woman she later asks to tie her shoelaces.

Eudora Welty has said that this story would not have been the same had the old muddle-headed woman been white, and surely she is right. The sense of the inspirited nature of our world here is a black understanding. Phoenix Jackson has a natural and unconsciously articulated empathy with all living things that is hard to find among the whites of her country. During her journey she apostrophizes foxes, owls, beetles, jack rabbits, coons; she speaks to the thorn bush as if it were sensate, and the scarecrow lives for her.

Phoenix Jackson is triumphantly herself, but she is seen with something of the general vision of the folktale – and that folktale vision was beginning to preoccupy Eudora Welty deeply. Confronting animate nature, following her instinctual knowledge, being true to her ideal, the old black woman represents the best part of us all, just as the protagonists of myths and legends tend to do. It is right that *A Curtain of Green* ends with this story; 'A Worn Path' is a miracle of humane literary art – complete, but pointing forward to other achievements.

3

'PASSIONATE THINGS, IN SOME ESSENCE, ENDURE'

I

IN AN essay written in 1944, 'Some Notes on River Country' – one of her very finest – Eudora Welty says:

> A place that ever was lived in is like a fire that never goes out. It flares up, it smolders for a time, it is fanned or smothered by circumstance, but its being is intact, forever fluttering within it, the result of some original ignition. Sometimes it gives out glory, sometimes its little light must be sought out to be seen, small and tender as a candle flame, but as certain.[1]

This beautiful simile owes something to the River Country's Natchez Indians' belief that their nation would decline if their sacred fire were allowed to go out, an idea which came to haunt Eudora Welty. Her journeys round Mississippi had opened up to her not just its present life but its past as well, which also turned out to be demanding and multifarious.

Mississippi, as we know the state now, is an area of 47,716 square miles, for the most part undulating wooded or farmed land. Geographically, the state divides into the coastal strip; the 'piney

---

1. Eye p. 286.

woods' which occupy most of its southern half; the western loess uplands which stretch from Louisiana north to Tennessee; the immensely rich alluvial Delta, lying to the west of the loess region (this is the great cotton country, not to be confused by the non-Southerner with the literal delta of the Mississippi as it flows into the Gulf of Mexico); the Bermuda-grass-covered 'prairie section' of farmland in the north; and, in the north-east, the red sandy-clay hills that border on Alabama (the country of 'Death of a Traveling Salesman' and *Losing Battles*). Tishomingo County, perhaps the poorest part of the whole State, lies here; it was here that Eudora Welty first felt deeply stirred to be the writer she has become.

In pre-Columbian times three main Indian 'nations' lived in this whole region, perhaps as many as 30,000 people altogether: the Chickasaws, the Choctaws and the Natchez. The first Europeans to interest themselves in it were the Spanish under the now fabled leadership of Hernando de Soto, but the first real colonists were the French. They founded the city now called Natchez, under the name of Fort Rosalie, in 1716; in 1729 it was attacked by the Natchez Indians, who massacred or took prisoner virtually all its inhabitants. The French retaliated, but continuous trouble with the indigenous peoples led to waning enthusiasm for maintaining the colony. After the British victory over French and Indians in the wars of 1754–63, Britain became the owner of the whole area, which was included in their colony of West Florida. During the American War of Independence, however, the original discoverers, the Spanish, took it over, and it did not join the United States until 1795 (as a result of the Treaty of San Lorenzo).

Three years later the Territory of Mississippi came into official being, with Natchez as its capital (changed in 1802 to the neighbouring village of Washington). Indian lands lay to the north; later these were ceded to the state by Andrew Jackson's Indian wars. By this time, however, the territory was too large for easy administration, so it was split up into Mississippi (statehood 1817) and Alabama (statehood 1819).

Now economic development of the land began in earnest, with the construction of communication systems and the intensification of the profitable cotton-growing. For the success of this, 'Negro' slave labour was imported. A new capital was founded, called after Andrew

Jackson (1822). Despite the fact that by now over half the population of the State was black (the highest proportion of any Southern State), administrative control was entirely in white hands. Consequently, in 1861, after Abraham Lincoln took office, there was overwhelming support here for Secession; indeed, Mississippi was the first State to secede after South Carolina, and it was a Mississippian, Jefferson Davis, who became President of the Confederate States of America. (Allen Tate wrote a fine life of him, and his statue, outside the Capitol in Montgomery, Alabama, gives a very good idea of this indomitable man.)

After the defeat of the South in 1865 Mississippi passed a law abolishing slavery, but refused to give black people the right to vote. The impositions of Reconstruction did not make the white Mississippians look the more favourably on repudiation of their past, or on radical change to the fabric of their society. Looking back, the tragic distress and violence that came to so terrible and bloody a head in the early 1960s seem to have been utterly inevitable.

Eudora Welty, like her friends, is intimately familiar with all this history; one way or another, it finds its way into her fiction. Her *œuvre*, however, follows a probably unconscious logic. Perhaps because she recoiled from so much and such widespread illiberal Southern preoccupation with the Civil War ('I hate the Civil War, and everything to do with it,' she told me memorably, and was to reiterate the sentiment later in different forms) she brought herself to write about this definitive period only in 1951, in 'The Burning', a story she does not like – indeed, virtually rejects. In her journeys into the Mississippi past her mind preferred to go back to the years of evolution, before the region had consolidated its strands and factions to become a secessionist State. But there is another, more personal reason for her creative attentions: she fell in love with the loess country, and it is this district that is above all else responsible for the three mythico-historical stories: the novella *The Robber Bridegroom*, written contemporaneously with the stories in *A Curtain of Green* (though published a year later), and two stories in *The Wide Net* (1943), 'First Love' and 'A Still Moment'.

Perhaps everyone needs a region that is near enough to their own to be reached easily and often, yet sufficiently distinct from it to become special, a spiritually fruitful alternative. Jackson is a manageable distance from the uplands of Mississippi, but even now you can feel a thrill of discovery as you leave Hinds County and go towards the loess region, which reaches out to the earliest recorded past and beyond, inspiring atavistic emotions.

Loess, which has made the land what it is, can best be described by Eudora Welty herself:

> Loess has the beautiful definition of aeolian – windborne. The loess soil is like a mantle; the ridge[s were] laid down here by the wind, the bottom land by the water. Deep under them both is solid blue clay, embalming the fossil horse and the fossil ox and the great mastodon . . .[2]

An old highway cuts through this luxuriant country; this is the Natchez Trace, connecting Mississippi's Natchez with Tennessee's Nashville. It must have been forged through the forest first by buffalo, then by Indians. The settlers and traders who first used the Trace often found it a dangerous route, with its wild animals, Indians, and people living outside the law, operating as bandits. The section of the Old Natchez Trace country that inspired Eudora Welty lies between Natchez itself and Vicksburg, where the great loess bluffs had so important a part to play in the Civil War siege.

'First Love' describes the 'great world of leaves' through which the Trace makes its way, the 'dense cane brake, deep down off the Trace – the densest part, where it grew thick and locked as some kind of wild teeth' – and shows how, in winter, the Trace is a sequence of 'glassy tunnels' through which travellers 'followed one another like insects going at dawn through the heavy grass'.

In 'A Still Moment' Audubon reflects:

> All life used this Trace, and he liked to see the animals move along it in direct, oblivious journeys, for they had begun it and made it, the buffalo and deer and the small running creatures before man ever knew where he wanted to go, and birds flew a great mirrored course above.[3]

---

2. Eye p. 288.
3. C.S. p. 193.

In this country geography was to assert itself to shape history: in the mid nineteenth century the Mississippi River changed course. Justifications of communities disappeared, and with them the communities as such. Thus Rodney's Landing – a centre of commerce, built before the American War of Independence to receive ocean-going ships from Britain – was abandoned, to be 'caught up' in the rampant foliage of this hot, humid terrain:

> I have never seen, in this small section of old Mississippi River country and its little chain of lost towns between Vicksburg and Natchez, anything so mundane as ghosts, but I have felt many times there a sense of place as powerful as if it were visible and walking and could touch me.
>
> The clatter of hoof and the bellow of boats have gone, all old communications. The Old Natchez Trace has sunk out of use; it is deep in leaves. The river has gone away and left the landings. Boats from Liverpool do not dock at these empty crags. The old deeds are done, old evil and old good have been made into stories, as plows turn up the river bottom, and the wild birds fly now at the level where people on boat deck once were strolling and talking of great expanding things, and of chance and money. Much beauty has gone, many little things of life. To light up the nights there are no mansions, no celebrations. Just as, when there were mansions and celebrations, there were no more festivals of an Indian tribe there; before the music there were drums.[4]

Exactly so! This country is a reminder of the mutability of all human cultures, of how one period's hub of business can be another's arcane yet awesome ghost town, and of how quickly, once decline has begun, dwarfing, silencing Nature takes over. It can also act as a palimpsest of Mississippi – and Southern – history.

The Natchez nation (probably about 6,000 in all), a Muskogean-speaking, agricultural, artistic, sun-honouring people, lived between the Yazoo and Pearl Rivers in five villages. In the essay quoted above, Eudora described her own intimations of them:

---

4. Eye p. 287.

The heat moves. Its ripples can be seen, like the ripples in some vertical river running between earth and sky. It is so still at noon. I was never there before the river left, to hear the thousand swirling sounds it made for Rodney's Landing, but could it be that its absence is so much missed in the life of sound here that a stranger would feel it? The stillness seems absolute, as the brightness of noon seems to touch the point of saturation. Here the noon sun does make a trance; here indeed at its same zenith it looked down on life sacrificed to it and was worshipped.

It is not strange to think that a unique nation among Indians lived in this beautiful country. The origin of the Natchez is still in mystery . . . they were envied by other younger nations – the Choctaws helped the French in their final dissolution. In Mississippi they were remnants surely of medievalism. They were proud and cruel, gentle-mannered and ironic, handsome, extremely tall, intellectual, elegant, pacific, and ruthless. Fire, death, sacrifice formed the spirit of the Natchez' worship. They did not now, however, make war.[5]

In *The Robber Bridegroom* the final proof of the stepmother, Salome's, wickedness is that she deliberately, and to her Indian captors' faces, blasphemes against the sun. In the fierce cold of the winter in which 'First Love' takes place:

The Indians could be heard . . . sending up placating but proud messages to the sun in continual ceremonies of dancing. The red percussion of their fires could be seen night and day by those waiting in the dark trance of the frozen town [Natchez itself].[6]

The decimation and eventual disappearance from any main road of history of this matrilineal people, with their remarkable social structure – Great Sun at the head, male and female Suns as an aristocracy, Nobles, Honoured People and Stinkards – is a tragic story, involving the cynical manipulation of inter-Indian feuds by both the French and the British, and massacres of and by the Indians themselves. (By the time of 'A Still Moment' they are still dangerous, with

5. Eye p. 293.
6. C.S. p. 153.

their 'new guns', but have obviously been dispersed, and robbed of effective centres.)

In *The Robber Bridegroom* – set 'just before 1798' – Clement Musgrove speaks of 'the land which the King of Spain granted me', not far from Rodney's Landing, with the Mississippi River a mile to the back, and the Old Natchez Trace a mile to the front. Rodney's Landing itself has at least three fair-sized inns, with 'the flourish of carriages hurrying through the streets after dark'. In 'First Love' the Natchez of 1807 sustains a comfortable, moneyed class and is even more sophisticated:

> People now lighted their houses in entertainments as if they copied after the sky ... their minuets skimmed across the nights like a pebble expertly skipped across water.[7]

But reminders of the pre-Territory days when the town belonged to Spain can easily be found – for instance, in the puncheon table in the room where the protagonist, the hotel boot-boy Joel, sleeps:

> He began to keep his candle-stick carefully polished, he set it in the centre of the puncheon-table, and at night when it was lighted all the messages of love carved into it with a knife in Spanish words, with a deep Spanish gouging, came out in black relief, for anyone to read who came knowing the language.[8]

How could it not be possible that such abundance of life is not, in some way, still present today? The contemporary traveller on the Trace will be aware above all of the prolixity of plant life that Eudora Welty lovingly itemizes in her writings – the ferns, the Cherokee roses, the magnolias and their cousins, the cucumber trees; and here and there, perhaps, a mimosa tree 'with its smell in the rain like a cool melon cut' – and of the birds that move among all these, including (just possibly) the ivory-billed woodpecker in which Audubon delighted (both in reality and in 'A Still Moment'), which ate (eats?) the swamp-land grapes by the bunch, and delivers 'a mournful and very piteous cry' if caught. The evocation of the natural wealth of this countryside

---

7. C.S. p. 161.
8. C.S. pp. 155–6.

is central to *The Robber Bridegroom*, 'First Love' and, above all, 'A Still Moment', at the very heart of which is an exploration of our complex relation to Nature.

In *The Robber Bridegroom* Rosamond rejoices:

> How beautiful it was in the wild wood! Black willow, green willow, cypress, pecan, katalpa, magnolia, persimmon, peach, dogwood, wild plum, wild cherry, pomegranate, palmetto, mimosa, and tulip trees were growing on every side, golden-green in the deep last days of the Summer. Up overhead the cuckoo sang. A quail with her young walked fat as the queen across the tangled path. A flock of cardinals flew up like a fan opening out from the holly bush. The fox looked out from his hole.[9]

But of course these plants, these birds and animals, which our predecessors saw and knew, are our logical conductors back to them; they are what we have in common, not least in how they address our imagination or psyche. They can lead, therefore, into the fusion of the historical and mythic which is the vision of the past we all hold. Place, for obvious reasons, is to a great extent responsible for this fusion, this vision.

II

I can see and hear Eudora Welty now, on that June day in 1978, asking, 'Would you like me to drive you to Vicksburg?', her enthusiasm for the River Country lighting up her face. I can see and hear – at her birthday celebrations – a youngish publisher from New York telling me how, as a result of reading the stories, she had discovered the area herself, and how much it had come to mean to her. (She later sent me a card insisting: 'You must hie yourself to Rodney as soon as you can.' I did.) And I see again too the cool, ordered room of my first 'interview' with Eudora Welty – on a morning even hotter than the day before, when I had journeyed down from Memphis. We began, I recall, by talking of the preservation, the ensured survival of history by means of myth and legend. What had been tentatively present in

---

9. R.B. p. 77.

my mind was drawn out and given shape by Eudora Welty as she spoke.

She pointed out that the elements of traditional folktales, out of which – indeed, *upon* which – each one is built, would have been of the utmost familiarity to their original audiences over the centuries. It is distance – of both time and space – that has given them the patina of the mysterious. Take the regular features of the 'household tales' collected by the Brothers Grimm – forest, river-ford, mill, woodcutter, miller, boatsman, castle, baron, bailiff, servant, goose-girl, swineherd. If they knew about anything, the original German-speaking story-tellers and hearers would have known about these. That is not to say that these 'properties' themselves do not contain deep psychic elements, which have, thanks to their conservation in the stories, survived their familiarity; but these psychic elements existed, were part of the audience's daily doings. The very word 'forest' would have evoked danger (wolves, bandits, pathless wilderness with no way out); a goose-girl would have suggested innocence and sexual vulnerability; a river the boundary between the known and the unknown, and so on. Eudora Welty, who had studied folktales all her reading life, believed that Americans – and perhaps the tradition-minded Southerners most of all – had access to similar worlds, if perhaps by her time at one remove, but that they had been insufficiently tapped. For its dwellers and travellers the Old Natchez Trace country had been exactly what the land of Hessen had been for those whose folktales were collected by the Grimm Brothers, or the Norwegian mountains for the communities who supplied Asbjørnsen and Moe. Here, after all, were forest, river, foresters, planters, flatboatmen, bandits, foreigners, profuse animal and plant life, etc. Eudora Welty felt, therefore, that fairytale (rather than the conventional historical novel, which borrows from works of bourgeois origin) would be the most appropriate instrument for discovering and revealing the most vital aspects of this region's historical past (which can stand in for all pasts elsewhere) – especially as it was already rich and proud in accumulated lore. Perhaps the only important departure from the genre as customarily articulated would be in the rendering of the setting. First, because you could not take for granted contemporary readers' knowledge of the places (on the contrary, for most, they would be remote and almost exotic). Second, because our post-Romantic sensibility demands attention to background of a kind foreign to the folktale. Indeed, interest in folklore and interest in Nature historically coincide – dating from the very years in which *The Robber Bridegroom* takes place.

In the lore of a region certain personages survive as legends, and so it is in the Old Natchez Trace country. It was only natural that Eudora Welty should, in these years, develop a certain imaginative intimacy with some of the more celebrated figures.

The flatboatman Mike Fink in *The Robber Bridegroom* was a sort of Southern Paul Bunyan, boastful, preternaturally strong, working the Ohio and Mississippi Rivers. (Stories about his life, of which there were at least eleven versions), were collected only five or so years after his death. Then there were the Harpe (sometimes Harp) brothers, bandits who operated on the Trace in the last years of the eighteenth century, and whose sadistic cruelty has been documented in Southern records. Little Harpe features in Eudora Welty's novella – he carries (as in recorded reality) his brother Big Harpe's head, in a trunk, preserved in the region's famous blue clay.

The politician and one-time Vice President Aaron Burr (1756–1836) has cast his ambiguous personality over all American historical mythology, and to some extent the same is also true of the bird artist John James Audubon (1785–1851). There was also the bandit John A. Murrell (fl. 1804–44), and the evangelist Lorenzo Dow, 'a wild and strange and really half-mad preacher' (to use Eudora Welty's own words), whose passionate sermons were often delivered from horseback.

Indians, Mike Fink the flatboatman, Burr, and Blennerhassett, John James Audubon, the bandits of Trace, planters, and preachers – the horse fairs, the great fires – the battles of war, the arrivals of foreign ships, and the coming of floods: could not all these things still move with their true stature into the mind here, and their beauty still work upon the heart? Perhaps it is the sense of place that gives us the belief that passionate things, in some essence, endure. Whatever is significant, and whatever is tragic in its story live as long as the place does, though they are unseen, and the new life will be built upon these things – regardless of commerce and the way of rivers and roads, and other vagrancies.[10]

So why should not these men and women, these incidents – however tall the stories – speak across the gulf of time to very different societies – just as, say, Robin Hood and Rob Roy have done?

In an interview with the University of Alabama's *Comment* magazine (1965), Eudora Welty said:

> I had been working for the WPA or for the Mississippi Advertising commission. In the course of my work I had to do a lot of reading on the Natchez Trace. I'm not a writer who writes fiction by research, but reading these primary sources, such as Dow's sermons, Murrell's diary and letters of the time, fired my imagination. I thought how much like fairy tales all of those things were. And so I just sat down and wrote *The Robber Bridegroom* in a great spurt of pleasure.[11]

Certainly her joy in creating the novella is palpable.

Yet the fairytale, being concerned with nothing less than survival itself, is always supremely serious. It is not usually connected with the post-Romantic business of jubilation. And in fact the story to which Eudora found herself turning in order to show the quintessence of the Natchez Trace country is one of extreme sombreness. It is not the least dualistic feature of the novella that something so high-spirited should have come directly from something so troubling.

III

In his authoritative study of the significance of fairytales in our lives, *The Uses of Enchantment*, Bruno Bettelheim associates the Grimm Brothers' 'The Robber Bridegroom' with their 'Fitcher's Bird', with Perrault's 'Bluebeard' and with a lesser-known tale from Romania, 'The Enchanted Pig'. All feature the female not being allowed to 'inquire into the secrets of the male' (as will Eudora Welty's novella), thus dealing with 'sexual-temptation' and 'the destructive aspects of sex'.

---

10. Eye p. 299.
11. C.E.W. p. 24.

In Grimms' disturbing story, a miller, deciding that his pretty daughter should be married, finds a socially presentable and apparently rich man who professes himself willing to be her husband. The girl, however, feels an inexplicable revulsion against him, and tries to get out of going to his house, which lies in the middle of the forest. But her suitor insists that she visits him that very Sunday. He will strew ashes through the wood to ensure that she does not lose her way.

On Sunday, then, despite feeling apprehensive, the girl sets out, having first filled her pockets with peas and beans, which she drops along the path, ash-strewn as promised. Eventually, right in the forest's depths, she comes to a little house, with a birdcage hanging above the door. The bird sings out:

'Turn again. bonny bride!
   Turn again home!
Haste from the robber's den,
   Haste away home!'

Despite this warning she enters the house, which turns out to be quite empty except for an old woman who, asked where the bridegroom is, tells her that her wedding can only be with death. She then hides the girl behind a cask so that she can watch what happens when the inhabitants return.

A band of robbers, with her husband-to-be prominent among them, arrives; they have a girl with them and they proceed to force wine on her until she falls down dead. The bridegroom himself tries to take a gold ring from her finger, but it eludes his grasp by flying up in the air and landing on the lap of his fiancée in her hiding place. The robbers search high and low for the ring, but the old woman prevents them from looking behind the cask, and in the end she is able to administer a sleeping potion to them all, enabling herself and the girl to escape. Of course the ashes on the forest path have blown away, just as the bridegroom intended, but the peas and beans have sprung up, and the girl returns to her father's house quite safe. She tells him what has happened, and they hatch a plan.

The wedding goes ahead, and at the feast everyone tells stories. The bride is asked for hers by the groom himself:

'I can tell you a dream I dreamed,' she complies. 'I dreamed I was going through a wood and walked on and on until I came to an empty-looking house. There was above the door a caged bird who cried out:

> "Turn again, bonny bride!
>   Turn again, home!
> Haste from the robber's den,
>   Haste away home!"

I only dreamed that, my love! . . . '

And on she goes, through the whole ghastly sequence of events, producing the dead captive's ring as proof that what she is telling is the truth. So the robber gang, and the bridegroom with them, are brought to justice.

This story obviously derives from the ignorance and the so often justifiable fear girls must have in a traditionally structured society of men, whose bidding they are supposed to do unquestioningly but from whose nature – including physical make-up – they have been kept, protected. It suggests, too, the cruelty of male sexual dominion as commonly accepted, which here takes the form not only of pre-meditated death to the central character but also of death to the captive, whose ring, a clear genital symbol, flees for safety to the lap of the nearest young female, the heroine. Yet punishment comes the men's way through female determination and bravery: the bride survives, and her foreboding is vindicated.

Yet in Eudora Welty's story based on this, sexuality, including uninhibited male sexuality, is celebrated. This may sound contradictory, and in one way it is; doubleness is of *The Robber Bridegroom*'s very essence. But like all good fairytales, it is also totally logical.

In the novella the miller becomes Clement Musgrove, an 'innocent planter' who increases his riches and property through good sense and industry; the daughter whom he wishes to marry well has a name and a character: Rosamond, beautiful, independent, wayward, given to extravagant if guiltless fantasies (for in her heart she is truthful); 'she has every fairy-tale property', says her creator. And the Robber Bridegroom is Jamie Lockhart. When he first appears at an inn on Rodney's Landing, he does Clement Musgrove a good turn

– indeed, he saves his life from the murderous attention of a fellow-guest: 'He was remarkably amiable to see. But by his look, nobody could tell what he would do.'[12] Indeed not! That is the point. Clement Musgrove decides that Jamie would make a good, suitable husband for Rosamond, but perhaps he should have trusted his ignorance, for this charming, brave and seemingly kind man is also (as in Grimm) a robber. (Or is it better that he did *not* trust his ignorance, for in truth Jamie does turn out to be an excellent and loving husband for his daughter?) The complexity does not end here. In her lecture on the book Eudora Welty said:

> The Robber Bridegroom, the double character of the title, owes his existence on the one side to history – the history of the Natchez Trace outlaws – and on the other side to the Brothers Grimm.[13]

So the doubleness of Jamie's behaviour and way of life is in part mimetic of the doubleness of his origins, and the relation of this quality to Rosamond is the opposite of what one might expect. (Or is it? This questioning of each statement is obligatory, and comes easily when we consider this novella. Everything – including every standard reaction to the conventional ingredients of fairytale – demands a second, and usually contradictory, look.) For it is the *robber* side of Jamie that is attractive to Rosamond, with which she falls in love; the polite, virtuous suitor brought home by her father bores her stiff. And her abduction and deflowering – which should be the tale's dark and frightening heart, if we were expecting Eudora Welty's story to be *like* the Grimms' tale (as opposed to be interesting kin to it) – prove to be nothing of the kind:

> [Jamie] rode right up to her, and reached down his arms and lifted her up, pail of milk and all, into the saddle with scarcely a pause in his speed.
>
> Up the ridge they went, and a stream of mist made a circle around them. Then it unwound and floated below in the hollows. The dark cedars sprang from the black ravine, the hanging fruit

---

12. R.B. p. 14.
13. Eye p. 303.

trees shone ahead on their crests and were hidden again by the cedars. The morning sky rolled slowly like a dark wave they were overtaking, but it had the sound of thunder. Over and over, the same hill seemed to rise beneath the galloping horse. Over and under was another sound, like horses following – was it her father, or an echo? – faster and faster, as they rode the faster. . . . Red as blood the horse rode the ridge, his mane and tail straight out in the wind, and it was the fastest kidnapping that had ever been in that part of the country.

Birds flew up like sparks from a flint. Nearer and nearer they came to the river, to the highest point on the bluff. A foam of gold leaves filled the willow trees. Taut as a string stretched over the ridge, the path ran higher and higher. Rosamond's head fell back, till only the treetops glittered in her eyes, which held them like two mirrors. So the sun mounted the morning cloud, and lighted the bluff and then the river, shining beneath another river of mist, winding and all the colors of flowers.

Then the red horse stood stock-still, and Jamie Lockhart lifted Rosamond down. The wild plum trees were like rolling smoke between him and the river, but he broke the branches and the plums rained down as he carried her under. He stopped and laid her on the ground, where straight below, the river flowed as slow as sand, and robbed her of that which he had left her the day before.[14]

Pathetic fallacy is proudly and joyously apparent in this rhapsodic passage (from that unspilled pail of milk onwards): the exuberance of Nature in the Trace country must logically include the exuberance of lovemaking between a young man and a girl, and the natural world as it moves into morning anticipates and counterparts the sexual act. The passage has also, as befits its setting, an eighteenth-century robustness and honesty reminiscent of a tradition of English attitudes to sex that Evangelicism and its descendant, Victorianism, all but extinguished. Consider the exultant quality of Elizabethan love poetry, which is also present in that passage:

---

14. R.B. pp. 63–4.

When as the rye reach to the chin,
And chopcherry, chopcherry ripe within,
Strawberries swimming in the cream,
And school-boys playing in the stream;
   Then O, then O, then O, my true love said,
     Till that time come again,
   She could not live a maid. (George Peele)

(Eudora Welty has judged this to be a happy parallel.)

But 'robbed her', says the text; Jamie is thus now a robber in a double sense, and his being so seems a matter for rejoicing. What is meant by this?

It is interesting to reflect that *The Robber Bridegroom* is Eudora Welty's first treatment of the coming together of the sexes. (All the couples in *A Curtain of Green* are established ones.) In her presentation of Jamie and Rosamond, does not Eudora Welty combine three elements? First, there is her own humanistic attitude; second, there is the (eighteenth-century) sexual mores that must be present in most pioneering communities, who cannot afford undue attention to bourgeois niceties about chastity; and last, but by no means least, there is what she perceives as the atavistic acceptance of sexuality that folktales embody and impart. This novella is, to an important degree, an anti-bourgeois tale. Far more morally repellent than any enticement and consent, as depicted here, is the acquisitive materialistic approach to sex and marriage – the whole business of dowries, finding suitors, arranging 'good' matches. That, surely, is why Rosamond prefers the free ranging 'robber' Jamie to someone who is more conventionally proper. That is why his kidnapping and seduction of her do not constitute a crime ('robbery') except in the eyes of polite society – in contrast to so much propriety-honoured practice. You could say that the real crime that Eudora Welty takes from the Grimms' tale is the (innocent?) father's willingness to marry his daughter off to a man against whom (rightly, as it proves) she has conceived an intense revulsion.

But honesty compels one to admit that sexuality does have a dark, destructive side. Jamie Lockhart is given an evil double, Little Harpe. His desire is a force of alarming cruelty, echoed in the feelings that consume stepmother Salome and her factotum, the sorry Goat. It is the shadow of the joyous libido of Jamie and Rosamond, and one to be constantly aware of. Moreover, Rosamond has her double too, in Goat's piteous, helpless sister.

The Robber Bridegroom – like the original fairytale and those related to it – derives its being from doubleness as a fact of existence, from the perpetual presence of shadow in all areas of life. In her lecture to the Mississippi Historical Society Eudora Welty said that it was 'not a *historical* historical novel':

> For while Jamie Lockhart leads a double life by hero's necessity, clearly this isn't the only aspect of duality in the novel. Crucial, or comical, scenes of mistaken identity take place more or less regularly as the story unwinds. There's a doubleness in respect to identity that runs in a strong thread through all the wild happenings – indeed, this thread is their connection, and everything that happens hangs upon it. I spun that thread out of the times. Life was so full, so excessively charged with energy in those days, when nothing seemed impossible in the Natchez country, that leading one life hardly provided scope enough for it all. In the doubleness there was narrative truth that I felt the times themselves had justified.[15]

And perhaps this doubleness should be adduced further to the dualism of those cultures from which the white South so largely derived: Scottish and 'Scottish-Irish'. (Look at so many Southern place names, examine the surnames in a Southern telephone directory – and what name could be more Scottish than Jamie Lockhart?) Eudora Welty must have given thought to this inheritance. The Calvinistic teaching of the Damned and the Elect imposed on all life a black-and-white pattern, often tragically encompassing the flesh-and-blood black-and-white, and not only in the Southern states. . . . So if the sense of doubleness gives *The Robber Bridegroom* its infectious enthusiasm for the rich possibilities inherent in just being alive, it also reminds one of the dark corollaries to human operations.

The very doubleness with which the novella concludes is itself ambiguous:

---

15. Eye p. 310.

Jamie Lockhart was now no longer a bandit but a gentleman of the world in New Orleans, respected by all that knew him, a rich merchant in fact.[16]

... the outward transfer from bandit to merchant had been almost too easy to count it a change at all, and [Jamie] was enjoying all the same success he ever had. But now, in his heart Jamie knew that he was a hero and had always been one, only with the power to look both ways and to see a thing from all sides.[17]

The successful businessman has been a hero of post-pioneer America, the successor of the frontiersman, and just as the frontiersmen included mythologized outlaws, whom society has taken to its heart, so have the businessmen too. Often morality and practice are interchangeable; it is merely the side of the law that is different – maybe the double-identitied robber and the double-identitied merchant are spiritually symbiotic.

The Robber Bridegroom is deftly worked; its chain of doubleness – including many disguises and mistakes of identity – proceeds with an irresistible liveliness towards the 'eucatastrophe' (to use J.R.R. Tolkien's unbeatable term) proper to the fairytale, that chord of triumphant happiness which resolves all discordant strife: Rosamond and Jamie, in a deft symbolic touch, become the contented parents of twins – and Rosamond herself had been a twin; her brother died when they were children on the Indian-beset journey through the wilderness to the Natchez Trace country. So, with doubleness, new life opens.

The novel provides, wholly organically, prophetic truths not just about the South, but about America itself. Indeed, no less than 'The Hitch-Hikers', or 'Keela, the Outcast Indian Maiden', it is a cultural paradigm.

Central to the book in this respect is the passage in which Clement Musgrove finds himself alone in the forest and, placing stones around him in a small circle, tries to appraise his situation:

'What exactly is this now?' he said, for he was concerned with the identity of a man, and *had* to speak, if only to the stones. 'What

16. R.B. p. 183.
17. R.B. p. 184.

is the place and time? Here are all possible trees in a forest, and they grow as tall and as great and as close to one another as they could ever grow in the world. Upon each limb is a singing bird, and across this floor, slowly and softly and forever moving into profile, is always a beast, one of a procession, weighted low with his burning coat, looking from the yellow eye set in his head.' He stayed and looked at the place where he was until he knew it by heart, and could even see the changes of the seasons come over it like four clouds: Spring and the clear and separate leaves mounting to the top of the sky, the black flames of cedars, the young trees shining like the lanterns, the magnolias softly ignited; Summer and the vines falling down over the darkest caves, red and green, changing to the purple of grapes and the Autumn descending in a golden curtain; there in the nakedness of the Winter wood the buffalo on his sinking trail, pawing the ice till his forelock hangs in the spring, and the deer following behind to the salty places to transfix his tender head. And that was the way the years went by.

'But the time of cunning has come,' said Clement, 'and my time is over, for cunning is of a world I will have no part in. Two long ripples are following down the Mississippi behind the approaching somnolent eyes of the alligator. And like the tenderest deer, a band of copying Indians poses along the bluff to draw us near them. Men are following men down the Mississippi, hoarse and arrogant by day, wakeful and dreamless by night at the unknown landings. A trail leads like a tunnel under the roof of this wilderness. Everywhere the traps are set. Why? And what kind of time is this, when all is first given, then stolen away?'[18]

On its most literal level this must be taken as an anticipation of the imminent changes in the Mississippi Territory in 1798; the Spanish would withdraw, ambitious settlers would come from other States; the Mississippi itself would become the great American commercial artery; the plantations would grow, requiring the 'special institution'

---

18. R.B. pp. 141–3.

of slavery. Clement delivers himself, then, of an elegy for loss of innocence, a melancholy fanfare for the imminent age of business and industry. 'The time of cunning has come,' he says sadly. 'Cunning is a world I will have no part in.' Commerce will no longer be for the innocently industrious. He stands despondent before the future (for all that it is gleefully presented in his last sight of Jamie and Rosamond), knowing that simpler values, closer to the original nature of things, will go under.

Two ripples advance down the river towards the planter, preceded by an alligator. An alligator represents – better perhaps than any other creature – the primeval, life before man. And those ripples, taken in this context, flowing first parallel, then converging, can represent the dual nature of the urban-originated culture that will succeed the alligator – on the one hand benign with material improvement, on the other malign with greed, competition, and the destruction of the organic community.

But before giving vent to his ideas about the future, Clement Musgrove concentrates on his immediate surroundings, deep in the forest off the Natchez Trace. In this concentration, redolent of a *participation mystique*, he comes near to bestowing on the natural world – shown as a deeply satisfying and beautiful round of distinctive seasons, rhapsodized in terms reminiscent of the Song of Songs – a prelapsarian condition (even though, of course, according to Christian myth, seasons are a consequence of the Fall). The singing birds on the branches of the trees, the beasts moving in continuous profile, suggest some ultimate Platonic absolute.

With industrialization humankind began to think of itself living in Historical Time as opposed to the purely Natural or Seasonal Time. (The nineteenth century was the first to call itself proudly by its enumeration.) Thinking about times past had given Eudora Welty a heightened awareness of approaches to Time passing; so Clement Musgrove, father of a fairytale heroine and, at his creator's confession, not a fanciful or even a particularly imaginative man, acts as a seer in *The Robber Bridegroom*, perceiving a major and probably irreversible change in sensibility between his own period and the future he can read from the ripples on the river.

IV

The contrast between *The Robber Bridegroom* and its successor, the story 'First Love' – which concerns Natchez and the Trace country some years later, in January 1807 – is immediately evident in their opening sentences.

> It was the close of day when a boat touched Rodney's Landing on the Mississippi River and Clement Musgrove, an innocent planter with a bag of gold and many presents, disembarked. (*The Robber Bridegroom*)[19]

> Whatever happened, it happened in extraordinary times, in a season of dreams, and in Natchez it was the bitterest winter of them all. ('First Love')[20]

The first is a statement of total objectivity. Of necessity, a fairytale's extraordinary events can convince only if they are narrated in an impersonal manner, and linked to a matter-of-fact presentation of the world both teller and audience share. Hence the devices used here – the adjective 'innocent' (relating a major character to a single quality) and the signalling of an all-important detail (the bag of gold) – follow the genre's long-established rule of selectivity; they name only what directly furthers the line of the story, and have nothing to do with the interior life of either narrator or characters. 'First Love', on the other hand, acknowledges from the very outset the limitations of objectivity; doubt is expressed about arriving at precise knowledge of events, the ability of all humans to create their own worlds is attested ('a season of dreams'), and even the sentence's one factual constituent – the unprecedented severity of the winter – is accorded a part-subjective qualifier, for 'bitterest' takes one into the realm of personal reaction.

The Robber Bridegroom was 'not a *historical* historical novel'; 'First Love' and 'A Still Moment' – despite, or perhaps because of, their concern with internal life – stand far nearer to history. Their personages – Burr, Audubon, Dow and Murrell – are anyway far more extensively

---

19. R.B. p. 1.
20. C.S. p. 153.

documented than those in the earlier work. Similarly, while there is no record of a deaf boy idolizing the fallen Burr as he awaited trial ('First Love'), and while it can never be proved that Audubon, Dow and Murrell ever did meet up on the Natchez Trace ('A Still Moment'), the narratives of the two stories are plausible, even possible.

For all its exuberance, *The Robber Bridegroom* does not suggest that people from the past can endure in our own time, for its characters, away from the scenes in which we see them, are too incomplete. (If we tried to carry them over into life, there would be unanswerable questions that could not be asked, such as: How is it possible for someone to be thoroughly delightful and a successful bandit? How can Jamie's 'taking' of Rosamond not be an unpalatably aggressive act, even though its accomplishment may have differed from its intention?) But in the stories we feel that Eudora Welty really has apprehended what is significant and what is tragic from earlier lives in the country she was coming to love so much. The natures of the historical people they deal with – and of the records which can convey us to them – must account for this; Mike Fink and Little Harpe, on the other hand, belonged too much to the one-dimensional world of unadulterated folklore.

Not that 'First Love' and 'A Still Moment' are unrelated to the fairytale – and not only because there is something legendary ('larger than life') as well as qualities of their period about their characters. The very shape, the very narrative movement of these tales, exemplify that most vital element of fairytale and myth, correspondence to shape and movement within the psyche – so that at their end we seem to have been about fundamentally existential business concerned with nothing less than survival itself. In the historical situations she chose here Eudora Welty found perfect objective correlatives for some of her most profound and most demanding preoccupations. She gave to the Natchez Trace her own inner inquiries, and received from it intimations of lives which she then endowed with life, paying attention to the flesh as well as the minds and hearts. 'First Love' and 'A Still Moment', then, surpass in scope and in execution (though in no way diminish the achievements of) even the best productions of *A Curtain of Green*, just as they surpass *The Robber Bridegroom* and the other stories in *The Wide Net* (even its splendid and lovable title story), and therefore have a chapter to themselves.

V

Eudora Welty also wanted to write about the present life of her River Country. While her photographs show a haunted land from which the throb of contemporary life has departed, they belong to a 'now' in which the very abandonment of towns and the consequent dominion of Nature are undeniable factors. The contemporary does not mean only the new and progressive (though the word has come to be used as though it did); it must also mean what the new and progressive have bypassed. What would it be like to grow up, to have your significant learning experiences, in a place where notions of fierceness or exigence turned the mind instinctively backwards? Or where no human upheaval, no surge of history-in-the-making, could ever be so terrible or so determinant as a natural one – winds, fires, floods?

The first predicament is one with which Europeans tend to be more familiar than Americans, and we can understand the affinity Eudora Welty felt for Irish writers, such as her friends-to-be Elizabeth Bowen and Mary Lavin, or think of that virtually contemporaneous presentation of poor, forgotten, sun-baked southern Italy, Carlo Levi's *Cristo si è fermato ad Eboli* (Christ Stopped at Eboli) as we read her fictive presentations of the Old Natchez Trace country today: 'The town was still called The Landing. The river had gone, three miles away, beyond sight and smell, beyond the dense trees. It came back only in flood, and boats ran over the houses.'[21] And the town cemetery:

> was a dark shelf above the town, on the site of the old landing place when the ships docked from across the world a hundred years ago, and its brink was marked by an old table-like grave with its top ajar where the woodbine grew. Everywhere there, the hanging moss and the upthrust stones were in that strange grave-yard shade where, by the light they give, the moss seems made of stone, and the stone of moss.[22]

This, in 'At The Landing', is Rodney, a place of rushing carriages and busy inns when last visited in *The Robber Bridegroom*. And the girl

---

21. C.S. p. 241.
22. C.S. p. 243.

whose daily landscape this ghost town forms is Jenny Lockhart, a descendant, one assumes, of Jamie and Rosamond, who were left in an upsurge of prosperity and success at the fairytale's end. Now the Lockhart name is attached to a pitiable specimen of degeneration like the albino Mag, tending her flowers with a jack-knife, or to the house where she lives, the very pattern of decay (albeit of a certain splendour):

> The Lockhart house stood between two of the empty stretches along the road. It was wide, low, and twisted. Its roof, held up at the corners by the two chimneys, sagged like a hammock, and was mended with bark and small coloured signs. The black high-water mark made a belt around the house and that alone seemed to tighten it and hold it together ... [It] was a beautiful doorway to see, with its fanlight and its sidelights, though they were blind with silt. The door was shut and the squirrels were asleep on the floor of the long cage across the front wall. Under the forward-tilting porch the clay-coloured hens were sitting in twos in the old rowboat.[23]

The closely related short stories 'At The Landing', 'The Wide Net', 'The Winds', 'Asphodel' and 'Livvie' are from the collection *The Wide Net*, to which should be added its remaining story, 'The Purple Hat', which, although it is set not in the Trace country but in New Orleans, is indisputably a product of the *genius loci*.

These stories are related not only because of shared place, but because of their shared preoccupation with sexual emotion. The Eudora Welty who wrote them was in her early to mid thirties; as an individual and as a writer she was obviously concerned with desire and love – in herself, in the lives of those around her, in life in general. If in *The Robber Bridegroom* the Natchez Trace country gave the opportunity both for paeans to sexual attraction and for delineations of its darker, predatory aspects, in these stories sex seems multifaceted, not susceptible to the reductions of either jubilation or fear.

'The Wide Net' is a comedy which can, I think, be related to the mistaken-identity comedy in *The Robber Bridegroom*, though it is far

---

23. C.S. p. 245.

more affecting because it is so much more truly human. For that reason it stands somewhat apart from the other four stories; there is a closer kinship between these. In each the elemental power of the land counterpoints the rise of emotion and desire in the human protagonists. For a time the former is dominant, then it subsides to leave an uneasy state of balance – or tension – between them, as in 'The Winds'.

When Josie wakes in the night the commotion she hears seems at first to be sounds of joy, from 'the Old Natchez Trace and Lover's Lane'. In fact a storm has arisen, and her father is taking her from her bed, as he will take her younger brother Will from his, for temporary safety from the thunder, the lightning 'flowing like the sea', and the potentially destructive wind. But the tempestuous weather turns Josie's thoughts above all else to Cornella, the 'cousin or niece' of the family opposite, on whom she has a passionate crush, and whom she perpetually honours in her mind, so well-stocked with fairytales: 'But she only had to face the double-house in her meditations, and then she could invoke Cornella. Thy name is Corn, and thou art like the ripe corn, beautiful Cornella.'[24]

When the storm's over, and Josie goes out to see what it has left in its wake, she comes across a scrap of paper with Cornella's name on it, a discovery so momentous that she has to find a special hiding place for it. What the paper says is what her heart has been saying before the storm, and throughout its course: '"O my darling I have waited so long, when are you coming for me? Never a day or a night goes by that I do not ask When? When? When?"'[25]

The feeling of geographical actuality is strong in all these stories, but in none more so than 'Asphodel', where the setting is that curious ruin, Windsor Castle. High on a bluff, it now consists of twenty-two Corinthian columns but was once a five-storeyed mansion whose tower Mark Twain used as a navigation landmark when he was a Mississippi river pilot. In the story its columns have dwindled to six; three 'old maids', assembled like choric figures from a Greek tragedy, tell of the ghastly, doomed marriage between Miss Sabina (newly dead) and Mr Don McInnis (vanished), whose proud old families came

---

24. C.S. p. 216.
25. C.S. p. 221.

from opposite sides of the Old Natchez Trace – 'actually situated almost back to back on the ring of hills, while completely hidden from each other, like the reliefs on opposite sides of a vase'.[26] One notes the Greek reference again; Windsor Castle/Asphodel was built out of the South's infatuation with Graeco-Roman culture, and this story is permeated by a sense of the Greek – is a pocket Aeschylean tragedy with an appropriate satyr-play as a coda. The tragedy is this: Miss Sabina, possessed of an Amazonian strength of mind, such as certain Southern upper-class women encouraged in themselves to counteract the general cult of the 'belle', drove Mr Don McInnis out of her family home, in which they had been living, because she was so fed up with his infidelities. ("How can I hate him enough?" she said over and over. "How can I show him the hate I have for him?"[27]) Mr Don decamped to Asphodel with a girlfriend; the house burned down, to Miss Sabina's gratification, though this event also unhinged her. Nemesis struck from within. The three women relate, in extended stichomythia, a lifetime of obsessional, unhappy tyranny which reached a horrible apotheosis only a matter of days earlier. Miss Sabina – old now and crazy – entered the post office 'bent upon destruction', proceeding to bully the postmistress and customers, and to tear up letters: 'A fury and a pleasure seemed to rise inside her, that went out like lightning through her hands.'[28] (We are reminded of the fire that consumed Asphodel itself.) She then laid about her wickedly with a stick until she had a stroke and dropped down dead.

But 'Asphodel' does not end with this hubris; the three old maids are interrupted in the midday calm that follows their storytelling by an apparition out of the tangle of vines: a bearded old man, 'buck-naked', followed by a troupe of goats. Of course he suggests Pan, but the women are not in any real doubt that he is Mr Don McInnis, one of Pan's avatars! Pan, Dionysus, the intense midday sun, the prolix vines, billygoats with beards blowing in the wind, and horns – the force that delivers these is what the women both fear and desire. And lest it be

26. C.S. p. 201.
27. C.S. p. 203.
28. C.S. p. 206.

thought that Eudora Welty views the chorus only as a passive, interpretative body, one must add that it was this trio who told Miss Sabina of Mr Don's infidelities, and so set the whole course of action in train.

In 'Livvie' we are concerned with a young black girl, who at sixteen marries a much older man – 'dignified, for he was a coloured man that owned his land and had it written down in the courthouse'[29] – who takes her off to his 'nice house, inside and outside both', twenty-one miles from her home, set in deep country off the Natchez Trace, a long way from any neighbours. Jealous and possessive of his young wife, Solomon eventually takes to his bed, keeping Livvie virtually as a servant, a prisoner in the house. She makes 'a nice girl to wait on anybody'. Most of the time, old Solomon sleeps.

But a day comes when Livvie *does* go out, as a result of the marvellously described visit from a cosmetics firm representative, Miss Baby Marie, who senses that Solomon is dying. Livvie walks out on to the Trace, the new purple lipstick fresh and bright on her mouth, and there, on the opposite side, stands a man who is immediately drawn to her: Cash, one of Solomon's own field-hands. They walk, they wordlessly express their mutual attraction – and when they return to Livvie's house, they enter the room where Solomon is asleep:

> . . . in his dreams he might have been an ant, a beetle, a bird, an Egyptian, assembling and carrying on his back and building with his hands, or he might have been an old man of India or a swaddled baby, about to smile and brush all away.
>
> Then without warning old Solomon's eyes flew wide open under the hedge-like brows. He was wide awake.
>
> And instantly Cash raised his quick arm. A radiant sweat stood on his temples. But he did not bring his arm down – it stayed on the air, as if something might have taken hold.[30]

Was he going to strike the old man, his boss, dead? Who can say? Here is another instance of one laden moment containing many truths and possibilities, of which only some can find realization in what follows.

---

29. C.S. p. 228.
30. C.S. p. 238.

What does happen is that Solomon recognizes Cash and, understanding the currents that have passed between the two young people, delivers a sort of blessing upon them which makes his wife sob, and in which he movingly asks for forgiveness: "'God forgive Solomon for carrying away too young girl for wife and keeping her away from her people and from all the young people would clamour for her back.'"[31] Then he dies – and the released couple break into a dance.

Cash, young, black and poor, resembles the previous story's semi-aristocratic old Mr Don McInnis in one thing: his unashamed male sexuality. Even the guinea pig he keeps in his pocket seems to personify the liveliness of the male member also, so to speak, kept there. And in 'At The Landing' – set in an intimately felt present-day Rodney's Landing – we meet yet a third manifestation of male power, Billy Floyd.

Billy Floyd is a young man to whom Jenny, encountering him in the countryside around the Landing, has been drawn for some time, but whom her grandfather (with whom she lives) dislikes intensely; indeed, he goes so far as to forbid her to see him. Billy is a constant flesh-and-blood testimony to the presence of the atavistic (which forest and river, with their respective controls of the destiny of the place, also proclaim). An old lady has told her that Billy Floyd may have

> the blood of a Natchez Indian, though the Natchez might be supposed to be all gone, massacred. The Natchez, she said . . . were the people from the lost Atlantis, had they heard of that? and took their pride in escape from that flood, when the island went under. And there was something all Indians knew, about never letting the last spark of fire go out.[32]

Jenny's grandfather is haunted by the notion that the river which has forsaken the Landing will return; the night before he dies, he dreams that it does so. But it returns in the form of a flood from which Floyd has to rescue Jenny in his boat. Then:

> He took hold of her, put her out of the boat into a little place he made that was dry and green and smelled good, and she went to

31. C.S. p. 239.
32. C.S. p. 254.

sleep. After a time that could have been long or short, she thought she heard him say, 'Wake up.'

When her eyes were open and clear unto him, he violated her and still he was without care or demand and as gay as if he were still clanging the bucket at the well.[33]

Naturally we think back here to Jenny's ancestors, Jamie Lockhart and Rosamond Musgrove. Jenny, like Rosamond, appears to enjoy an experience which has been given (out of male desire for gratification) without her assent. Later, after Billy has gone away, she searches for him, makes her way through the whole lush wilderness to the banks of the real river, and finds there a group of fishermen who know where he is – he is out on the dangerous waters of the river, but he will return shortly. These men go on to take Jenny to a houseboat where, one by one, they rape her. When an old woman inquires about her, she is told simply: 'She's waiting for Billy Floyd.'

This is perhaps Eudora Welty's most obscure story, certainly as far as the ending is concerned, and the author herself has criticized this. Does Jenny's ultimate fate have something to tell us about the white race's guilt and weakness with respect to the red, Billy Floyd's people (he rides a red horse too)? It is not clear.

What is to be made of this group of Natchez Trace stories? They are puzzling and not one of them is wholly satisfactory. First, because place is overpowerful; one feels that the characters, for all the thought and feeling accorded them, arose after, and as a result of, the author's fascination with River Country, and are consequently dwarfed by it, interesting us most when they are in direct juxtaposition with it. Secondly, the sexual content does not seem to be completely under the author's control. Part of the point of these stories is their demonstration of the wantonness in male sexual conduct, counterpointed by the troubling wantonness of nature (fire, flood, etc.). But it is a wantonness for which the women appear to have a curious relish that rather vitiates any more complete picture. One feels the cruelty of the act dissolve in the rather rhapsodic treatment of Livvie, or of Jenny's capitulations. Moreover, the animalistic behaviour eclipses other aspects of the men concerned, preventing any overview of them.

33. C.S. p. 251.

What comes over best in these stories – particularly in 'Livvie', which seems considerably the most complete – is the feeling of loneliness of the woman denied experience. And in the terrible wait of the repeatedly raped Jenny, we have a poetic, disturbing image of vulnerability.

But 'The Wide Net' itself is a beautiful work, beautiful alike in its humanity and in its art. A tall story – owing much to one told Eudora Welty by the friend to whom she dedicated it – it is also characterized by a simplicity which ensures that its people, while they are admirably representative, are superior to and illuminated by its events.

A little bored by the way his young wife carries on about her pregnancy, William Wallace Johnson goes out for a night with the boys, and does not come back until early morning. His wife decides to teach him a lesson: she leaves a note, the exact content of which we never read, but the gist is that she is going to do away with herself – drown herself in the Pearl River. William Wallace rouses the friend he has been out on the town with, and they decide that with the help of various neighbourhood families, and with the use of old Doc's wide net, they will go down the Old Natchez Trace to the river, and drag it all the way to Dover, to see whether they can find Hazel.

The search, for all the appalling possibility of Hazel's drowned body, is the greatest fun, and everybody enjoys himself, notably the young members of the retinue – the black boys Sam and Robbie Bell, the energetic Rippen brothers, Brucie and Grady (who counts all the cars of the passing train and has a sty – 'Sty, sty, git out of my eye, and git on somebody passin' by'). Morning turns into a glorious day, though in the afternoon a storm will break, there will be heavy rain on the river, and lightning will strike. But while the sun is out, there is a contagious radiance: they catch 'more shoes than I ever saw got together in any store', and a great deal of fish; they find an alligator and a long eel; William Wallace dives and dives, gaining the depths, 'so dark that it was no longer the muddy world of the upper river but the dark clear world of deepness . . .'. Half-naked, they all sit on the bank and cook and eat catfish (that famous Southern speciality), and William Wallace – who has lost his wife, and might come across her body sooner or later – stretches himself out in 'the glimmer and shade of trampled sand', and exclaims contentedly:

'There ain't a thing better than fish,' and then makes everybody laugh by doing a comic dance with a catfish hooked to his buckle-belt.

Does William Wallace know what we soon suspect? – that Hazel was teasing him in that letter, and has never gone anywhere near the river? Surely he does – and Eudora Welty has herself said as much, in an interview with *Comment* magazine (16 October 1965): 'I don't think he thought she was down there. But she could have been.' And certainly it turns out that the oldest member of the party, Doc with the net, never thought it likely:

> 'Who says Hazel was to be caught? . . . She wasn't in there. Girls don't like the water – remember that. Girls just don't haul off and go jumping in the river to get back their husbands. They got other ways.'[34]

And so it turns out. When the long, adventurous, fruitless day is over, William Wallace gets back to his house:

> He went up on the porch and in at the door, and all exhausted he had walked through the front room and through the kitchen when he heard his name called. After a moment, he smiled, as if no matter what he might have hoped for in his wildest heart, it was better than that to hear his name called out in the house.[35]

The voice, of course, is Hazel's. Their reconciliation is affectionately spirited, charged by a delightfully erotic sense that some sort of justice has been done.

Why does this story succeed where the others in this group do not? Principally because in 'The Wide Net' the people stand at the very centre of one's attention. Place is extraordinarily tangible – the river, its denizens and surprises, the river town of Dover after the rain, the hill in the evening with the fragrant honeysuckle – but it is place as part of the experiences of its inhabitants. And the people themselves – unintellectual, lively, quick in their responses – are caught with a joy in their being, served by an intently watchful eye and vigilant ear. So when the moments of illumination do come – the appearance of the

---

34. C.S. p. 186.
35. C.S. p. 187.

famous King of Snakes ('in an undulation loop after loop and hump after hump of a long dark body') and the advent of the storm – they visit and temporarily translate *real* human beings, whom we have seen going about their business as their seemingly unremarkable selves.

Nor must the mythic quality of 'The Wide Net' be ignored. Whereas in 'Asphodel' the Greek parallels seem perhaps overdeliberate, too much in conscious control, in this story they come to the mind naturally, suggested by events. There is a sense in which William Wallace and his company are Jason and the Argonauts, embarked on their quest. Certainly the whole journey down the river is a rite of passage: William Wallace temporarily released from domesticity and marriage, the men bonded in adventure, tests of prowess (all those necessary yet symbolically significant dives into depths!) and irresponsibility – until the female, in the form of Hazel's mother, asserts itself. Thus the reconciliation is also a restoration of the male–female balance. This is surely what causes that sense of happiness we take away from 'The Wide Net'; we are happy to feel ourselves kin to these muddled, ordinary enough people, because (as in William Wallace's dives) we salute the hidden profundity of their yearnings, and recognize them as our own.

'Asphodel', 'The Winds' and 'At The Landing' show that Eudora Welty had not yet arrived at a creative relationship between her own naturally introverted temperament and the demands of the exterior. If violence is to be addressed, the introspective mode of, say, 'At The Landing' is not sufficient. We feel nagged by a need to understand Billy Floyd (and his peers) in action, and that understanding is withheld from us. 'The Wide Net', on the other hand, is Chaucerian in its sense of human foible, shared experience and kinship (whether literal or otherwise), and it is surely ancestor to *Losing Battles*.

VI

So far Eudora Welty has been presented as a figure on her own, a traveller analogous to those essential solitaries, the salesmen or itinerants of her early stories, the eye behind the camera, the rapt mystic of the layered moment. But she is someone who greatly (and, it would appear, easily) enjoys other people's company, and has maintained friendships all her long life.

The young woman who wrote these stories, and attained success in the larger, literary world, had a firm place in her native community that was perhaps unusual among writers. Too often, the pattern for the artist who is not from a metropolitan area – for Americans perhaps more than most others – is that they move away from the society of their youth, and in a different milieu associate principally with others connected with the arts. Mark Twain turned his back on Hannibal, Missouri; Willa Cather did not live among the Swedish and Czech emigrants who people her earlier novels. Those of the 'revolt from the village' (Sherwood Anderson and others) rarely stayed in that 'village'. The peregrinations and deracinated lifestyles of the Lost Generation – a mere ten years Eudora Welty's seniors, after all – are too well known to need further comment. Katherine Anne Porter's life was a restless one; indeed, in our knowledge of it there are lacunae where she chose silence to cover wild experiences. And of the Southerners who were most famous in the 1940s Allen Tate followed – if briefly – a Lost Generation way of life before attaching himself to universities; Robert Penn Warren also became an academic, for much of the decade in Minnesota; Faulkner, his spells in Hollywood notwithstanding, was indeed of Mississippi, but something of a recluse, certainly not easily placed with regard to his neighbours. Carson McCullers led a bohemian existence in New York City. But Eudora went on knowing her friends and her family's friends from earliest days, and one hastens to say that they included many remarkable and unusual people. Their unusualness was not necessarily of the kind that made them establish themselves in New York City and earn national or international reputations, though some of them (the composer and conductor Lehman Engel, for instance) did exactly that.

Eudora Welty has said that she has always been a shy person, shy physically, and that this was often a factor inhibiting certain relationships. She is distinguished by a considerable refinement, of manners, interests, cast of mind. But she is also lively and amusing, and this combination of refinement and spiritedness remains one of her most individual and noticeable qualities.

Gossip, serious interest in culture (all her set kept up with what was happening in New York, and made regular stays there), excursions into the Mississippi countryside, the development of liberal views, inventive frivolity (making 'spoof' advertisement photographs, for example, of high fashion) – here was a real community of spirit on which Eudora Welty was to draw for her later work, as well as for her own sustenance. (Indeed, even a book set in a different atmosphere from her own, like *Losing Battles*, must derive some of its spiritual or emotional solidity from her sense of belonging to friends and family.)

Eudora Welty's photographs show a continuum of happy socializing from the mid 1930s on. One can see quite easily the currents of sympathy flowing between these Jacksonians: Charlotte Capers (later Director of the Mississippi Archives, whose entertaining conversation I have listened to with such pleasure); Hubert Creekmore, writer, translator, the 'boy up the street' who told Eudora Welty where to send her story 'Death of a Traveling Salesman', 'a very talented and wonderful person', she has said, and her photographs of him somehow convey this; Nash K. Burger, who became editor of the *New York Times Book Review*; Lehman Engel, who came back to Jackson every year from New York; Rosa Wells, John Fraiser Robinson, Willie Spann; Frank Lyell, who became Professor of English at the University of Texas; the painter Helen Lotterhos . . . a number of these names are recognizable from the dedications of Eudora Welty's books. *Delta Wedding*, for example, is dedicated to John Fraiser Robinson (who, having supplied her with the anecdote that gave rise to 'The Wide Net', was the dedicatee of that story too); while *The Golden Apples* is dedicated to Rosa Wells and Frank Lyell.

By the time *The Wide Net* was published, Eudora Welty was enjoying a certain reputation and security of position. This was due, she will often say, to the appearance in her life of two men of remarkable judgement: John Woodburn and Diarmuid Russell.

Eudora Welty had submitted her early stories to magazines herself:

[An] old friend, Hubert Creekmore . . . knew all about sending stories out. He was a writer who started before I did, and published many good novels and poems. I wouldn't let him read anything I wrote but just asked him: 'Hubert, do you know where I

can send this?' – and he said to John Rood of *Manuscript*. So
I sent it off and John Rood took it, and of course I was flabber-
gasted. So was Hubert![36]

This was 'Death of a Traveling Salesman'. After that her stories were
accepted for that distinguished periodical *The Southern Review* (published from Baton Rouge by the Louisiana State University Press,
though in no sense an organ for it), then under the editorship of Robert
Penn Warren and Albert Erskine. Katherine Anne Porter was one of its
advisers. The part played in the second phase of the Southern Renaissance by the *Review*, with its strong New Criticism affiliation, is immense; it seems only right that fine work like 'A Piece of News', 'A
Memory' and 'The Hitch-Hikers' should have first appeared in its
pages.

But Eudora Welty found it quite another matter to interest national
magazines. A young editor from Doubleday, John Woodburn, passed
through Jackson and stayed at the Weltys' house, taking a number
of her stories back to New York. He tried to get Doubleday – and others
– to publish them, but with no success. Then he recommended them to
a friend who was opening an agency: Diarmuid Russell, son of the distinguished Irish poet 'A.E.', Yeats's great friend. Eudora Welty says:

> I was his first client, I think. . . . He wrote me when he first opened
> the agency, just as he wrote to lots of young writers whose works
> he'd read that he liked and whom he thought might not have an
> agent. And I had had some stories in the little magazines and the
> quarterlies. He wrote and asked if I would like him to be my agent.
> I'd never heard of a literary agent, but I liked his letter so much that
> I wrote back by return mail and said, 'Yes! be my agent!' Well, his
> first letter showed me what he was like. And also his second
> because when I wrote and said, 'Yes, be my agent,' he wrote back
> and said, 'Now don't be too quick. You don't know anything about
> me; I may be a crook for all you know.' He spent about a full year
> or maybe two full years trying to get my stories in national circu-
> lation magazines and finally made it with the *Atlantic*.[37]

36. C.E.W. pp. 85–6.
37. C.E.W. p. 173.

The *Atlantic* took two stories, 'A Worn Path' and 'Why I Live at the P.O.', which appeared in the issues of February 1941 and April 1941 respectively. Even today, after so much else that Eudora Welty has published, their outstanding imaginative excellence holds firm; they have passed into general literary currency.

Eudora Welty often speaks of her luck in having had publishing friends, but one must also invert her statement: what luck for a young agent or a young editor to come across 'A Worn Path'!

With the appearance of her stories in national magazines, New York publishers became interested, and Diarmuid Russell was now able to sell a collection of her stories, *A Curtain of Green*, to John Woodburn at Doubleday. Her delight can easily be imagined:

> And, you know, for Doubleday to publish a book of short stories by an unknown writer was really extraordinary in those days. Or, maybe, at any time for anyone to. So when John moved to Harcourt, Brace I moved with him, because it was to him that I had the allegiance.[38]

The book she took to Harcourt, Brace was *Delta Wedding* (1946). She was to stay with them for her next three books; then came the fifteen years occupied with the writing of *Losing Battles*. During this time almost everyone she had known at Harcourt, Brace left. So she turned to Random House, where Albert Erskine, formerly of *The Southern Review*, now was: 'when I came to Random House it was another full circle'.

Eudora Welty calls John Woodburn 'marvellous'; of Diarmuid Russell she has said: 'I just can't tell you what it meant to me to have him there. His integrity, his understanding, his instincts – everything was something I trusted.'[39]

Critics and other writers had not been slow to recognize the quality of her work (though as was to be expected, there were dissident, unappreciative voices such as Diana Trilling, with her almost violent animus against anything Southern, who gave a harsh and extremely unperceptive review to *The Wide Net* and later to *Delta Wedding*).

---

38. C.E.W. p. 186.
39. C.E.W. p. 185.

Robert Penn Warren, for instance, wrote an essay, 'The Love and the Separateness in Miss Welty', for the prestigious *Kenyon Review* (Spring 1944), treating with the analytic seriousness one associates with the New Criticism, both the preoccupations and the artistic methods of her writing, establishing emphases that seem today to have been astonishingly prescient. While Eudora Welty remained a very private person, averse to any literary life as such, naturally her confidence was enormously boosted by support and serious consideration from outside. Here too may be another explanation of the shift in her work that *Delta Wedding* marks.

In her first two collections of stories, and in her novella, Eudora Welty's work is, to an interesting degree, the fruit of an empathic curiosity; from a sheltered life she went out to poor parts of her own State, discovering people and modes of life she had scarcely suspected in her professional-class youth. Her discovery of the past, often so present and powerful, was also a reaching out to what was challenging and different, to the violence and vision of a society whose history had come to some sort of end.

But with *Delta Wedding*, her first full-length novel, the second phase of her work begins, and curiosity yields to deeper and wider knowledge. Not that curiosity disappears – on the contrary, it is ever-present. But on one level Eudora Welty must have appeased some hunger of mind and spirit, and was now ready to bring her scrutiny and understanding to bear on a whole field of life. It is surely significant that whereas the stories in *A Curtain of Green* and *The Wide Net* focus primarily on individuals detached from their society (though the society is never absent), the works of her second phase have wide canvases (even the classically circumscribed *Optimist's Daughter*) with strong evocations of community, yet their major portraits are ampler, deeper, more complex.

While this development must be due principally to a process of individuation, one must obviously not underestimate the enormous change in the world in which Eudora was now writing – more specifically while she was working on *Delta Wedding*. On 7 December 1941 the Japanese attack on Pearl Harbor precipitated US entry into the Second World War, and the shadow over life that had been evident for so long now became omnipresent. Chestina Welty had once written on the back of a photograph of her young sons scrambling over the relics of war at Vicksburg: 'May these boys never know closer contact with a cannon,' but her prayer for peace was not granted: Walter Welty went on active Pacific service. Everywhere relatives and friends were in danger; if this obviously darkened Eudora Welty's picture of life, it also made her value with more urgency and strength kin, all dear ones, community, civilization itself.

Her private involvement and obligation apart, she took on a number of wartime journalistic assignments to earn money, and as a burgeoning writer she now had a greater choice of these. During the summer of 1944 she worked for the *New York Times*. As the editor of its *Book Review*, Robert Van Gelder, later reported:

> she turned out splendid reviews of World War II battlefield reports from North Africa, Europe and the South Pacific. When a churlish *Times* Sunday editor suggested that a lady reviewer from the Deep South might not be the most authoritative critic for the accounts of World War II's far-flung campaigns, she switched to a pseudonym, Michael Ravenna.[40]

And Michael Ravenna was to be respected, quoted, and called upon to give opinions. However, he was away visiting the front whenever his appearance on radio shows was requested.

The war was, of course, an upheaval in American lives, if not quite to the degree that it was to the British, and it is as such that Eudora Welty, so naturally a peaceful and family-orientated person, speaks of it in conversation. The inroads its demands made on Americans were of particular relevance to the Southern situation; after the service given by so many black citizens, the culture of segregation increasingly became perceived as the injustice and evil anachronism it was.

When Eudora Welty returned to Jackson from New York, it was *Delta Wedding* that absorbed her working life. No writing could be more assured than 'First Love' and 'A Still Moment'; their artistry is that of genius. But they stand very much as articulations of private epiphanies; from *Delta Wedding* on, Eudora Welty has confidence in

---

40. C.E.W. p. 33.

the validity of a more encompassing vision, and also in her powers to serve it. She now emerges as she must have felt: as a tested writer addressing fellow-citizens.

VII

Characteristically, *Delta Wedding* began as a short story. Eudora Welty submitted 'The Delta Cousins' to Diarmuid Russell; he wrote back saying that what she had written was Chapter Two of a novel. Respecting his advice, she thought about his remark and decided he was right. It is not surprising, however, that the key to *Delta Wedding*'s preoccupations is to be found in that second chapter, which centres round her Fairchild aunt's gift of a night-light to Dabney Fairchild, the bride-to-be. The night-light is surely reminiscent of Keats's Grecian Urn:

> Aunt Primrose lighted the candle inside and stepped back, and first the clay-colored chimney grew a clear blush pink. The picture on it was a little town. Next, in the translucence, over the little town with trees, towers, people, windowed houses, and a bridge, over the clouds and stars and moon and sun, you saw a redness glow, and the little town was all on fire, even to the motion of fire, which came from the candle flame drawing.[41]

Dabney is thrilled, but as she runs up the front steps to greet her mysterious, powerful Uncle George, and goes towards her fiancé, Troy Flavin, she lets the precious object drop, and it shatters into fragments. That breakage means so many things: the fragility/destructability of the Old Southern past, represented by the aunts; and of the feminine, represented by Dabney herself as she comes into contact with the two most ineluctably male persons in her world – the one a spiritual outsider, the other a literal one. The night-light was a little piece of fantasy, a 'pretty' – for town and fire were never thus – and our fantasies, too, can be shattered through a sole act. But the night-light itself depicts – albeit in a pleasing way – conflagration, destruction. Although the Delta world is one of river and well-watered fields, the

---

41. D.W. p. 46.

possibility of fire must never be forgotten. And fire burns inside everyone of us: we are a temple for it, as the night-light was for the candle. George is burning – for his wife, for other women, for life; Dabney, still not out of her teens, fresh, innocent, is also burning – for Troy Flavin . . . The lyrical manner, the very real charm, of *Delta Wedding* must not blind us (as apparently they did some of its earlier critics) to its essential sombreness.

'The day was the 10th of September, 1923.' Eudora Welty went to enormous trouble over this date; having decided on the 1920s, when she had been near enough in age to the little girl Laura, who is to be our principal conductor into the Delta world, she realized she had 'to pick a year when all the men could be home and uninvolved', with no claims from war or flood – a year that could, in its lack of external pressure, show both the strengths and the essential precariousness of such a society as the Fairchilds' Shellmound.

We enter the Delta with motherless Laura McRaven, travelling on the train officially called the Yazoo–Delta but generally known as the Yellow Dog, to stay with her mother's large family, the Fairchilds, for Dabney's wedding to the estate overseer.

And then, as if a hand reached along the green ridge and all of a sudden pulled down with a sweep, like a scoop in the bin, the hill and every tree in the world and left cotton fields, the Delta began. . . . Thoughts went out of her head and the landscape filled it. In the Delta, most of the world seemed sky. The clouds were large – larger than horses or houses, larger than boats or churches or gins, larger than anything except the fields the Fairchilds planted. . . . [Laura] watched the Delta. The land was perfectly flat and level but it shimmered like the wing of a lighted dragonfly. It seemed strummed, as though it were an instrument and something had touched it. Sometimes in the cotton were trees with one, two or three arms – she could draw better trees than those were. Sometimes like a fuzzy caterpillar looking in the cotton was a winding line of thick green willows and cypresses, and when the train crossed this green, running on a loud iron bridge, down its centre like a golden mark on the caterpillar's back would be a bayou.

When the day lengthened, a rosy light lay over the cotton . . .
In the Delta the sunsets were reddest light. The sun went down
lopsided and wide as a rose on a stem in the west, and the west
was a milk-white edge, like the foam of the sea. The sky, the field,
the little track, and the bayou, over and over – all that had been
bright or dark was now one color. From the warm window sill
the endless fields glowed like a hearth in firelight, and Laura,
looking out, leaning on her elbows with her head between her
hands, felt what an arriver in land feels – that slow hard pounding in the breast.[42]

None of Eudora Welty's descriptions of the Mississippi landscape
is more beautiful than this, not even those evocations of the Trace,
in reality of far more immediate beauty to the eye of the traveller. The
beauty here derives in part from the child's excitement, from her
enthralled gratitude. But by making Laura arrive at the Fairchilds' at
sunset – as in the external world of distances and train timetables she
would have done, journeying from Jackson – Eudora Welty has created a strong picture, which will never fade, of a society standing at the
fierce end of something, of things coming to a close even though the
light is fiery and impressive.

The Delta epitomizes the Old South – the huge plantations, the rich
landowners, the overseers, the black people working the fields. Land,
money, white power – and the black workers who made all that possible, and still constitute a considerable percentage of the rural population. Culturally they could be said to be the victors of the contained
struggle, for, defying the State penitentiary and the multiple cruelties
of life in such a system, they have given their passionate music not just
to their own people, or to the South, or to America, but to the entire
world – for the Delta, that strange triangle some way north of Jackson,
with Tennessee's Memphis at its apex, is 'the land where the Blues
began'.

Met at the station by a family Studebaker crammed with children
(including the 'baby') and dashingly driven by fourteen-year-old
Orrin, Laura is plunged into a benevolent bustle, among which move

42. D.W. p. 4.

her cousins' parents, Battle and Ellen, repositories of order and kindness. Ellen – particularly seen by herself, creating islands of quiet amid the hurly-burly of preparations – is reminiscent of Mrs Ramsey in Virginia Woolf's *To the Lighthouse* (a novel Eudora Welty greatly admires, and has written about; reading it was a revelation for her, she has said). These fictional women share a wholly feminine capacity to receive and contain the needs and confusions of others, particularly those who are dependent on them. Of Ellen riding through the countryside it is said: 'The repeating fields, the repeating cycles of season and her own life – there was something in the monotony itself that was beautiful, rewarding – perhaps to what was womanly within her.'[43]

Nevertheless – and despite the insistent loveliness of much of the writing about the pattern of life at Fairchilds – we read only superficially (as Diana Trilling must have done) if we are not aware all the time of the pressures from without, and the disruptions from within, threatening, almost certainly eventually combining to destroy this seemingly impregnable, peaceful place; even Ellen's calm (she is now with child yet again, in tune with nature's cycles) will not quite prevail against them.

Outside, the very sight of Man-Son picking cotton is enough to disturb Dabney, who feels obliged to nod 'sternly' to him. She cannot forget that Man-Son was one of the 'two little Negroes' who 'had flown at each other with extraordinary intensity here on the bank of the bayou', and had had to be parted, their knife opportunely caught in the air by her Uncle George. Then there is the old black woman, Partheny, with her far from comforting magic. They are animated by forces quite outside any Fairchild jurisdiction, and acknowledge quite alien codes.

Nor have the Fairchilds jurisdiction enough even to settle the world as they feel it should be. The Great War killed the talented Uncle Denis, but even before his death he had made a misalliance, itself a surrender to non-Fairchild forces, the result of which was his half-idiot daughter Maureen, with her strange broken speech and widely directed spite. (She is at the centre of the novel's recurring anecdote, an illuminating paradigm of what patrimony cannot control.)

---

43. D.W. p. 240.

Maureen is an outsider, albeit from within. Dabney's husband-to-be, Troy Flavin, from the red-clay hills of north-east Mississippi (the country of 'Death of a Traveling Salesman'), is another kind of outsider; his practical, laconic obstinacy is needed by this Delta family to ensure the probity of their inheritance, but they cannot resist looking down on him, with his hill-country ways and his touching pride in his mother's traditional patterned quilts. (The marriage will surely not be an altogether satisfactory or easy affair; in Troy again we sense a foreign code that will operate against the family's traditions.)

No character is more important to the novel's meaning than Laura's uncle, George Fairchild. Now a lawyer in Memphis, he retains the closest relationship with his family, from nine-year-old Laura upwards – a relationship which extends even to his loved dead brother, Denis. But there is something different, unfamilial, about him; he lacks the others' tribal simplicity of vision. Dabney realizes this early on: 'George loved the *world*, something told her suddenly. Not them!' [the Fairchilds] 'Not them in particular.'[44] She has just remembered seeing him at a picnic:

> Perhaps the heart was always made of different stuff and had a different life from the rest of the body. She saw Uncle George lying on his arm on a picnic, smiling to hear what somebody was telling, with a butterfly going across his gaze, a way to make her imagine all at once that in that moment he erected an entire, complicated house inside his sleepy body. It was very strange, but she had felt it. She had then known something he knew all along, it seemed then – that when you felt, touched, heard, looked at things in the world, and found their fragrances, they made a sort of house, within you, and all else, the other ways to know, seemed calculation and tyranny.[45]

Of these last George can always stand acquitted; his vital capacity for empathy with a diversity of others does not make him a comfortable member of the group, and some of his ways of expressing that

44. D.W. p. 37.
45. D.W. pp. 33–4.

empathy are discomfiting. We have to believe him when he tells Ellen that, obeying the urge of the moment, he made love to the wild, lost girl of the woods whom she also encountered by chance. When we meet George, his wife Robbie has run away; later they are reconciled, but in choosing her, and in his dealings with her, George departs from the solid (at least in their own eyes) Fairchild values.

Robbie is socially another outsider, whose very existence is a disturbance to the Fairchilds' older values; in her beats the pulse of the modern age. As a wedding is the centralizing event in the book, this outsider's reflections on traditional marriage, traditional attitudes to the relationship between the sexes, is of central importance:

> And of course those women knew what to ask of their men. Adoration, first – but least! Then small sacrifice by small sacrifice, the little pieces of the whole body! Robbie, with the sun on her head, could scream to see the thousand little polite expectations in their very smile of welcome. 'He would do anything for me!' they would say, airily and warningly, of a brother, an uncle, a cousin. 'Dabney thinks George hung the moon,' with a soft glance at George, and so, George, get Dabney the moon! Robbie was not that kind of woman. Maybe she was just as scandalous, but she was born another kind. She did want to ask George for something indeed, but not for the moon – not even for a child; she did not want to, but she had to ask him for something – life waited for it. . . . What do you ask for when you love? If it was urgent to seek after something, so much did she love George, that that much the less did she know the right answer.[46]

Even though this novel moves through Shellmound, the family home, and Marmion (Uncle Denis's place), with all their antebellum furniture and portraits; through the vast endless-seeming cotton-fields and the township named for the Fairchilds themselves, the work is totally opposed to the power of possessions – opposed in a non-revolutionary sense, maybe, but opposed none the less. Perhaps that is why the strongest thematic images concern those for whom possession is not possible – the wild girl of the woods, and Maureen who, though she

---

46. D.W. p. 146.

has inherited property, will never be able to appreciate it, let alone manage it.

Towards the end of the novel the Fairchilds assemble for the wedding photograph (Eudora Welty the photographer is constantly present in this book). The professional photographer tells the group that his work has also included pictures of a young girl killed on the railroad track:

> 'Train victim. . . . Ladies, she was flung off in the blackberry bushes. Looked to me like she was walking up the track to Memphis and met Number 3.'
> . . . the light flashed for the picture.
>   Ellen looked at the bride and groom, but if the first picture showed her a Mitchem Corners choral singer, then the second showed her seeing a vision of fate; surely it was the young girl of the bayou woods that was the victim this man had seen.[47]

Fate, reality, the violence of the world beyond the Delta property, break in – even when we are wishing them elsewhere – disrupting even the carefully planned conventional serenity of an official wedding photograph.

Over and over again the story is told of how Uncle George had to stop and rescue Maureen, who had got her foot stuck on the wooden crossing of the railroad track, while the train – the very Yellow Dog on which Laura arrived at Fairchilds – came ever nearer. His wife Robbie cried out that he had never have done the same for her. Everyone's version of what happened is different; the exact truth of the situation will never be known. But in every version its symbolic properties are bold and resonant enough. George, Robbie and Maureen all exist at tangents to the family and its view of life, but help to define it even while they expose its limitations. An accident to any one of this trio would impair the health of the whole, yet there is something that tends towards the violent, the 'accidental', in each of them. And the Yellow Dog/Yazoo–Delta train is the force of the external modern world that can be ignored only on peril of death.

Like all Eudora Welty's major fiction, this novel insists on

---

47. D.W. p. 218.

complexity, on pluralism even inside the single person. Perhaps no scene is more compelling than Robbie's walk in the 'boiling sun', reflecting on the deficiencies of the Fairchild view of men and women, a dissension with which the reader must sympathize:

> In Robbie's eyes all the Fairchild women indeed wore a mask. The mask was a pleading mask, a kind more false than a mask of giving and generosity, for they had already got it all – everything that could be given – all solicitude and manly care. Unless – unless nothing was ever enough – and they knew. Unless pleading must go on forever in life, and was no mask, but real, for longer than all other things, for longer than winning and having.[48]

She breaks off from such percipient thoughts because of the heat – she wants shade – and she sees a little cotton shed to take refuge in.

> But when she stepped into the abrupt dark, she jumped. There was a Negro girl there, a young one panting just inside the door. She must have been out of the field, for sweat hung on her forehead and cheeks in pearly chains in the gloom, her eyes were glassy.
> 'Girl, I'm going to rest inside, you rest outside,' said Robbie.
> Like somebody startled in sleep, the girl moved out a step, from inside to outside, to the strip of shade under the doorway, and clung there. Her eyes were wild but held a motionless gaze on the white fields and white glaring sky and the dancing, distant black rim of the river trees.[49]

This passage brings us a fresh realization of the disturbing coexistences of ordinary life, and of the extreme difficulty (and danger) of simplifying things with ready moral judgements.

Delta Wedding is full of marvellous insights, many of them furthering Eudora Welty's vision of the layered richness of the 'still moment'. 'A moment', reflects Ellen Fairchild, 'told you the great things; one moment was enough for you to know the greatest thing.'[50] No less worthy of admiration is its design, moving from Laura's arrival to the

---

48. D.W. p. 147.
49. ibid.
50. D.W. p. 240.

last night of her stay, with Troy and Dabney returned home, and George and Robbie about to go back to Memphis. But perhaps the execution of that design is less complete than it is in the later fiction. In the novel's overall movement there is rather too little overt tension for its theme to emerge as sharply above its context as it should, and again, there is insufficient concentration on one viewpoint. We forsake Laura for Ellen, for Dabney, for Robbie, and a certain dissipation of attention results. While it would be wrong to call this strongly felt and thought novel apprentice work, one can certainly avow that thereafter, in her longer novels, Eudora Welty repeated none of its comparative shortcomings, so writing it *was* a kind of apprenticeship, after all. All her later productions are consistently and organically true to the laws of their own being.

VIII

Delta Wedding is more overtly metaphoric of the South than any of Eudora Welty's later novels. After finishing it, she probably felt – as the South moved perceptibly into a new phase of its history with the end of the Second World War – that no metaphor could ever be complete enough, at least not without being reductive in a way totally inimical to her art; therefore, one should not be attempted. This surely endorses my view that it is right to look on the Southern writer as a member of a country rather than a region. By analogy, no British or French novelist would be expected to produce, in a novel of any depth or individuality, something which answered the 'British' question or the 'French' one, even supposing (a difficult supposition) such a question to be identifiable. It would be expected that the novelist would write out of her or his personal literary make-up, and make a contribution to truth through the complex validity of that individual work of fiction. Nevertheless there are, of course, novels which do seem peculiarly expressive of the prevalent condition of a society at one particular time – in British fiction I think of Angus Wilson's *Late Call* or V.S. Naipaul's *The Mimic Men* – though their power derives from a genuine matching of real creative interests to the cultural dilemma in question.

Non-Southerners, however – it must be conceded – increasingly expected the Southern novelist to tackle what they saw as the

'Southern subject', summed up as 'the officially sanctioned separateness and inequality of the races'. Southern writers, therefore, often confronted a double expectation of their work: those who knew them and knew the South would look to some fulfilment of personal vision (which would, of course, take in on some level the general Southern scene). Those from outside would expect a direct treatment of the question, tantamount to a statement of position. There was a feeling that it was necessary to know exactly where William Faulkner or Eudora Welty or Allen Tate stood. There was even a feeling – not usually articulated – that Southern writers should not be read unless their credentials were clear, otherwise there would be a danger of a sort of moral contagion.

Almost thirty years after *Delta Wedding* was published in summer 1973, the novelist Alice Walker asked Eudora Welty: 'Did you think there was anything wrong with Mississippi (in terms of race) in those days, when you were young? Did you see a way in which things might change?' Her reply – made as a private individual – is highly illuminative of her position and practice as a writer:

> Well, I could tell when things were wrong with people, and when things happened to individual people, people that we knew or knew of, they were very real to me. It was the same with my parents. I felt their sympathy, I guess it guided mine, when they responded to these things in the same way. And I think this is the way real sympathy has to start – from direct feeling for something present and known. People are first and last individuals, and I don't think of them in the mass when I feel for them most.[51]

Eudora Welty's parents' commitment to humane democratic values gave her the best start in life; made it impossible for her to assent to a segregated society. Her natural feeling for individual predicaments – which first received artistic expression in her many, many photographs of poor country black and white people – meets an impenetrable denial of itself in the form of the thwarting or inadmission of any fellow-human being. At the same time her dissociation

---

51. C.E.W. p. 134.

from thinking about people 'in the mass' (perhaps a little disingenuous in political terms) signals her artistic behaviour as a novelist – and the position to which that behaviour will lead. She is not going to desert her own territory to deal with mass psychology, mass movements. To do so would be to cease to exist as the novelist she is.

In that interview Alice Walker also asked her: 'Over the years have you known any black women? Really known them?' She answered:

I think I have. Better in Jackson than anywhere, though only, as you'd expect, within the framework of the home. That's the only way I'd have had a chance, in the Jackson up until now. Which doesn't take away from the reality of the knowledge, or its depth of affection – on the contrary. A schoolteacher who helped me on weekends to nurse my mother through a long illness – she was beyond a nurse, she was a friend and still is, we keep in regular touch. A very bright young woman, who's now in a very different field of work, began in her teens as a maid in our house. She was with us for ten years or more. Then she went on to better things – her story is a very fine one. She's a friend, and we are in regular touch too. Of course I've met black people professionally, in my experience along the fringes of teaching. Lecturing introduced us. The first college anywhere, by the way, that ever invited me to speak was Jackson State [a black university established in the days before desegregation] – years ago. I read them a story in chapel, as I remember.[52]

Eudora Welty's honesty – the supreme importance of this quality is something she stresses in this interview – is nowhere more apparent than here. She does not lay claim to intimacies she has not had, and nor to knowledge either, but answers feelingly about her experiences. She does not indulge in generalized rhetoric, and by implication, makes us realize anew just how difficult the social climate was – the more difficult for a woman, because of its traditionalism – blocking so many possible or burgeoning cross-race meetings.

We are left in no doubt about Eudora Welty's passionate belief in the huge importance of deep friendships between the races, and social

---

52. C.E.W. pp. 136–7.

cultural exchanges between the two communities. As well as speaking at black Jackson State in the days before desegregation, she was also the first speaker before a black-and-white audience at Millsaps College.

The period in which Eudora Welty produced her main body of work – 1949–72 – saw the most radical changes and upheavals in Southern life since the Secession and the Civil War. With hindsight, it seems inevitable that this should be so; it did not necessarily seem so inevitable at the time.

The South, of all areas of the United States, had been the biggest beneficiary of the 'New Deal'. That meant that while many grave problems remained, it recovered most quickly from the Depression. The Federal payment allocated in this period to poor black people – the kin of all those photographed by Eudora Welty – brought home to them just how shockingly ill-paid they had been before. At the time of American entry into World War II the Southern black people were perhaps aware as never before of the injustices of the society they had been living in – and determination that it must be transformed grew, considerably reinforced by the whole matter of black service in the forces and involvement in the war machine. Black soldiers, expected to fight against an enemy rightly vilified for its racism (Nazi Germany) and carrying out their duties with enthusiasm and courage, found that prisoners of war could enjoy privileges denied to them because of their colour. Both the Truman and the Eisenhower administrations had to address this situation in both the 'North' – cities like Detroit saw increased resentment and violence – and, with far more diffidence and difficulty, in the South.

This was the period of persistent and successful campaigning by the NAACP (National Association for the Advancement of Coloured Peoples), founded in 1900, and of general agitation that segregation should end in schools (and if in schools, why not elsewhere?). Nowhere was resistance fiercer or more obsessional than in the Deep South, Mississippi and Alabama. There was a resurgence of the Ku Klux Klan; there was the growth of White Citizens' Councils, which sought to preserve the Southern status quo against outside influences.

Despite the fact that Lincoln had been a Republican, and therefore the white South had a Democrat allegiance by tradition, it was the Democrats (mostly Northern Democrats) who attracted black voters and concerned themselves with attempting a racially just and equal society. As we have seen, Eudora Welty worked for Adlai Stevenson in his bid to be President, against Eisenhower, and he would undoubtedly have been a far more active enthusiast for black rights than the man who defeated him.

The problems of the South, as such, are not tackled directly in Eudora Welty's great works of fiction (though she produced powerful and disturbing work on the 'Southern subject' in stories such as 'Where is the Voice Coming From?', 'Keela, the Outcast Indian Maiden' and 'The Demonstrators'). Some explanation or justification for this will be provided later in my consideration of Eudora Welty's 1965 essay 'Must the Novelist Crusade?'. Nevertheless, there are some features of her art, even in the first of her major books, which are worth considering in this context.

I believe she is a far more revolutionary writer than she is generally considered (and consciously – indeed, determinedly – so, though she has preferred not to vaunt her claims). Her profound humanism has led her to eschew all ways of reducing human beings to stereotypes, to embodiments of this quality or that. Releasing her people from the strict definitions of sociopolitical confrontation – particularly her fellow-white Southerners, whom she knows the best – she is able to present their depths and secret intuitions.

Eudora Welty has delivered Southern literature from an obligation to follow the pervasive myths about its history and make-up. One can search the pages of her work in vain to find any reference whatsoever to the glories of the antebellum South, any championing of Agrarianism (other than a heartfelt reverence for the countryside and the work that sustains it), or any possible flirtation with the desirability of segregationalist culture. She has quite simply and radically ignored the idea that the South is under a peculiar obligation to respect and exculpate itself for its past. A further radicalism is to be found in her treatment of a powerful and familiar aspect of the South, its Fundamentalist/Evangelical religion. In *Losing Battles* much is made of the Baptist–Methodist rivalries (albeit primarily in social terms), and in Uncle Nathan a tragic man is given over to a fierce and inexorable

God, as he might be in the pages of Flannery O'Connor. The historically placed Lorenzo Dow apart (a wonderful portrait indeed), it is hard to think of other characters, either black or white, who are vessels for Southern religion.

Eudora Welty's fascination with myth – with the whole mythopoeic mythological cultures of the Classical and Celtic worlds – may represent her search for an alternative vision of human existence to that of Fundamentalist Christianity. She did not experience this at first hand; and so it does not require a dissociation from Christianity in a broader sense. In *One Writer's Beginnings*, published in 1984, she was to declare of herself as a young woman: 'I painlessly came to realize that the reverence I felt for the holiness of life is not ever likely to be entirely at home in organized religion.' But it is out of her reverence for the holiness of life that her great work has been written. That is the credo – more inclusive in width and depth than a straitened political or religious one – which animates and sustains her classic works.

PART TWO

THE CLASSIC WORKS
AND AFTER

4

'FIRST LOVE' AND 'A STILL MOMENT'

I

'FIRST LOVE' tells of the change that comes over Joel Mayes, 'a deaf boy twelve years old', during the severe winter weather of late January 1807. Joel has been in Natchez since the summer, following a hazardous journey from Virginia during which he lost both his parents, and nearly lost his own life too. He lives at the hotel, where he 'does' the boots, sleeping in a 'dark little room' behind the saloon bar beside the puncheon table. 'It was in his own room, on the night of the first snowfall, that a new adventure began for him.'[1] This sentence has a fairytale ring, yet the word 'adventure' is too subjective for a fairytale. The story is concerned with the expansion of a boy's soul – with what is, in effect, his deliverance from the limitations and prison of both his circumstances and his being.

To his room come two men; they are to come night after night, and it does not take him long to recognize them from the posters everywhere in the town: one is Aaron Burr, on trial for conspiracy against the US government; the other is Burr's friend and accomplice Harman Blennerhassett. The moment Burr raises his right arm, 'a tense, yet gentle and easy motion', becomes for the boy (as yet unnoticed) 'like the first movement he had ever seen, as if the world had been up to that night inanimate'. And in a sense, it is. 'First Love'

---

1. C.S. p. 156.

marks a significant development of Eudora Welty's concept of the crucial moment.

Here, Burr is responsible for the sudden intensification of Joel's world. Eudora Welty is, of course, reaching across her story to readers (particularly American readers) who will project mythic qualities on to him. The eminent officer in the War of Independence, Burr obtained the same number of votes as Thomas Jefferson in the presidential election of 1800, but it was Jefferson who was chosen to be President by the House of Representatives. Burr went on to be defeated again, as gubernatorial candidate for New York. Blaming his enemy, the Federalist leader Alexander Hamilton, for this, Burr challenged him to a duel, and Hamilton died. Burr then fled to the Southwest, where his activities led to charges of treason against the US government. He and his fellow-conspirator, Harman Blennerhassett, were quartered in Natchez for trial in neighbouring Washington, by this time the Territory's capital.

Joel could not have known any of this, but he intuits some of Burr's attributes by paying rapt attention to him; indeed he senses (and readers sense with him) the wild turn that Burr's life will take after his trial. (Burr was to serve a long exile in England and France, and nurture many improbable and improvident schemes before returning to the United States.)

Joel is almost literally enthralled by Burr. The disgraced politician fills the great gulf of need in his orphaned and perforce silent life; he wants to serve him, be of use to him:

> [Burr and Blennerhassett] came to his room every night, and indeed Joel had not expected that the one visit would be the end. It never occurred to him that the first meeting did not mark a beginning. It took a little time always for the snow to melt from their capes – for it continued all this time to snow. Joel sat up with his eyes wide open in the shadows and looked out like the lone watcher of a conflagration. The room grew warm, burning with the heat from the little grate, but there was something of fire in all that happened. It was from Aaron Burr that the flame was springing, and it seemed to pass across the table with certain words and through the sudden nobleness of the gesture, and touch Blennerhassett.[2]

2. C.S. p. 158.

The use of fire here intensifies the legendary aspect of 'First Love'. In 'Death of a Traveling Salesman' Sonny went to 'borry some fire'; the Natchez Indians (who are on the margins of this very story) believed that fire was sacred. Here fire, which makes survival possible, gives comfort and epitomizes our most passionate energies, is embodied in a single human being – and Joel goes out to him, as he would to the element itself, knowing that he will be able to manage no dialogue, no relationship. All he has to bestow is his own fire-like capacity for devotion.

Love makes Joel follow the course of Burr's doomed sojourn in Natchez; he watches him as he is taken up by Natchez society, he accompanies the crowds to his trial, and then witnesses his escape from Natchez in disguise – the once mighty man now obliged (as a consequence of own misjudgements) to flee in 'mock Indian dress and with the boot polish on his face'.

> Joel followed him on foot toward the Liberty Road. As he walked through the streets of Natchez he felt a strange mourning to know that Burr would never come again by that way. If he had left in disguise, the thirst that was in his face was the same as it had ever been. He had eluded judgment, that was all he had done, and Joel was glad while he trembled. Joel would never now know the true course, or the true outcome of any dream; this was all he felt. But he walked on, in the frozen path into the wilderness, on and on. He did not see how he could ever go back and still be the boot-boy.[3]

Love has brought the twelve-year-old into the 'real' adult world, where fantasies must be acknowledged for what they are, and pain must be confronted. In this 'bitterest' winter Joel has found the fire he was in need of, and it has not only kept him alive, it has ensured his entry into life proper. The story thus tells of his arrival at a level of psychic health, at a stable ego, at a plane that can involve worry and sadness, but is always preferable to other more protected levels. In presenting this it has performed the function of the fairytale, and the depth of its quasi-realistic treatment of people and place drives it far deeper than *The Robber Bridegroom*, or such a comparatively crude excursion as

---

3. C.S. p. 167.

'Asphodel'. Its especial imaginative conviction derives from Joel's disability (his deafness) and his hero Burr's manifest character defects. These mirror the inevitable deficiencies and restrictions of our own personalities, and those of any human being in whom we place our trust.

The last paragraph of all tells of the posse coming along the Liberty Road to capture the escaped Burr. As for Joel: 'He walked on. He saw that the bodies of the frozen birds had fallen out of the trees, and he fell down and wept for his father and mother, to whom he had not said good-bye.'[4] Thus 'first love' and its concomitant, necessary sorrow have unlocked in Joel the grief for his parents to which he has hitherto been unable to give vent.

Joel's impaired condition returns us to Eudora Welty the photographer taking pictures of casualties of the Depression, though in no spirit of sociological patronage or false pity; it returns to the sick Bowman in 'Death of a Traveling Salesman', trying more truly to discern the couple's hospitality and, above all, to that fine 'photographer's' story 'The Key'. All apprehension is impaired, is the lesson Eudora Welty wishes to teach us, since we can never communicate with others on all levels, with all modes of being. In 'The Key' the young man witnessed and attempted to reach the deaf-and-dumb couple; now in 'First Love' we, as the deaf boy, have to make sense of and gain the attention of the whole hearing, noise-making world:

> . . . his eyes were for something else, something wonderful. He saw the breaths coming out of people's mouths, and his dark face, losing just now a little of its softness, showed its secret desire. It was marvellous to him when the infinite designs of speech became visible in formations on the air, and he watched with awe that changed to tenderness whenever people met and passed in the road with an exchange of words. He walked alone, slowly through the silence, with the sturdy and yet dreamlike walk of the orphan, and let his own breath out through his lips, pushed it into the air, and whatever word it was it took the shape of a tower. He was as pleased as if he had a little conversation with someone.[5]

4. C.S. p. 168.
5. C.S. p. 154.

And then, watching Burr and Blennerhassett at their middle-of-the-night rendezvous:

> ... the breath of their speech was no simple thing like the candle's gleam between them. Joel saw them still only in profile, but he could see that the secret was endlessly complex, for in two nights it was apparent that it could never all be told.[6]

Eudora Welty herself has said:

> ... there was another reason for making the boy in 'First Love' a deaf character: one of the other characters – Aaron Burr – was a real person. I couldn't invent conversation for him as I could for an imaginary character, so I had him speak in front of a deaf boy who could report and interpret him in his own way.[7]

Invention would have been the more difficult, she could have added, since Burr was a famous rhetorician and wit. But without giving us a word from him, Eudora Welty convinces us of two things: first, that Burr is a man in the grand manner, the public arena in life is his natural habitat; second, that through this very propensity to grandeur, he is now doomed.

Burr exhibits that doubleness that had interested Eudora to such an extent in *The Robber Bridegroom*: the man of intellect, the political genius, the distinguished soldier and servant of his country, whose middle age was characterized by enormous recklessness, bad judgement and vanity – his subversion, however understandable, of Jefferson; the duel which brought about Hamilton's death; the grandiose and impracticable plans he allowed himself to entertain. We know from what Joel simply but attentively sees that as well as his remarkable qualities, Burr possesses attributes that will not serve him or others well:

> Always he talked, his talking was his appearance, as if there were no eyes, nose, or mouth to remember; in his face there was every subtlety and eloquence, and no features, no kindness, for there was no awareness of the present.[8]

---

6. C.S. p. 158.
7. C.E.W. p. 84.
8. C.S. p. 159.

He flirts with the women at Natchez soirées, argues with Blennerhassett – who, with his wife, joined him from Ireland, and whose diaries of this wintry month Eudora Welty drew on; we see him lying down on the puncheon table and sleeping, his face full of his own dark and destructive past, and we know then – through Joel – of the unsatisfactory years stretching ahead for him.

In *The Robber Bridegroom* Rosamond applied an ointment to Jamie's face, and his disguise (of berry juice) came off; she could then see who he was – or rather, one half of who he was. Joel needs no recipe; his intent gaze is enough.

> This was Burr's last night: Joel knew that. This was the moment before he would ride away. Why would the heart break so at absence? Joel knew it was because nothing had been told. The heart is secret even when the moment it dreamed of has come, a moment when there might have been a revelation. . . . Joel stood motionless; he lifted his gaze from Burr's face and stared at nothing. . . . If love does a secret thing always, it is to reach backward, to a time that could not be known – for it makes a history of the sorrow and the dream it has contemplated in some instant of recognition. What Joel saw before him he had a terrible wish to speak out loud, but he would have had to find names for the places of the heart and the times for its shadowy and tragic events, and they seemed of great magnitude, heroic and terrible and splendid, like the legends of the mind.[9]

This leads to another important theme of the story: the opening out of a moment into a palimpsest of such dimensions that life's truths seem held in it.

There are three such moments for Joel, before the last of them at the puncheon table. The first is when he sees Burr raise his arm, and his love began. The second follows on from the entrance into 'his' room of Blennerhassett's wife (and, according to history, his niece also; Joel's fixity of gaze gives him knowledge that they are in some way blood-kin). Her playing of the violin has an extraordinary effect on Joel, which

---

9. C.S. p. 165.

he cannot understand; he can tell, though, that she is manifesting some deep force behind life, neither moral nor analysable. He knows 'a sensation of pain, the ends of his fingers were stinging. At first he did not realize that he had heard the sounds of her song [on the violin], the only thing he had ever heard.'[10] Is this to be taken literally? Almost – as people can experience temporary silence or sightlessness at times of emotional climax. The moment when it is as if Joel hears (as once he did, before his traumatic journey from Virginia) has a strange result:

> For a moment his love went like sound into a myriad life and was divided among all the people in his room. While they listened, Burr's radiance was somehow quenched, or theirs was raised to equal it, and they were all alike.[11]

The third moment is a sensing of the terrible powers which propel us all without our conscious knowledge, powers which have already been expressed in the intensity of that winter. The winter weather, after all, contains the whole story; the first and last sentences are imbued with its inexorability, and the prose throughout appears to be engaged in a struggle with some great force beyond Joel, Burr, Blennerhassett, Natchez, even the Trace and Wilderness themselves, a force that can transform the world, paralyse activity, take lives – and for which Nature is an inadequate term.

II

'"Inhabitants of Time!"' shouts Lorenzo Dow, the Man of God in 'A Still Moment'. '"The Wilderness is your souls on earth."' For this half-mad preacher, time and space are merely the context in which the testing of souls, the sorting out of the Elect from the Damned, is done; just as the Wilderness, with the Trace running through it, is a no-man's-land between two places of habitation.

Eudora Welty brings three men together to a spot on the Trace at some date in 1822 (certain historical liberties have been taken). She knew Lorenzo Dow from his volumes of sermons, sermons which

---

10. C.S. p. 164.
11. ibid.

(as we have seen) were often delivered from horseback, as (to himself) here. Some of the sentences which have attracted most critical attention in this story, as showing the complexities of the author's intellectual position – those on Love and Separateness, for example – are in fact his own, sometimes used verbatim.

John A. Murrell (here called James), the bandit whose appalling activities, pre-eminently slave-stealing, had the whole South as theatre, is known from the writings of the man responsible for his capture and ten-year imprisonment, Virgil A. Stewart – *A History of the Conviction, Life, and Designs of John A. Murel [sic]* (1835) – and from the popular Southern romantic novelist William Gilmore Simms (1806–70), who wrote about him in two of his most successful books.

As for John James Audubon, he was one of the outstanding Americans of his time; *The Birds of America* (1827–38) has been called 'the most magnificent monument raised by art to science'. Eudora Welty had access to his posthumously published *Journals* (1929) and *Letters* (1930).

These three men owe something of both their posthumous public stature and their fascination and significance in this story to that doubleness their times seem to have peculiarly encouraged. One of the trio, Lorenzo Dow, actually believes in dualism; it permeates his whole reception of the world. As he moves along the Trace he sees, between its high banks, 'dusky shapes', those of the saved and (duskier still) those of the damned. His inner ear continually hears promptings to a course of action to save himself from mortal danger, though even here a duality is in operation: 'Each time when he acted so it was at the command of an instinct that he took at once as the word of an angel, until too late, when he knew it was the word of the devil.'[12] His every movement – along the Trace, as elsewhere – is informed by opposition to his being: 'Lorenzo well knew that it was Death that opened underfoot, that rippled by at night, that was the silence the birds did their singing in.'[13] On horseback he is 'turning half-beast and half-divine, dividing himself like a heathen Centaur'.[14]

---

12. C.S. p. 190.
13. ibid.
14. C.S. p. 190.

Eudora Welty tells us how important to him his 'despair' is, 'as well as his ecstasy', and points out that 'he had no way of telling whether he would enter [a] sermon by sorrow or by joy'. Yet, paradoxically, his desire to serve his dualistic creed (or vision) – for in a faith like his, intellect and emotion are one – has dulled him to the other antitheses of existence:

> To transmute a man into an angel was the hope that drove him all over the world and never let him flinch from a meeting or withhold goodbyes for long. This hope insistently divided his life into only two parts, journey and rest. There could be no night and day and love and despair and longing and satisfaction to make partitions in the single ecstasy of this alternation.[15]

At the end of the story he is to be obsessed by another division: between Love and Separateness. In a sense this debate is itself a dramatization of the doubleness of his mythopoeic personality; adept at saving himself, happy with Peggy, his loving wife in Massachusetts, fearing her death as well as his own, and reminded of her when he looks at natural beauties such as flowering trees – indeed, a tender man rather than otherwise – he is committed to a religion of great ferocity, preaching distrust of what pleases the senses, renunciation of the warm and sheltering, and a continual awareness of life as a battleground. This division in him, we assume, was the engine that drove him to his achievements as a preacher – achievements which torridly survive to this day; and it is certainly what creates the agony of his thoughts with which this story concludes.

Murrell might seem to belong to the same dark company as Little Harpe (he who was the good-hearted Jamie Lockhart's shadow) in *The Robber Bridegroom*. As a young man he used to waylay travellers with a cry of 'Stop! I'm the Devil!'; he believed that he was a very instrument of Evil, serving its cause both outwardly – kidnappings and murders – and inwardly, reciting stories of his crimes to himself and to imminent victims, stories in which he was gradually revealed as the all-powerful destructive perpetrator. He built a horrifying reputation for himself as highway robber (on the Trace and elsewhere; he was a

---

15. C.S. p. 194.

wanted man in eight States), as horse thief (hence the H.T. branded on his thumb) and slave-stealer. (He would steal and sell the same slave time and again, killing him when he had become too widely known for use.) Yet he moved through his terrible life in a state of unbearable loneliness; here, depraved as he is, he is possessed by a need for communication, company, even acceptance. (We think of Milton's Satan, knowing what he has forfeited by his rebellion, yet grieving at his loss.) Maybe Murrell's waylaying and murdering of people is a fearsome perversion of his need for them. Moreover, is there not a spiritual dimension to his acts?:

> Lorenzo might have understood . . . that Murrell in laying hold of a man meant to solve his mystery of being. It was as if other men, all but himself, would lighten their hold on the secret, upon assault, and let it fly free at death. In his violence he was only treating of enigma.[16]

Certainly in this possessed man's literal vision (but is he any more possessed than the virtuous Lorenzo Dow?) Eudora Welty reveals doubleness: 'blinking into a haze', he will see 'whiteness ensconced in darkness', light that only turns one deeper into self.

Besides, this man knows fear, and his fear – this is crucial to the meaning of the whole story – is of the present, of any given minute in which he is situated. He has to protect himself from its naked power by remembering what he has already done, and by thinking of what he will do afterwards – in both cases deeds of destruction: 'Destroy the present! – that must have been the first thing that was whispered in Murrell's heart – the living moment and the man that lives in it must die before you can go on.'[17] And again, terrifyingly:

> This man going forward was going backward with talk. He saw nothing, observed no world at all. The two ends of his journey pulled at him always and held him in a nowhere, half asleep, smiling and witty, dangling his predicament.[18]

Beyond his period and outside this story John James Audubon's fame

---

16. C.S. p. 192.
17. ibid.
18. ibid.

is, of course, very different from Dow's or Murrell's. Audubon is not merely celebrated outside the South – indeed, outside America; he has been a means by which his time and place have gained the interest and admiration of the rest of the world. *The Birds of America* is not only an extraordinary contribution to both natural history and to art, it is an intensely American contribution. The landscape against which his birds, rendered with such intense accuracy, are placed is always virginal, mysterious – the wilderness given a near-mystical loveliness that never, however, removes it from reality. Yet no sooner has one written the word 'American' than an aspect of Audubon's doubleness appears: born in Haiti, illegitimate, he was educated in France. The disciple of both Rousseau and Buffon, he studied natural history and art under the quintessentially French Jacques David. He put it about that he was the Lost Dauphin (son of Louis XVI and Marie Antoinette). Thus this very American art has French antecedents, both spiritual and literal, and for part of his life he was concerned with himself more as a member of French royalty than as anything else:

> Audubon in each act of his life was aware of the mysterious origin he half-concealed and half-sought for. People along the way asked him in their kindness or their rudeness if it were true, that he was born a prince, and was the Lost Dauphin, and some said it was his secret, and some said that that was what he wished to find out before he died. But if it was his identity that he wished to discover, or if it was what a man had to seize beyond that, the way for him was by endless examination, by the care for every bird that flew in his path and every serpent that shone underfoot.[19]

So his quests for wildlife are at once services to art and science and a means of vindicating himself, of making the myth he'd encouraged about himself seem the truer, giving a psychological edge to all his now famous journeys: 'Not one was enough; he looked deeper and deeper on and on, as if for a particular beast or some legendary bird.'[20] In other words, he is trying to find a singleness behind the doubleness, and attaining in so doing a (fairly explicit) Platonism of vision:

19. C.S. p. 197.
20. ibid.

O secret life, he thought – is it true that the secret is withdrawn from the true disclosure, that man is a cave man, and that the openness I see, the ways through forests, the rivers brimming light, the wide arches where the birds fly, are dreams of freedom? If my origin is withheld from me, is my end to be unknown too? Is the radiance I see closed into an interval between two darks, or can it not illuminate them both and discover at last, though it cannot be spoken, what was hidden and lost?[21]

The three men cannot exactly be said to *meet* in this place ('a great live-oak at the edge of a low marshland') and at this time (the hour of sunset), for meeting implies communication, acknowledgement, mutual statements of identity, tacit or otherwise – whereas in this case:

There was a little space between each man and the others, where they stood overwhelmed. No one could say the three had ever met, or that this moment of intersection had ever come in their lives, or its promise fulfilled.[22]

But it is none the less a convergence that becomes something rather more because of the arrival, witnessed by all three men, of a 'solitary snowy heron' coming 'to feed beside the marsh water'. It does not draw them together so much as – simply by being its compelling, independent and beautiful self – relate the three more nearly to one another, in their human complexity and limitation.

The eyes of the three men, which have seen the sunset in the west, turn to the bird, and become 'infused with a sort of wildness' – wildness in the sense that each makes a primeval return to the domain of the bird. In the paragraph which is surely the climax of the story, the one which celebrates and shows forth the stillness of its title, Eudora Welty writes:

What each of them had wanted was simply *all*. To save all souls, to destroy all men, to see and to record all life that filled his world – all, all – but now a single frail yearning seemed to go out of the three of them for a moment and to stretch toward this one snowy, shy bird in the marshes. It was as if three whirlwinds had drawn

21. C.S. p. 195.
22. C.S. p. 196.

together at some centre, to find there feeding in peace a snowy heron. Its own spiral of flight could take it away in its own time, but for a little it held them still, it laid quiet over them, and they stood for a moment unburdened . . .[23]

In a very real sense, the snowy heron *is* the eponymous still moment. For not only can its peaceful being stand for some immeasurable, eternal quiet behind all existence, it also constitutes a dimension in which three men so diverse and so separate in their preoccupations can converge. And so its occurrence, in this spot on the Natchez Trace, is an embodiment of Time itself – of Time that is double in nature, transcendentally beyond human recording yet manifesting itself to us in identifiable minutes. Audubon reflects: 'It was as if each detail about the heron happened slowly in time, and only once.'[24]

And the individual responses to the snowy heron? It effects a caesura in their obsessed, near-solipsistic thoughts. Lorenzo's first reaction is delighted wonder. The Man of God goes out to it with the same rapture (we conjecture) as he went out to his young wife, saying to himself: 'Nearness is near, lighted in a marsh-land, feeding at sunset. Praise God, His love has come visible.'[25] In his dualistic vision he inclines instinctively to place the bird among the emanations of God's goodness.

When Murrell looks at the bird, it is to think again about the ambitious scheme he has been entertaining, which also manifests doubleness. He, the notorious slave-stealer and slave-killer, will instigate what he calls 'The Mystic Rebellion', whereby he will cause insurrection among bondmen. Again, though, his rebellion is essentially the same as that of Milton's Satan: he will incite a company to liberate themselves, but not into freedom. In his fantasies, slaves bow down before him, and on the banner they will all follow will be an 'awesome great picture of the Devil'.

But the bird's inscrutable reality breaks into even this compulsive dream. Solitary as it is, the heron brings home to Murrell his own loneliness, and he finds himself overtly desiring communication with

---

23. ibid.
24. ibid.
25. C.S. p. 195.

others (with society in general, and with the two individuals he has just encountered). Perhaps the bird signifies the end of his criminal career, and this still moment is the moment of his capture, of his having to confess. Or perhaps, above all else, it is the moment when he at last makes contact:

> His look pressed upon Lorenzo, who stared upward, and Audubon, who was taking out his gun, and his eyes squinted up to them in pleading, as if to say, 'How soon may I speak, and how soon will you pity me?' Then he looked back to the bird, and he thought if it would look at him a dread penetration would fill and gratify his heart.[26]

Meanwhile, Audubon is taking out that gun.

Audubon has responded to the snowy heron for what it is, as the others have not and could not. His first and instinctive response is to watch it, 'steadily, in his care noting the exact inevitable things. When it feeds it muddies the water with its foot'.[27] Even before its appearance he has been 'looking with care' all about him (the only one of the three who does so), rejoicing to be out on the Trace after his protracted, oversophisticated stay in Natchez, acclimatizing himself to the 'great abundance', and being able again to 'see things one by one'. This very day he has been pleased to see a flock of purple finches overhead, and to note 'the soft *pet* of the ivory-billed woodpecker'. And when the heron comes into view, he, alone of the three, appreciates its extreme vulnerability, fragility coexisting with strength:

> The bird was defenceless in the world except for the intensity of its life, and he wondered, how can heat of blood and speed of heart defend it? Then he thought, as always as if it were new and unbelievable, it has nothing in space or time to prevent its flight.[28]

Already possibly, even in the moment's stillness, he knows what he will do: 'And he waited, knowing that some birds will wait for a sense of their presence to travel to men before they will fly away from them.'[29]

---

26. C.S. p. 196.
27. ibid.
28. ibid.
29. ibid.

So it is Audubon, the naturalist, whose career and art depend on wildlife, who kills the snowy heron, who brings the still moment to its end. Lorenzo Dow is horrified; in his eyes, as he meets them, Audubon sees 'horror in its purity and clarity' for the very first time in his life. Murrell merely withdraws from the deed, pleased that it has brought this encounter to a close; he can now go on his dark, self-dramatizing way again.

Why did Audubon kill the heron? On one level the answer is easy to state – and state it Eudora Welty does (though in such a tone that we do not take it for a complete explanation):

> [Audubon] tightened his hand on the trigger of the gun and pulled it, and his eyes went closed. In memory the heron was all its solitude, its total beauty. All its whiteness could be seen from all sides at once, its pure feathers were as if counted and known and their array one upon the other would never be lost. But it was not from memory that he could paint.[30]

One inference to be made is that it is art and science which are most ruthless in their power over living beings – more so than religion (Dow) and political action (Murrell, however darkly, can be said to represent this). Audubon's absence of malice, his lack of cruelty, only compound the chill horror of what he has done. He has killed in a noble cause, he will turn his action to humankind's good (maybe even to the heron-kind's ultimate good) by what he will proceed to do – and already we can see a scientifically exact, artistically living painting, with the Natchez Trace landscape numinously in the background. But – to offset this – he has taken a unique life; that heron whose miraculous beauty and innocence so moved him can never exist again, has been taken out of time and space.

Is Eudora Welty here projecting, presenting in heightened form, guilt which she knew when she was waiting for that right moment as a photographer, that instant when to click the shutter, which also told her a 'storyteller's' truth? Are the exploitations, the deprivations of individual freedom, caused by the disinterested activities of art and science, really more utterly destructive than those of religion (which,

---

30. C.S. p. 197.

after all, seeks to save all souls) or of politics (which, however murky, offers its adherents parts to play)? The story forces us to confront this dreadful possibility. When the heron is dead – while Lorenzo knows fear, and Murrell feels glad to be on his way again – Audubon has 'his head still light in a kind of trance'. He moves back into the forest reasonably contented – not that he is not ambivalent, even a little uneasy, about what he has done:

> What he would draw, and what he had seen, became for a moment one to him then. Yet soon enough, and it seemed to come in that same moment, like Lorenzo's horror and the gun's firing, he knew that even the sight of the heron which surely he alone had appreciated, had not been all his belonging, and that never could any vision, even any simple sight, belong to him or to any man. He knew that the best he could make would be, after it was apart from his hand, a dead thing and not a live thing, never the essence, only a sum of parts; and that it would always meet with a stranger's sight, and never be one with the beauty in any other man's head in the world. As he had seen the bird most purely at its moment of death, in some fatal way, in his care for looking outward, he saw his long labour most revealingly at the point where it met its limit.[31]

This is a difficult passage. On the one hand, Eudora Welty suggests that no art (or science) can match the perfection of the living thing. For that reason it would seem a doomed venture which does not justify the extinction of a life in its cause. On the other hand, her admiration for Audubon's achievements here is obvious (as we know it is in life); it is capable of bringing us to a more informed and penetrating vision, especially if we take it at the 'point where it met its limit'. In that sense, therefore, it would seem to vindicate the ruthlessness it requires. . . . Nevertheless, I do not think this adds up to a satisfactory reading of the story – do not think that its lesson is that Audubon's later rendering of the snowy heron will compensate – indeed, redeem – its unmerited death.

While Eudora Welty's own art may have important qualities and

---

31. C.S. p. 198.

procedures in common with Audubon's, it is not to be identified or confused with his. In her story she remains apart from him, even where she is explaining the workings of his mind most sympathetically, and she chooses to end not with his reconciliation to what he has done but with the anguish of Lorenzo Dow.

By calling the story 'A Still Moment', and by identifying that moment with the living being of the heron, Eudora Welty is positing a reality beyond that of any human endeavour and interpretation – and how the quotation above insists on the partial and doomed nature of any attempt to map or reproduce that reality! Eudora may forgive Audubon as Audubon; she may admire his art as the best possible outcome of his particular credo, and of the behaviour that goes with it; she may even share – vicariously – his acceptance of his limitations, and rejoice that out of them may come accurate and beautiful portraits of birds. But she ascribes no absolute qualities to him or his position, no qualities more positive than those which balance best against those of the other men. The most important truth in the story is the fact of the heron's mysterious, peaceful being. Against that – and against the destruction of that being – we must make our judgements, state our preferences, seeing the moral and metaphysical deficiences of them all.

In identifying the heron with a moment of Time that is outside clock Time, and the killing of it with a reinstatement of the latter in all its restrictiveness, the whole story can be seen as a confrontation by temporal, spatial humanity of the non-temporal, non-spatial dimension behind existence. Religion, the pursuit of virtue, politics, blind violence, the pursuit of evil, art and science – all in their various ways, pay homage and point to this, while revealing themselves impotent – one is tempted to say useless – before it. Better, perhaps, just to accept the snowy heron with wonder, and try to emulate its harmony with the laws of its being.

But while this idea may be what we ultimately preserve from the story, what we immediately take away from its concluding paragraphs is an expression of ontological despair – or outrage. The terms of the debate roused in Dow's head by the heron's death derive from the actual sermons and writings of the preacher himself:

157

The hair rose on his head and his hands began to shake with cold, and suddenly it seemed to him that God Himself, just now, thought of the Idea of Separateness. For surely He had never thought of it before, when the little white heron was flying down to feed. He could understand God's giving Separateness first and then giving Love to follow and heal in its wonder; but God had reversed this, and given Love first and then Separateness, as though it did not matter to Him which came first. Perhaps it was that God never counted the moments of Time; Lorenzo did that, among his tasks of love. Time did not occur to God. Therefore – did He even know of it? How to explain Time and Separateness back to God, Who had never thought of them, Who could let the whole world come to grief in a scattering moment?[32]

Lorenzo's way of dealing with these devastating thoughts – and with the touching picture of the heron that comes into his mind immediately after them – is to retreat (the only apt word) into the harshnesses of dualistic religion: the beauty of the heron was a temptation away from God, on whom his mind should have been fixed, a diversion of maybe devilish origin; therefore the bird itself must be upbraided as 'Tempter!' Only thus can he banish sorrow, the memory of beauty and intellectual agony.

Perhaps the only resolution lies in art such as this. The tension between our intimations of transcendental truths and earthbound reality has to be recognized: those moments when – however fleetingly – reconciliation is presented to us must be venerated. 'A Still Moment', springing logically from Eudora Welty's interest in the Natchez Trace and the people who knew it, is also the culmination of all those moments of revelation, in life and in art, that had fascinated her for so long. It is a mystical work, a work literally of ecstasy, and so consummate is the art which expresses it that it remains unsurpassed in all her later work, though it has pointed the way to important elements in it. This is already, I believe, the domain of W.B. Yeats and 'The Tower', and even if Eudora Welty would not seem to agree with the great poet's proud lines here, she surely would have seen her art as kin to their spirit:

---

32. ibid.

Death and life were not
Till man made up the whole,
Made lock, stock and barrel
Out of his bitter soul,
Aye, sun and moon and star, all,
And further add to that
That, being dead we rise,
Dream and so create,
Translunar Paradise.[33]

In one sense there could be no going on from this story. 'The moment stops.' Early in her career, then, Eudora Welty attained a literary plane that Yeats reached in old age, and Rilke – in the *Sonnets to Orpheus* and the last of the *Duino Elegies* – comparatively late.

What she did was to take 'A Still Moment' and the truths she had explored and realized in it into other kinds of work. Now she had to bring together the human truths learned from her early travels and stories and the metaphysical truths learned here. *The Golden Apples*, *Losing Battles* and *The Optimist's Daughter* – particularly, perhaps, the first, which is, in essence, a sequence of apprehensions and epiphanies – contain its findings; these shine out, touching every corner, in these later, ampler, warmer works.

---

33. *Yeats's Poems*, Macmillan (1989), ed. A. Norman Jeffares, p. 306.

5

THE GOLDEN APPLES

I

ASKED IN an interview in July 1977 about her own favourites among her books, Eudora Welty replied:

I think really that book of stories called *The Golden Apples* is, on the whole, my favourite. Somehow that's very close to my heart. It has some of the stories I most of all loved writing. And then it excited me, because I discovered only part way through that the stories were connected. All this time in the back of my head these connections had worked themselves out.[1]

The Golden Apples, then, is not a novel in the normal sense (though according to Eudora Welty, thesis-writers regularly attempt to prove that it is); it is a sequence of stories, each, with the exception of the last, independent in itself, though shedding light on the others. Though three – 'June Recital', 'Moon Lake' and 'Music from Spain' – are of particular complexity and subtlety, and repay careful study on their own, *The Golden Apples* demands to be considered as a unified whole; Diarmuid Russell spoke aptly when he told Eudora Welty: 'I think this is a very, very good *book*'[2] (emphasis added), and Eudora Welty

---

1. C.E.W. p. 192.
2. ibid.

herself said that in working on it 'the interconnections of the book fascinated [me]'. She felt there was something 'coming from them as a group with a meaning of its own'.[3] Of course, what she implies is true: we do not here, as we would in an orthodox novel, follow characters on straight lines of development towards some artistically logical point of departure; rather, we encounter them – now in the foreground, now in the distance – at those moments of visionary truth with which short stories in general, and Eudora Welty's in pre-eminent particular, are concerned. Nevertheless, each story creates demands that are met not merely by later stories (which may satisfy our questions on this point or that) but by the totality of the work, which gives us the appropriate larger intellectual and emotional context in which to see characters and events.

The Golden Apples is given primary unity by both place and time. Place is a town called Morgana, situated somewhere in the Mississippi Delta – and its intimately bound neighbour, MacLain, seven miles away. This is farming country, with thick woods (Morgan's Woods) to hand, and with a lake, Moon Lake, some four miles distant. Roads go out from Morgana to Vicksburg and Jackson; both places make themselves felt at certain points. (Jackson, where the gubernatorial inauguration takes place, also houses the state mental hospital, to which Miss Eckhart is consigned; Vicksburg, where pleasure is to be had at a sufficiently safe distance from home – Ran MacLain's activities with Maideen, and Virgie with Mr Nesbit – and where the Mississippi is impressively in view, is 'nineteen miles over the gravel and the thirteen little bridges and the Big Black'.) The slow Y. and M.V. train calls on its way south from Memphis, Tennessee at Morgana – which does not, however, have a proper station – you jump down on a summer's day from the train to find the town across the yard, with the 'oaks like the counted continents against the big blue'. The town is on the Big Black River, and there are small hills nearby.

It is a common enough practice in the Delta for a place name to be made from the surname of a prevailing family (Morgan) with the suffix 'a'. And we meet the Morgans who gave their name to the town, just as we are to meet the MacLains of MacLain. But Eudora Welty

---

3. C.E.W. p. 43.

also liked the imaginative association of Morgana with Fata Morgana, the Italian name (equivalent to our Morgan le Fay of Arthurian romance) for a misleading vision, originally as seen at sea from the coast of Calabria:

> I was drawn to the name because I always loved the conception of *Fata Morgana* – the illusory shape, the mirage that comes over the sea. . . . My population might not have known there was such a thing as *Fata Morgana*, but illusions weren't unknown to them, all the same – coming in over the cottonfields.[4]

(Cotton-fields can seem like a sea. 'The world shimmered,' thinks Virgie Rainey, looking at them. And again, just as the Sicilian fishermen depended on the sea for their livelihood, so this community relies on cotton.)

We are presented with a very considerable cross-section of this community. The MacLains – of the Courthouse in MacLain – and the Morgans, who own Morgan's Woods, stand at its social apex, and the significantly named King MacLain – both sorry provincial satyr and a character who invites, however ironically, comparisons with other kings, with Zeus/Jupiter – is pivotal throughout. To the MacLains is ascribed a Southern Civil War past; King's grandfather is buried in the Confederate section of Cedar Hill, the town cemetery, though by now what exactly he did in the War has been generally forgotten. Then come the families who form the bulwark of small-town life: the Morrisons (Wilbur Morrison is editor of the local newspaper, *The Bugle*); the Carmichaels (Drewsie Carmichael, the bank manager, becomes Mayor); the Starks (the businessman Comus Stark has married into the Morgan family; his wife is Miss Lizzie). Important tradespeople in Morgana/MacLain are Billy Hudson of the Stores, whose daughter, Miss Snowdie, becomes King MacLain's wife; and Old Man Moody, who runs the Seed and Feed. A little further out of these concentric social rings are the Raineys, who have come to Morgana from North Mississippi, smallholders who sell their produce; Old Fate (Lafayette) Rainey goes round the town with his blue wagon calling out his wares: 'Milk, milk/Buttermilk,/Fresh dewberries

---

4. C.E.W. p. 88.

and/Buttermilk.' After the MacLains, the Raineys are to be our most consistent concern.

Beyond these families are the poorer, sprawling country people: the Sojourners, the Sissums, the Holifields, the Nesbitts. Also dropped into the community are various outsiders: transients such as Mr Voight, the commercial traveller who rooms at Miss Snowdie's, or (not transient – not by intention, anyway) Miss Eckhart, another roomer, the German piano teacher. Morgana must also be at least 40 per cent black; part of it is known to the white townspeople as 'niggertown' (and do not let us pretend that in such communities the word 'nigger' is not still used! I have heard it, quite often, with my own ears). Some of the black people we meet are attached to white households: Plez, his hat always full of roses, belongs to the Raineys'; the talkative, credulous, sensitive Juba to the Starks'. Some of the black people, however, lead lives that are totally mysterious to the white population; among those helping out at the Moon Lake camp, for example, are Elberta and her son, Exum.

And there will be additions to the ranks of the town dead in Cedar Hill cemetery.

Time as well as place holds the sequence. Just as Eudora Welty indulges in no formal geographical or sociological description, so much of the chronology has to be deduced, though clearly it had a very precise existence in the writer's mind. (Part of the reason why it has to be inferred is that while the stories are, in fact, in chronological order, they make intricate use of memories, flashbacks and retrospective anecdotes, according to their individual artistic needs.)

The opening story, 'Shower of Gold', told by Mrs (Katie) Rainey, mother of a small boy and a 'baby girl', concerns the birth of the MacLain twins. They arrive, she relates, on 1 January, and given the sense of propitiousness she is imparting, it seems fair to surmise that this New Year's Day was also the first day of the century. This inference certainly pertains. Victor, Katie's small boy, grows up enough to be sent to France in the First World War, to meet his early death (some time between 1916 and 1918). By the last story in the book this tragedy is mentioned as having occurred in 'the other war', the *Second* World War having only recently ended. This last story in the sequence

('The Wanderers') concerns Katie's death and funeral. Thus the happenings of the whole book are contained between Katie Rainey's young motherhood and her burial: between 1900 and 1946.

Eudora Welty has said of *The Golden Apples*: '[The stories] are about human relationships in their beginnings and changes among the characters in their different times, all within the frame of Morgana.'[5] This, like her comments on the *Fata Morgana* motif, helps to give us a key to the secondary and profounder unity of the stories – unity of theme (or, better, of intertwined themes). We alight now on this person at such a time, now on another in a different situation and in a different year; we should not expect novelistic progression here. But every time we alight it is to explore, to attempt to hold the fleeting moment and go in and in, there to discover correspondences both elaborate and simple.

This kind of unity between characters – and between what befalls them – is emphasized, shown for the living force it is, by mythology. The mythological reference of *The Golden Apples*, taken from the Classical and Celtic cultures, is extensive and complex, though there is unity here too. When we approach this subject we should remember Eudora Welty's own words in her interview with John Griffin Jones:

> . . . equivalents . . . are all apart from my intention. I used [myths] in the way I think life does. Life recalls them. These likenesses occur to you when you are living your life. They are plucked out of here and there because they seem to apply. I wanted to show mainly in [*The Golden Apples*] something about illusion in our lives. . . . Everybody was sort of trapped in their own dream world [in Morgana], or were apprehensive of leaving, of getting outside of it; all but Virgie who really was and is a courageous and fine person.[6]

In other words, received myths, as universally recognized dramatizations of human desires, are necessary for her purpose here, if the people of Morgana are to stand for others everywhere. Eudora Welty belongs, after all, to a generation who took into their mature

---

5. Afterword to *Morgana: Two Stories from 'The Golden Apples'*, illustrated by Mildred Nungester Wolfe, University Press of Mississippi (1988).
6. C.E.W. p. 332.

lives Freud's and Jung's revelation that myth is central to human interconnectedness (to employ her own term) when it was still comparatively new to our awareness. And her use of myth here – and, for that matter, her use of other interconnections too – is as intricate as it is in the work of post-Freudian, post-Jungian writers such as Joyce, Eliot, Lawrence, O'Neill or Faulkner, who, with the older Rilke and Yeats, provide the only true points of comparison for *The Golden Apples*.

Like *The Waste Land* or *Mourning Becomes Electra*, the work signifies through its title the appropriate areas in which our imaginations should be exercised – areas rather than area, for the golden apples belong to several myths, to more than one culture. There are the golden apples guarded by the Hesperides, which constituted Hercules' Eleventh Labour. There are the fruits of the Garden of Eden (which, it must be recalled, were never actually called 'apples' by the Hebrew scribes). In the text itself, however, mythological apples are overtly referred to only once; Eugene MacLain, an exile from Morgana in San Francisco, thinks: 'Was it so strange, the way things are flung out at us, like the apples of Atalanta perhaps, once we have begun a certain onrush?'

In the classical myth Aphrodite gave Melanion three golden apples which he had to let fall during the course of his chariot race against Atalanta, so that she would stoop and pick up each of them, and he would win. These apples would seem to be what distract us from any goal, from any race-winning, however intent on it we may believe ourselves to be. But while Eudora Welty is too scrupulous an artist to have introduced such allusions were they not germane to an understanding of the whole, there is a further and even more pervasive – if less direct – reference to the fabulous fruit. 'The Golden Apples' was the title Eudora Welty originally chose for the wonderful second story, which we now know as 'June Recital', and here we find a central character haunted by – and quoting from – a strange gnomic poem whose author it is not difficult to identify as W.B. Yeats. In fact, if we trace the lines we come to 'The Song of Wandering Aengus', from *The Wind Among the Reeds* (1899), and find that it does indeed deliver those golden apples of the title. Moreover, the poem sets up other echoes:

I went out to the hazel wood,
Because a fire was in my head,
And cut and peeled a hazel wand,
And hooked a berry to a thread;
And when white moths were on the wing,
And moth-like stars were flickering out,
I dropped the berry in a stream
And caught a little silver trout.

When I had laid it on the floor
I went to blow the fire aflame,
But something rustled on the floor,
And someone called me by my name.
It had become a glimmering girl
With apple blossom in her hair
Who called me by my name and ran
And faded through the brightening air.

Though I am old with wandering
Through hollow lands and hilly lands,
I will find out where she has gone,
And kiss her lips and take her hands;
And walk among long dappled grass,
And pluck till time and times are done
The silver apples of the moon,
The golden apples of the sun.[7]

Yeats has taken archetypal images in their Celtic forms – sun, moon, gold, silver, apples, the wanderer – and made out of them a concentrated lyric which seems to articulate a personal (and a supra-personal) position. This is Eudora Welty's own achievement: a new and powerful fusion of archetypes.

In the case of *The Golden Apples* the word 'myth' operates in a double sense – to refer to the traditional bank of story, Classical and Celtic (and even at one point, at Miss Eckhart's insistence, Germanic) from which Eudora Welty draws meaning, and to the patterns she herself makes from her people, their situations, responses and actions. Few who know 'June

7. *Yeats's Poems*, p. 93.

Recital' will not have imported it – whole, with all its organically related components – into their own imaginative experience, where it can be drawn on for help and knowledge – just as Eliot's 'Death by Water' of Phlebas the Phoenician, 'who was once as handsome and tall as you', or Faulkner's 'idiot' Benjy haunting the golf course in the hope of hearing his lost sister Caddy's name spoken, have become for us as powerful human icons as those preserved in the houses of Oedipus or Agamemnon.

II

In the first story 'Shower of Gold' Mrs (Katie) Rainey, addressing us as if we were interested visitors to Morgana who perhaps already know a thing or two about life there, begins her tale with the words 'That was Miss Snowdie MacLain', indicating the woman from the house across the road who has just come over to collect her butter. Then Mrs Rainey gives us Miss Snowdie's story – partly to explain why she has stopped letting her come over with the butter herself, as was her custom until the previous week – and what we learn affects our reception of everything else in the book (as much as an opening chapter would in a conventional novel). It also (involuntarily, as it were) establishes the mythological terms of reference.

Miss Snowdie Hudson, an albino 'as sweet and gentle as you find them', with some money behind her from her storekeeper father, had been the unexpected choice of wife of Mr King MacLain, a seasoned rake who already, 'so say several', had sired children, 'known and unknown', some of them apparently in the County Orphanage. Maybe Miss Snowdie's money had been an allure; certainly it built the house across the way from Katie Rainey's. King – the very name sets our imaginations working, especially when we think of his amorous career, free of any sense of obligation except to his own will – came to and from his wife, forsaking his legal training for a travelling job, once leaving her for over two years, maybe three. When he returned after this absence, it was to make Miss Snowdie pregnant. She came over to tell Miss Katie the news, just as she was milking: 'It was like a shower of something bright had struck her, like she'd been caught out in something bright.'[8]

---

8. C.S. p. 266.

And it is after this shower that the whole story is named. It is a sufficiently arresting image to exercise our curiosity, and we are thus asked to remember that it was as a shower of gold that Zeus came down to the imprisoned Danaë and impregnated her, the result being the hero Perseus. Mr King MacLain, his act of fathering over, disappears (in godlike style), leaving his hat on the bank of the Big Black River as if he has drowned himself: Miss Snowdie gives birth to twins. Doubleness was not left behind with *The Robber Bridegroom* (where, as we saw, Rosamond was herself a twin, and the mother of twins); it is a significant feature of all mythological systems, and twins are a frequent symbol. But while this departure from strict parallelism can (rightly) indicate to us that the MacLain twins are heroism fractured, divided, as their histories will testify, it also acts as a warning against any pedantically literal reading. The Zeus-like nature of King, his sexual 'shower-of-gold' attribute, can indeed mean that he is capable of siring a Perseus – but not, perhaps, here, on this occasion. We must be ready to look elsewhere.

The twins, Randall and Eugene, arrive on New Year's Day, nine months to the day after King's disappearance; what is more: 'They were both King all over again, if you want to know it.'

Mrs Rainey then moves forward about four years to a Hallowe'en ('only last week') – years in which King has been sighted, maybe apocryphally, here and there about the South. The day is to be significant in her own familial history, because it is the day her baby daughter Virgie swallows a button. Miss Katie goes over to Miss Snowdie's to help her cut out patterns for sewing. The twins are playing outside, wildly rollerskating all over the place, with Hallowe'en masks on: Eugene's a Chinaman's, Ran's representing a 'lady with an almost scary-sweet smile'. Although neither of the women inside hears or sees him, a man comes to the house, whom Old Plez ('one of Mrs Stark's mother's niggers') recognizes as King MacLain returned to his own again. King goes around the premises as if he is inspecting them, passing the fig tree that is to feature prominently later. Then his sons – who do not recognize him, for the very good reason that they have never seen him before – accost him, teasing him for a stranger, greeting him with 'How do you do, Mister Booger [Bogeyman]?' delivered in 'high birdie voices', and skating all round him, pulling faces.

It is (quite credibly) all too much for King MacLain, who turns about and goes away, not to reappear for many years. But with great pathos Miss Snowdie, hearing of his appearance, runs into the yard hoping to see him, and maybe it is her feeling of humiliation that makes her keep Katie at a distance from now on.

Mrs Rainey's concluding words are strange: 'But I bet my little Jersey calf King tarried long enough to get him a child somewhere. What makes me say a thing like that? I wouldn't say it to my husband, you mind I forget it.'[9] And now we realize that Mrs Rainey has a greater familiarity with and interest in King MacLain than she has chosen to reveal. When she advises her audience 'beware of a man with manners', is she thinking of herself? How does she know so much about the trysting-place deep in Morgan's Woods, where Snowdie was summoned to meet King MacLain after one of his disappearances?: 'I could have streaked like an arrow to the very oak tree, one there to itself and all spready.' Don't her grumbles about her husband mean something ('Fate Rainey ain't got a surprise in him')?[10] And how about her telling us that during this absence: 'I see King in the West, out where it's gold and all that.' And why does she say, at one point: 'it hurts my conscience being that lucky over Snowdie'. But there is also little doubt that she is versed in Morgana gossip, and when she says that King has 'tarried long enough to get him a child somewhere', she doubtless has a specific rumour in mind.

The history contained in 'Shower of Gold' was told by someone who, though concerned, was not directly involved. Voice is everything, including its hesitations, its evasions. In 'June Recital' the drama is presented through the eyes, ears and memories of a brother and sister, Loch and Cassie Morrison (children of local newspaper editor Wilbur Morrison), but the scenes which bring it to its final stages are but partially or inadequately apprehended by these witnesses; indeed (in Loch's case), key elements are not understood. At the centre of the story are Virgie Rainey and her old music mistress, Miss Eckhart, two linked outsiders, the younger an outsider by temperament, the older by origins (Germany) and preoccupation (classical music).

---

9. C.S. p. 274.
10. C.S. p. 264.

But the insiders of Morgana, though they play less active parts in the story, are important too.

In time we have moved about fifteen years on from 'Shower of Gold'; Mrs Rainey's young son Victor has been killed on the battlefields of France, and Virgie, only a button-swallowing baby in the previous story, is now sixteen, has left school and is earning her living as pianist at the Bijou cinema. The popular silent movies (which assist Loch's fantasies, as well as providing Virgie with a means of earning money), the tie-and-scarf dyeing, the bitter war memories now at last receding into the past, the hay-waggon-riding, the feeling that sexual emancipation is in the air, the new electric fan, the aeroplane that has flown over the town with the lady in it, and the Octagon Soap Coupons that Loch collects – with all these we have surely arrived at 1920, at the opening of a new period which, even in this comparatively isolated Delta town, seems to promise so much for the adolescents who figure so prominently in this story.

As far as place is concerned, however, the story has moved only one block on: to the house next door to that new one in which Miss Snowdie MacLain and her twins were living in 'Shower of Gold'. Husbandless, Miss Snowdie has now gone back to 'where she came from' – to MacLain itself – and her house is virtually empty now. (We learn in the last story that in fact Miss Snowdie spent all her own money trying unsuccessfully to track down her errant husband through a Jackson detective agency.) After several desultory occupants, it has been bought by a Miss Francine Murphy, whom people rebuke for letting the property go. Loch and Cassie's mother still calls it the 'vacant house' – and even now it is unlived in, except for Old Man Holifield, the nightwatchman at the cotton-gin who sleeps in one of the rooms during the day, and acts as a sort of caretaker. Unlived in, but not unloved; the boy Loch Morrison, viewing the house from the bedroom where he lies ill with a malarial fever, has 'wrapped it with a summer's love'. For him, everything about it is charged with a special interest. Ahead of him as he looks out is the big fig tree that King MacLain inspected on his Hallowe'en return all those years ago.

The big fig tree was many times a magic tree with golden fruit that shone in and among its branches like a cloud of lightning bugs – a tree twinkling all over, burning, on and off, off and on, the sweet golden juice to come . . .[11]

The magic fig tree reminds us not only of the mythic apple trees, it has discernible properties belonging to its own kind: figs, for obvious reasons, are emblematic in different cultures of both male and female genitalia. The admiring Loch is on the threshold of puberty. His observations of the goings-on in the house next door are symptomatic on one level of a (fairly cheerful) initiation into sexual relations. Figs are indeed the reason why Virgie comes back to the house, and Loch sees her eating them: 'They were rusty old fig trees, but the figs were the little sweet blue. When they cracked open their pink and golden flesh would show, their inside flowers, and golden bubbles of juice would hang, to touch your tongue first.'[12]

The central action of 'June Recital', the last act of its contained drama, takes place one hot summer day. Loch fastens his father's old telescope on 'the vacant house' to discover a double event: one upstairs (erotic, happy), one downstairs (destructive, unhappy, related to thwarted or suppressed sexual feelings). Upstairs, into the bedroom opposite his own, comes a girl, whom he recognizes as his sister's contemporary, Virgie Rainey, and a sailor, who make love on the old bed with its slipping-down mattress, while downstairs, into the parlour below with its piano and row of broken chairs, comes an old woman he first identifies as the sailor's mother. Her behaviour is certainly extraordinary by any standards; he watches her going about the room stuffing up every crack with rolled-up newspapers (by a nice irony, copies of his father's, *The Bugle*). Only after studying her for some time does Loch understand that she intends to burn the place down.

But in her going to and fro across the parlour she pauses to pick out part of a tune on the old piano, and Loch's sister Cassie, dyeing her scarves in the room next door which has a different view of the MacLains' old house, remembers it as Beethoven's 'Für Elise', the favourite of her old German piano teacher, Miss Eckhart, and the showpiece of her best pupil, Virgie Rainey. Through Cassie's memories we now appreciate the strangeness (and the aptness too) of the

11. C.S. p. 279.
12. C.S. p. 278.

present conjunction of Virgie, young and tumbling with her sailor in the upstairs room, and Miss Eckhart, who loved and believed in her, old and crazy and lethal below. Miss Eckhart, who used to lodge in that very house (as Miss Snowdie's roomer), whom no one much liked, whom people turned against on account of her alleged German sympathies in the War, had, we now learn, fought for Virgie to develop her musical talents, and had lost the battle.

'June Recital' is in four parts. The first is related through the keen, curious, bewildered eyes of Loch – who, against parental orders, climbs out of his bedroom window on to the branches of the hackberry tree ('skinning the cat') the better to see what is happening; the second through the reflections and memories of Cassie; the third through Loch again, though he is now ears as well as eyes. Miss Eckhart is caught in the act and arrested, but not until a visitor has appeared, whom Loch thinks he knows and takes (erroneously) for another former roomer of Miss Snowdie's. The fourth part continues the direct action, though our principal consciousness is again Cassie's, with whose thoughts – indeed, with whose future recurrent dream – the whole story ends.

Thus, through the occurrences of this late afternoon in high summer 1920, we understand a Morgana history which has taken some years to unfold – a history that emphasizes the inescapably restrictive and inward-turned nature of small-town life, which, for all its charm and its often very real warmth and mutual helpfulness, can (and does) maim, paralyse and kill. The story of Miss Eckhart especially manifests this truth; after all, she attempts an act of terrible revenge on the community, proof in itself of her ungovernable misery – Miss Eckhart with her alien language, religion (Lutheran) and traditions, and her concern with an art that is part of *Hochkultur* outside Southern life, outside America, as utterly remote from the interests of all around her as her punch and *Kuchen* are from their pies and cakes; Miss Eckhart with her enforced spinsterhood that protests against itself in her behaviour towards Mr Sissum at the shoe store. She is sweet on him, and after he is drowned in the big Black River, she does not see why she should deny her strong feelings for him. As in life, almost every character in *The Golden Apples* parallels at least one other, and often more than one: lonely Miss Eckhart parallels and contrasts with

Miss Snowdie, her landlady, whose husband was presumed drowned in the Big Black River.

Miss Eckhart lived, we learn, through Cassie, for her highly organized June public concerts and for her doomed hopes for Virgie Rainey ('"Virgie Rainey, *danke schoen*,"' she would say to her after her fine playing of a piece. 'But recital night was Virgie's night, whatever else it was.') Both these lifelines belong intolerably to the past now; wayward Virgie has (one might think) prostituted her gifts by becoming a cinema pianist (and often an inattentive one at that). Virgie, in her wilfulness as well as her abilities, parallels Miss Eckhart; the differences between them – in station, in generation and in emotional make-up – are emphasized poignantly by the fact that while her old teacher is engaged in destruction, Virgie is engaged in lovemaking. Perhaps this is a clue to what will save her from a life like Miss Eckhart's, with her unpopularity and her frustrated feeling for Mr Sissum: we are told that Virgie clicks her heels 'as if she were free, whatever else she might be. . . .', whereas Miss Eckart's lack of psychic freedom causes her to end, wretchedly, in the insane asylum at Jackson.

The fourth part of the story shows us, as witnessed by Cassie, the coming together of teacher and beloved pupil who, thanks to the former's attempted arson, has had to flee the house with her sailor:

> 'She'll stop for Miss Eckhart,' breathed Cassie.
>
> Virgie went by. There was a meeting of glances between the teacher and her old pupil, that Cassie knew. She could not be sure that Miss Eckhart's eyes closed once in recall – they had looked so wide-open at everything alike. The meeting amounted only to Virgie Rainey's passing by in plain fact.[13]

And later that evening Cassie, a sensitive and intelligent – albeit conventional – girl broods:

> . . . she thought back . . . again to Miss Eckhart and Virgie coming together on the dead quiet sidewalk. . . . They were deliberately terrible. They looked at each other and neither wished to speak. They did not even horrify each other. No one could touch them now, either.

---

13. C.S. p. 325.

Danke schoen. . . .That much was out in the open. Gratitude –
like rescue – was simply no more. It was not only past; it was
outworn and cast away. Both Miss Eckhart and Virgie Rainey
were human beings terribly at large, roaming the face of the earth.
And there were others of them – human beings, roaming, like lost
beasts.[14]

Principal among these frightening others, of course, is Mr King
MacLain, a figure with whom (in his homelessness, his individualism
and his passion) both Miss Eckhart and Virgie have patent affinities.
As in the previous story – and, for that matter, in the one that follows
– Mr King's appearance is quite abrupt and unexpected, perhaps even
by himself: an emanation of a god, indeed. Loch confuses him with an
elderly exhibitionist, Mr Voight (to whom indeed King is psychological kin – a grubby parallel here!). He arrives at the very moment of
conflagration, yet his reactions – for after all, the house has been his –
are those of someone in a different category of human being from the
norm, someone for whom property and community, and a whole network of needs and obligations, mean very little. '"All right, burn it
down, who's to stop you?" . . . [He] shook all over. He was laughing,
Loch discovered. Now he watched the room like a show. "That's it!
That's it!" he said.'[15] His is a strange mixture of heartless and con-
temptible insouciance, and admirable indifference to the conventions –
doubleness, the Janus head again. Loch, looking at King MacLain and
Miss Eckhart (believing they are Mr Voight and the sailor's mother),
thinks: 'It could be indeed that he knew her from his travels. He
looked tired from these same travels now.'[16] While Cassie, reflecting on
Miss Eckhart and Virgie, thinks: 'What she was certain of was the distance those two had gone, as if all along they had been making a trip.
. . . It had changed them.'[17]

In contrast Cassie and Loch, delightfully delineated (that is, delineated with clear delight on the author's part) belong – as far as this
story goes – to normal, domestic, societal life: she with her romantic

14. C.S. p. 330.
15. C.S. pp. 319–20.
16. C.S. p. 321.
17. C.S. p. 330.

summer waggon excursions out to Moon Lake, all rocking rides and singing, and her favourite songs ('By the light, light, light, light, light, of the silvery moon') and her receptiveness to poetry; he with his longing to have a bird, his taste for adventure and his rather male brand of curiosity; and their lost, early-childhood deep affection for each other. (Even if Eudora Welty had not admitted it later, one could perhaps have guessed that she herself and her brother Edward had gone into their making.) But maybe this summer day is an epiphany for both of them. Cassie is to be haunted not by the Miss Eckhart and Virgie whom she has seen but by the face of King MacLain, whom she has not seen this time, a face delivered to her by the poem she has been so moved by, a 'grave, unappeased, and radiant face', an extraordinarily powerful combination of attributes. In truth, that poem should have prepared her for its power; we are treated to four lines of it, three which describe wandering – virtually a condition of King's being – and a fourth of a strangeness which corresponds somehow to the events of the whole story: '*Because a fire was in my head*'. King is to be the Wandering Aengus of Cassie's Yeats poem, and perhaps it is fear of him which leads her into the prematurely old-maidish life we see her living at the end of the sequence. Loch, we are told, came back from the Second World War not to Mississippi but to New York City. ('"Likes it there. He writes us."') Perhaps some fear kept him away too.

In addition to Cassie and Loch we meet their parents, their mother a refined, artistic woman with a particular feeling for her son. In her – when we reread the story carefully – we can detect a sadness, a sense of a life out of joint with her dreams, which will at least partly explain her suicide, of which we learn in 'The Wanderers' and which is to astound everyone years later. Could her melancholy derive from an emotional source, and could her special attachment to Loch suggest a different father for him than her husband? '"He's been gone since you were born,"' says Cassie of King MacLain, while Mrs Morrison says his reappearance is 'as interesting as twenty fires'.

And then we think back to 'Shower of Gold' and remember Katie Rainey saying that she thought King had tarried long enough to sire a child. Who would be the right age among the characters we have subsequently met? Loch Morrison, exactly. Moreover, his mother has a curious special tenderness towards him, as if there had been something curious and tender about his begetting.

With this notion in our minds, we then remember King descending on one woman like a 'shower of gold', and think that this could have been repeated with another – that Mrs Morrison could subsequently have enjoyed the role of Danaë, in which case Loch has about him the aura of the hero, Perseus. It is an imaginatively exciting realization. Perseus cut off the Gorgon Medusa's head with the aid of a mirror, to prevent her baleful glare turning him to stone. And who is more Gorgon-like than poor old, malignant, once powerful Miss Eckhart, whom he too apprehends indirectly – through the telescope? Of Miss Eckhart's face when she is playing, we are told: '[It] could have belonged to someone else – not even a woman, necessarily. It was the face a mountain could have, or what might be seen behind the veil of a waterfall.'[18] While her love 'never did anybody any good'. Are these not qualities of a Gorgon, pointing out something anti-human in Miss Eckhart that we must deplore, however much we sympathize with her lot, and which Virgie Rainey is to redress in her own later life?

Of Katie Rainey, narrator of 'Shower of Gold', we hear that she could not control her children, let them run wild, and threw herself in a frenzy of grief on to her son Victor's coffin at his funeral. We also hear of the MacLain twins, regular figures on those hay-waggon rides. Ran and Eugene, we are told, always call out to Mrs Morrison '"Come on! You come with us!"'; we learn in the very next story that they are like King MacLain multiplied by two ('If it was Mr King, he was, suddenly, looking around both sides of the tree at once . . .') so this detail can also lead us into thinking about a sexual bond between the twins' father, and Cassie and Loch's mother.

Fire attempted and in the head, the fire of the sun as it beats down on the Mississippi town, and of the fever Loch Morrison is suffering, of unappeased heart and unappeased face – these masculine images dominate the story, give it its peculiar essence. Palliatives are to be found in the Yeats poem, in the moonlit starry night, in the waters in which the silver trout can appear, in the emanations of the feminine, in

18. C.S. p. 300.

the silver apples of the moon and the 'golden apples' of the sun, the prospect of fruit that can refresh and bestow joy.

The third story, 'Sir Rabbit', a short bucolic, erotic interlude, takes us forward in time to another dramatic, unheralded reappearance of King MacLain although, as in the previous tale, an eye is cast backwards to further Morgana history since the time of 'Shower of Gold'. We are given access to the memories of Mattie Will Holifield before her marriage to Junior, when she was Mattie Will Sojourner, of a large poor white family; we hear how she was accosted by the MacLain twins in the woods, and how they had boyish but none the less sexy sport with her. We are given a lively thumbnail sketch of Ran and Eugene's lives in these missing years, and we can find in them something of their father's sylvan lawlessness. We then move on to a Mattie Will married to a crass, chauvinistic Junior Holifield, who takes her hunting with his gun and his dog and 'a nigger' in those same Morgan's Woods, and witness the emergence of King MacLain. A row ensues, King 'peppers' Junior's hat with gunshot, and Junior, for all his macho airs, faints. While he is temporarily 'suspended dead to the world over a tree', King 'enjoys' Mattie. Having done so, he falls asleep snoring 'as if all the frogs of spring were inside him – but to him an old song'.

If readers had identified the poem haunting Cassie Morrison as Yeats's 'Song of Wandering Aengus', they might also recognize a Yeatsian reference in the description of Mattie succumbing to King:

> But he put on her, with the affront of his body, the affront of his sense too. No pleasure in that! She had to put on what he knew with what he did – maybe because he was so grand it was a thorn to him. Like submitting to another way to talk, she could answer to his burden now, his whole blithe, smiling, superior, frantic existence.[19]

This echoes another poem which has meant much to Eudora Welty, and played a part in the genesis of this book, 'Leda and the Swan', thus bringing home this seemingly slight story's thematic unity with the rest of the sequence:

---

19. C.S. p. 338.

A sudden blow: the great wings beating still
Above the staggering girl, her thighs caressed
By the dark webs, her nape caught in his bill,
He holds her helpless breast upon his breast.

How can those terrified vague fingers push
The feathered glory from her loosening thighs?
And how can body, laid in that white rush,
But feel the strange heart beating where it lies?
A shudder in the loins engenders there
The broken wall, the burning roof and tower
And Agamemnon dead.
   Being so caught up,
So mastered by the brute blood of the air,
Did she put on his knowledge with his power,
Before the indifferent beak could let her drop?[20]

Zeus disguised himself as a swan in order to mate with Leda, wife of the King of Sparta; from their union came the twins Castor and Pollux, and Helen of Troy. The poem, intended by Yeats as a tribute to the birth of Greek civilization, is, as he himself realized, more an expression of the violence in sexual possession whereby knowledge of the tragic possibilities of life passes from violator to victim. Eudora Welty keeps some aspects of this, but also softens it. King MacLain may in so many respects be a sorry and a selfish man (a telling comparison links him to a goose rather than a majestic swan), though he has already fathered his Castor and Pollux (Ran and Eugene) and maybe his Helen too (Virgie), but he is superior to the boorish Junior Holifield, and so his lovemaking can transform Mattie Will as her husband's cannot. The episode over, Mattie Will, reminding us of Mrs Rainey in the first story:

> could look away into the big West. She could see the drift of it all, the stretched land below the little hills, and the Big Black, clear to MacLain's Courthouse, almost, the Stark place plain and the fields, and their farm, everybody's house above trees, the

---

20. *Yeats's Poems*, p. 322.

MacLains' – the white floating peak. . . . And Morgana all in rays,
like a giant sunflower in the dust of Saturday.[21]

King, like the face of Cassie's dreams, is radiant – irradiating.

'Shower of Gold', with its image of a descent from the heavens
and its envisioning of a golden west, brings the element Air to mind
(associated with Gemini, the sign of the twins and Zeus/Jupiter/King's
own element). 'June Recital' has Fire at its centre, while the bedding in
the woods and the general acknowledgement of compelling animal car-
nality of 'Sir Rabbit' lead us to the element Earth. Central to 'Moon
Lake', as its title proclaims, is Water. Water is associated, as here, with
the moon, with femininity – and no story can be more redolent of the
feminine than this, with its cast of nubile girls at a summer camp, with
their swimming and rubbing of insect repellent on one another's young
bodies and their talks late at night in the tent, and with the supporting
cast of visiting organizers and matrons, such as Mrs Gruenwald, 'fatly
capering and leading them all [the girls] in a singing, petering-out string
down to the lake'. Of all the elements, water is the one which provides
us most often with a rite of passage – whether by immersion, that
simulacrum for drowning, death and resurrection, or by passing over it
on a boat (both of which we encounter in this story):

> Nina wondered if it was the slowness and near-fixity of boats out
> on the water that made them so magical. Their little boat in the
> reeds that day had not been far from this one's wonder, after all.
> The turning of water and sky, of the moon, or the sun, always
> proceeded, and there was this magical hesitation in their midst, of
> a boat. And in the boat, it was not so much that they drifted, as
> that in the presence of a boat the world drifted, forgot. The
> dreamed-about changed places with the dreamer.[22]

If 'June Recital' showed Loch burning in his masculinity in a sun-
dominated world, while fire crackled in the house opposite, 'Moon
Lake' centres on him diving into the depths of Moon Lake to come up
with an embodiment of the feminine, a girl to whom the primeval slime
is clinging.

---

21. C.S. p. 340.
22. C.S. p. 360.

Readers have already heard about Moon Lake: it was the destination of those hay-waggons on which the youth of Morgana, the MacLain twins and Cassie among them, went riding. 'And mightn't it be on the Moon? – it was a strange place, Nina thought, unlikely – and three miles from Morgana, Mississippi, all the time.'[23] By Moon Lake two linked sets of girls are camping: girls from Morgana's 'better' families, such as Nina Carmichael, the Mayor's daughter, and Jinny Love Stark, the sharp-tongued, strong-willed, at times somewhat spiteful daughter of the owner of Morgan's Woods, and girls from the County Orphanage. We should be on the alert here; has not Mrs Rainey already told us that 'children of his [King MacLain's] are growing up in the County Orphan's', while, Junior Holifield said to Mattie Will: '"And don't nobody know how many chirren he has"'? The two sets of girls are thus connected to each other not only by the lake itself, and by those activities arranged for them by the philanthropic organizers, nor even by the social obligations enjoined by these adults, but by the irresponsible Jovian progenitor King MacLain. And our attention is particularly directed to Easter (which turns out to be spelled as Esther), most recalcitrant of the girls, with her pert answers ('"I should worry. I should cry"'); of her appearance we read: 'Easter's hair was a withstanding gold. . . . [The Morgana girls] liked to walk behind her and see her back, which seemed spectacular from crested gold head to hard, tough heel.'[24] King must surely have had a part in her making – and with this youngest of his progeny we have arrived at another and a younger myth, for Easter's submersion and resurrection in the lake clearly bring to mind the world's most potent story, which lies behind her name.

With these girls – or, rather, not *with* them but *beside* them – is Loch Morrison from 'June Recital', three years on. He's there (under sufferance) as Boy Scout and Life Saver, and to play reveille and taps on his bugle for all the campers. Eudora Welty has admitted;

> My brother Edward was in fact a Boy Scout, who, one summer,
> acted as life guard and was beleaguered in a small camp for girls,
> but that was in a later year, in another camp, in another part of

23. C.S. p. 344.
24. C.S. pp. 346–7.

Mississippi. I brought him, along with his bugle, to 'Moon Lake', where I needed Loch. Like Loch exactly, I remembered, when Edward was at a stage when he could hardly endure the presence of girls, he lived surrounded by them, more or less at their mercy. Whatever happened at that camp, he was on hand, dwelling in boredom and disgust, but, as a Boy Scout, *prepared*. For Loch at Moon Lake I didn't change Edward a bit; he was perfect as he was. But as far as he ever mentioned, he was never called on to perform artificial respiration on anybody.[25]

In 'Moon Lake' Loch is called on to do just this, providing the story's reverberating climax; Easter, whose ways so confound the sheltered Nina and Jenny Love, has an accident: a black boy, Exum, causes her to fall off the diving-board. Exum is a delectable creation:

Eventually there was Exum wandering with his fish pole – he could dance on a dime . . . he used to work for a blind man. Exum was smart for twelve years old; too smart. He found that hat he wore – not a sign of the owner. He had a hat like new, filled out a little with peanut shells inside the band to correct the size, and he like a little black peanut in it. It stood up and away from his head all around, and seemed only following him – on runners, perhaps, like those cartridges for change in Spights' store.[26]

He is a counterpart, however, not so much to fellow-blacks such as Old Plez, who also delights in hats, but to King MacLain himself; both are eruptions of wilful Nature in the world of insiders, and the way Exum brings about the accident springs perfectly from his character:

Exum's little wilted black fingers struck at his lips, as if playing a tune on them. He put out a foolishly long arm. He held a green willow switch. Later every one said they saw him – but too late. He gave Easter's heel the tenderest, obscurest little brush, with something of nigger persuasion about it.[27]

---

25. Afterword to *Morgana*, p. 151.
26. C.S. p. 350.
27. C.S. p. 363.

(The comedy here is at the expense of the white gossips who circulate the story.)

It is Loch Morrison who has to rescue Easter – or rather, *find* her and rescue her, because for a while she vanishes. After repeated dives he is able to emerge holding her, 'her arm sliding through his hand'. They first join underwater, Loch 'snatch[ing] the hair of Easter's head', then come together in a perfect mimesis of sexual intercourse as Loch persists in his attempts to revive her while she is spread out on the table. It is possible that he is innocent of what he is about; bystanders, however, do not receive the performance innocently – among them (though in no way shocked) Ran MacLain, who has appeared in the woods, cap on his head, gum in his mouth, attended by his hunting dogs: 'Under his cap bill, Ran MacLain set his gaze – he was twenty-three, his seasoned gaze – on Loch and Easter on the table. He could not be prevented from considering them all.'[28] The confrontation gains in impact if we appreciate that he may here be looking at his own half-brother with their shared half-sister. At any rate, he salutes in them some kind of affinity with himself – a quality which the consciously respectable *bien-pensants* of Morgana, here represented by Jinny Love's mother, Miss Lizzie Stark, have denied, repressed.

That night, Loch alone in his solitary tent, knowing that a rite of passage has indeed been accomplished, beats his chest and, naked, capers in front of his mirror, armed with a lit candle – just as if he had literally succeeded sexually. The girls, witnessing him from the safety of their own tent, are unimpressed: 'Minnowy thing that matched his candle flame, naked as he was with that, he thought he shone forth too. Didn't he?'[29] But truly his hour has now come. Thanks to Easter, dredged up from the lake floor, from the very depths of the feminine, he has left the world of Nina and Jinny Love, and of his own uneasy self, and entered that of King and Ran MacLain. Easter, as well as living up to her name, is at one with those other female (Arthurian) manifestations of the lake, Morgan le Fay (a significant name in the context of this book) and Lancelot's Lady

28. C.S. p. 369.
29. C.S. p. 374.

of the Lake. Arthur received from the lake his sword Excalibur; Loch receives a power analogous to the sword, which his putative father and putative brother already possess. (Ran, looking at him, is described as 'seasoned'.) Yet there is, of course, ambivalence here; Loch's self-vaunting (considered conceited by the girls) has an uncomfortable aggressive aspect.

If 'Shower of Gold' is exempted as a prelude to the whole book, all the stories so far have been concerned with innocence – or, more precisely, with the end of innocence. Considering its lubricious matter, this may seem an odd term to use in connection with 'Sir Rabbit', but really Mattie Will is still very much an innocent; her time with King in Stark's Woods has awakened her, even enabling her to see the MacLain twins who accosted her in childhood more clearly:

> That day, with their brown, bright eyes popping and blinking, and their little aching Adam's apples – they were like young deer, or even remoter creatures . . . kangaroos. . . . For the first time Mattie Will thought they were mysterious and sweet – gamboling she knew not where.[30]

But in the fourth and fifth stories, each focusing on one of the MacLain twins, we are a very long way from innocence. Truly we can see that, by now, here, in Yeats's words, 'the ceremony of innocence is drowned'. We find ourselves deep in the pains – and in the so often defeating dullnesses, too – of experience.

The change 'The Whole World Knows' marks also enables us to review what has gone before in a new light.

There is a stylistic change too. Following Mrs Rainey's prologue, in her racy, homely voice, the stories have been rich-textured and closely worked, and though they probe characters' minds they do so by endowing often tangled thoughts with authorial order and clarity. Now in 'The Whole World Knows' the monologue is emotionally charged, spare of images, urgent in its vocabulary and rhythm, often exclamatory – Ran MacLain addresses his errant and unknown father in tones of anguished rebuke. We feel the dominating emotion right from the first:

---

30. C.S. pp. 340–41.

Father, I wish I could talk to you, wherever you are right now.

Mother said, *Where have you been, son?* – Nowhere, Mother. *– I wish you wouldn't sound so unhappy, son. You could come back to MacLain and live with me now.* – I can't do that, Mother. You know I have to stay in Morgana.[31]

After the femininity and the seeming triumph of the feminine in 'Moon Lake' come two stories where exploration of male sensibility and masculinity is dominant. Both the stories of the MacLain twins are anti-domestic, treating of men impatient of confinement, seeking ways to break out and somehow to meet the demands of their tormented psyches.

Ran is living as a roomer in his former home; Miss Francine Murphy has at last converted it into a real boarding-house, though it lacks proper cooling-fans and has clearly come down in the world from the smartish new house built for a family with Mr Eugene Hudson's money. The reason for Ran's sadness is that his marriage (for which he received no parental example) has gone wrong; his wife, Jinny Love Stark, who has grown into a high-spirited, lissom young woman, has been unfaithful to him with Woodrow Spights, his junior at the bank.

They say Jinny MacLain invites Woody out there [to her family house] to eat, a year younger than she is, remember when they were born. Invites under her mam's nose. Sure, it's Woodrow Spights she invites. Who else in Morgana would there be for Jinny Stark after Ran, with even Eugene MacLain gone? . . . At the Circle, at Miss Francine's, at Sunday school, they say, they say she will marry Woodrow: Woodrow'd jump at it but Ran will kill somebody first. And there's Ran's papa and the way he was and is, remember, remember? And Eugene gone that could sometimes hold him down. Poor Snowdie, it's her burden. He used to be sweet but too much devil in him from Time was, that's Ran. He'll do something bad. He won't divorce Jinny but he'll do something bad. Maybe kill them all. . . . And oh, don't you know, they run into each other every day of the world, all three. Sure, how could

---

31. C.S. p. 375.

they help it if they wanted to help it, how could you get away
from it in Morgana? You can't get away in Morgana. Away from
anything at all, you know that.

Father! You didn't listen.[32]

Whereas previous stories have offered epiphanies, 'The Whole World
Knows' admits us into obsession, grief, panic, despair. Ran's cry, in its
intensity, bewilderment and anger, is one of real universal application.
Is this what the romance of King's earlier wanderings, his Jovian
indomitability as a lover, the whole multiple and tempting satyr-plays
of 'Sir Rabbit' has come to, what it *had* to come to? Not only is the
tragedy the very masculine one of the searcher who can't find psychological ease for himself; the voice, too, is very male. We are near
such other masculine voices: the desperate Quentin Compson's in
The Sound and the Fury, or that of Thomas Wolfe's father-obsessed
Eugene Gant in *Look Homeward, Angel* (both novels 1929). The male
imbalance that has now occurred (ushered in by Loch's naked antics)
requires Virgie as we meet her in 'The Wanderers' to restore the needed
harmony. In these two stories violation of the feminine is as literally
true as it is spiritually true.

Ran's agonized voice has an agonizing story to tell. To compensate
himself for the betrayal by Jinny Love, he consoles himself with the
company (and the company only) of an eighteen-year-old girl,
Maideen Sumrall, one of the Sojourners (as he later learns), and thus
kin to Mattie Will of his boyhood woodland frolic. Maideen is sweet
and unformed and flattered by his attentions, but before long bores
him with her endless chatter of doings at the Seed and Feed where she
works, and of the women's magazines she reads. He has not so much
as kissed her when he takes her in his car to Vicksburg. And leaving
Morgana/MacLain for the first time in so long – readers have not yet
left it – he feels strangely excited.

After a visit to a squalid dive, a houseboat that acts as a speak-
easy, where they have rather too much to drink, Ran drives the two of
them past the memorial park, to a motel called Sunset Oaks. He has
brought his old pistol with him. In the bedroom he displays the pistol,

---

32. C.S. p. 379.

pointing it first in sorry theatre at Maideen, then turning it on himself, putting it in his mouth:

'Don't do it, Ran. Please don't do it.' Just the same.

I made it – made the awful sound.

And *she* said, 'Now you see. It didn't go off. Give me that. Give that old thing to me, I'll take care of it.'

She took it from me. Dainty as she always was, she carried it over to the chair; and prissy as she was, like she knew some long-tried way to deal with a gun, she folded it in her dress. She came back to the bed again, and dropped down on it.

In a minute she put her hand out again, differently, and laid it cold on my shoulder. And I had her so quick.[33]

And that, perhaps, should have been that – and they would have returned to Morgana, and put the whole melancholy episode behind them. This is not, however, what happens. We have a clue to the sad sequel to this night in Ran's impassioned cry: 'How was I to know she would go and hurt herself? She cheated, she cheated too. . . . Father, Eugene! What you went and found, was it better than this?'[34]

Not until the last story do we learn that Maideen, in terrible emulation of her lover, made an attempt on her life – and, unlike him, succeeded, to be found dead on the floor of the Seed and Feed. Ran, with his male brand of egotism, had not counted on that. This is a very dark story, with the climax appropriately taking place at night.

. . . the night descended like a bucket let down a well. . . . It was never dark enough, the enormous sky flashing with August light rushing into the emptiest rooms, the loneliest windows. The month of falling stars, I hate the time of year this is, Father.[35]

In 'The Whole World Knows' Jinny Love is twenty-five; in 'Moon Lake' she was (approximately) sixteen. This means that Ran MacLain is about thirty-two (that allegedly significant age – what the Germans call the *Christusjahr*). Ran says: 'To me ambition's always been

---

33. C.S. p. 392.
34. ibid.
35. C.S. p. 391.

186

a mystery' (though by the end of the book he has become Mayor and, correspondingly, a community figure). In 'Music from Spain' Eugene MacLain is in his forties; indeed, he ascribes the day's aggressive and restless activities to his age.

Eugene was the gentle, 'good' twin: the one who took music lessons where his brother wouldn't, a fast runner who earned himself the general nickname of Scooter. He has been 'a kind man, soft unto innocence', but that has ceased to be enough; life has forced from him other things as well as kindness. That this twin who was the closer to his mother, Miss Snowdie, had also much of his father in him is evident in the fact that he left Mississippi in his very early twenties, and didn't Katie tell us in 'Shower of Gold': 'I believe [King's] been to California. Don't ask me why. But I picture him there. I see King in the West, out where it's gold and all that.'[36] Well, now a son of his *is* out in the West – has been so without once coming back for almost twenty years. When as very small boys the twins wore their Hallowe'en masks, 'Eugene Hudson', we were informed, 'wanted to be the Chinaman and so Lucius Randall had to be the lady.'[37] San Francisco is proverbially famous for its Chinatown, and that is where Eugene ended up, just as Ran has ended up being a victim to women: to his wife, Jinny Love, and to the poor girl for whose suicide he is partly responsible.

'Music from Spain' is the only story of the sequence set outside Mississippi. Eudora Welty wrote it in San Francisco; she has called it something of a long love letter to the city:

> It came in [the creative burst of writing the story-sequence] last. I wanted to show somebody from Morgana who'd gone outside the local circle; and yet he was no better outside than he would've been inside. . . . I never knew for certain if I should include that with the other stories or not.[38]

A small private publisher, the Levee Press, issued it separately, before *The Golden Apples* was published. Although its difference from the other stories is considerable, heightened by the detailed yet medium-istic rendering of San Francisco itself, it is a vital and necessary part of

36. C.S. p. 268.
37. C.S. p. 269.
38. C.E.W. p. 332.

the whole. Not only does it show how Eugene, the 'missing' MacLain twin, has fared, everything that occurs in it is a kind of mirror-correlative for the rest of the sequence. It is written with a density unsurpassed even by 'June Recital' or 'Moon Lake', yet, more than any of the others, it is also an hallucinatory affair, an outer landscape transmuted into an inner luminous one. While it avoids the violent action of 'June Recital' or 'The Whole World Knows', it is a tragic production, with loneliness, frustration, incomprehension, incompleteness its dominant emotions. To a far greater extent even than its immediate predecessor it is a story of the male bereft of the female (for in 'The Whole World Knows', however unhappily, Jinny Love and Maideen are real, lively and compelling presences).

The theme, as well as the occasion for developing it, is declared in the opening paragraph:

> One morning at breakfast Eugene MacLain was opening his paper and without the least idea of why he did it, when his wife said some innocent thing to him – 'Crumb on your chin' or the like – he leaned across the table and slapped her face. They were in their forties, married twelve years – she was the older: she was looking it now.[39]

This is no *acte gratuit*, however much the slap may have surprised its perpetrator; it is a release of resentment and unhappiness, an expression of maleness thwarted, of masculine romanticism turned sour.

Everything in the story proceeds from this opening slap. Setting out on foot for work (at Bertsinger, Jeweller's), Eugene suddenly appreciates that there is no reason why he should go to work that day. If slapping his wife was a sort of moral holiday, why not have a more complete one? The whole city goes about its business, but he – who, when all is said and done is an outsider here, a Southerner in the West, whose clothes and gestures proclaim his origin – need not join in for once. And by chance his path crosses with that of another outsider, more thoroughly a stranger here – a real foreigner, a Spaniard, whom he has heard playing his guitar the previous night, and whom he rescues from what could have been a fatal accident:

---

39. C.S. p. 393.

The guitarist reached the curb and in entering the traffic – really, he was quite provocatively slow, moving through this city street – he almost walked beneath the wheels of an automobile.

With the other's sudden danger, a gate opened to Eugene. That was all there was to it. He did not have time to think, but sprang forward as if to protect his own. His paper flew away from him piecemeal and as he ran he felt his toes pointing out behind him. This did not surprise him, for he had been noted for his running when he was a boy back home; in Morgana, Mississippi, he was still little old Scooter MacLain.[40]

Eugene thus acts as his boyhood self would have done, but he cannot bring to the encounter Scooter MacLain's comparative freedom from unease and sorrow; instead, he confronts the stranger as someone who is all too conscious of being in his forties, has suddenly behaved un-kindly to a wife he has long been out of love with emotionally and sex-ually, has suffered the unspeakable pain of losing his little daughter, is now rather bored by his job, and not sorry to be giving him-self a break from it. (Thus, the mature Eugene imagines the walls of the marital bedroom softening and suffocating him, and 'a band of sunshine' on a step strikes him as being 'soft and level as little [daugh-ter] Fan's hair when she would go flying before him'.) For the rest of that day (many hours) Eugene and the Spaniard are in one another's company, all over the city – the one speaking no Spanish, the other no English – yet we have a sense of the men's need for one another in their isolation, their uncertainty, Eugene projecting on to the Spaniard his own predicament, even asking him to be a receptacle for it. Eugene even starts addressing him as if there has been a transposition of roles, as if the agonies and guilts are the other man's, not his own:

'Your little girl,' Eugene remarked aloud, 'said, "Mama, my throat hurts me," and she was dead in three days. You expected her mother would watch a fever, while you were at the office, not go to talk to Mrs Herring. But you never spoke of it, did you? Never did.'[41]

---

40. C.S. p. 401.
41. C.S. p. 413.

And later: '"You know what you did," Eugene said. "You assaulted your wife. Do you say you didn't know you had it in you?"'[42]

The two men – the foreigner very large, the Southerner/ San Franciscan small, neatly made, slight – execute a sort of slow protracted dance over the city, going to eat at a restaurant and leaving it, witnessing a street accident (a real one this time) in which someone ('a dumpy little woman' really *is* killed), walking city squares and passing many people of all kinds and ages on their way down to the embankment while the sun of the day gives way to rain, to the end of the beach and then up along a road on one side of which are rocks and the 'sea exploding straight under them'. And so to a cliff, to its top, where this strange ballet, in which both dancers are active and passive at one and the same time, comes to a kind of climax. Obeying a related impulse to the one which caused him to strike his wife, Eugene 'thrust both hands forward and took hold of the other man, not half compassing the vast waist'; the Spaniard, panicking, roars out loud, there is a chase for the hats that get dislodged by movement and the wind, then the Spaniard picks Eugene up, wheeling him, subjecting him to the control of his own great, strong arms, and all the victim (who has brought this on himself) can think is 'My dear love comes'. The strange duet is (mimetically) redolent of virtually simultaneous murderous aggression and (asexual) amorousness, but it ends anticlimactically, with the two men going to have coffee at a dull little neighbourhood café. In the same way Eugene's whole day of existential action and rebellion also ends bathetically: he finds his wife in the middle of a long, trivial gossip with that very Mrs Herring with whom she had been gossiping at the time of little Fan's fatal illness.

Eugene and the Spaniard have danced out, so to speak, the themes of the entire story sequence: the prolonged dialogue with someone whose language you cannot understand relates to Loch Morrison apprehending people he incorrectly identifies through his telescope held upside-down, and indeed to the general failures in comprehension that we have witnessed in Morgan's Woods, by Moon Lake, and at Sunset Oaks. The fusion of murderousness and love exhibited in the grotesque demonstrations on the clifftop is but an intensification

---

42. C.S. p. 419.

of what has characterized the relationship between Miss Eckhart and Virgie, or Loch and Easter, and – more obviously – Ran and both Jinny Love and Maideen Sumrall. Moreover, music has already been significantly identified with yearning, with aspiration – for Virgie and Miss Eckhart again, and for the orphan Easter, perhaps Eugene's half-sister, who wanted so much to be a singer – and here Eugene thinks back to his own lessons with the German woman, and turns out to have been quite musical all along. There is a further connection between Miss Eckhart and the Spaniard (whose name we learn only at the end: Bartolomé Montalbano) – both are foreigners, both (remembering the date of 'Music from Spain') from countries with whom the USA had broken off relations for reasons of war (Wilhelmine Germany, Franco's Spain). The Spaniard is in exile (and thus repeats the various different forms of exile in the entire book), and his music expresses this – at any rate, the only part of his music which, in concert, Eugene had admired:

> Only when the man at last played very softly some unbearably rapid or subtle songs of his own country, so soft as to be almost without sound, only a beating on the air like a fast wing – then was Eugene moved.[43]

The Spaniard appears to Eugene – and here he reveals himself as a true son of King MacLain, for all his twelve long years of domesticity – as gloriously detached: 'Eugene had been easily satisfied of one thing – the formidable artist was free. There was no one he loved, to tell him anything, to lay down the law.'[44] But is not such freedom another illusion, another *Fata Morgana* mirage so tellingly represented by the whole city-wide day-long wandering in the Spaniard's company? It is not as if he himself has been able to put aside the past, and Mississippi, just by being distanced from it for so long. He is reminded of an old picture associated with his father:

> Eugene saw himself for a moment as the kneeling Man in the Wilderness in the engraving in his father's remnant geography book, who hacked once at the Traveler's Tree, opened his mouth,

---

43. C.S. p. 411.
44. C.S. p. 406.

and the water came pouring in. What did Eugene MacLain really care about the life of an artist, or a foreigner, or a wanderer, all the same thing – to have it brought upon him now? That engraving itself, he had once believed, represented his father, King MacLain, in the flesh, the one who had never seen him or wanted to see him.[45]

And in some of the most beautiful and heartfelt passages in the entire book, he thinks back to his Mississippi life:

Now, too late when the city opened out so softly in beauty and to such distances, it awoke a longing for that careless, patched land of Mississippi winter, trees in their rusty wrappers, slow-grown trees taking their time, the lost shambles of old cane, the winter swamp where his own twin brother, he supposed, still hunted.[46]

That twin is still present within him, part of his being:

And Eugene felt all at once an emotion that visited him inexplicably at times – the overwhelming, secret tenderness toward his twin, Ran MacLain, whom he had not seen for half his life, that he might have felt toward a lover. Was all well with Ran? How little we know! For considering that he might have done some reprehensible thing, then he would need the gravest and tenderest handling. Eugene's eyes nearly closed and he half fainted upon the body of the city, the old veins, the mottled skin of pavement. Perhaps the soft grass in which little daisies opened would hold his temples and put its eyes to his.[47]

The last story, 'The Wanderers', attempts resolution of the themes of the other stories; I say attempts, not because it is not a beautifully realized and complete work but because irresolution is part of the meaning of the whole. Stasis, often of a very sad kind, is the lot of many of the characters who, united by the death and funeral of Katie Rainey, come together (as in *Delta Wedding*, for Dabney Fairchild's marriage, as for the ninetieth birthday of Granny Vaughn

---

45. C.S. p. 409.
46. C.S. p. 399.
47. C.S. p. 415.

in *Losing Battles*) – stasis and, worse, decline; while as for Virgie, courageously lighting out for new territory, who knows what her fortune will be?

With the urgent voice of Ran MacLain, the elemental aspect of the sequence might seem to have gone into abeyance. But with its enormous sky, flashing with shooting stars – 'The Whole World Knows' brings air to mind; while behind 'Music from Spain', behind the city of San Francisco, looms the spectre of fire:

> If like the curtains of the aurora borealis the walls of rooms would give even the illusion of lifting – if they would threaten to go up. That would be repeating the Fire – of course. That could happen any time to San Francisco. It was a special threat out here. But the thing he thought of wasn't really physical.[48]

'The Wanderers' returns to the other elements, the two associated with receptive femininity: water and earth. Water provides the river in which Virgie goes for her decisive, purgative, moonlit swim at the back of the MacLain place:

> In the middle of the river, whose downstream or upstream could not be told by a current, she lay on her stretched arm, not breathing, floating. Virgie had reached the point where in the next moment she might turn into something without feeling it shock her. She hung suspended in the Big Black River as she would know to hang suspended in felicity.[49]

This is indeed the element of metamorphosis; Virgie emerges from her immersion as if washed of the past. The vestigial mud that had clung to Easter does not cling to her.

> She felt the sand, grains intricate as little cogged wheels, minute shells of old seas, and the many dark ribbons of grass and mud touch her and leave her, like suggestions and withdrawals of some bondage that might have been dear, now dismembering and losing itself.[50]

---

48. C.S. p. 408.
49. C.S. p. 440.
50. ibid.

She is now ready for change and the future. As for earth, it is the element in which Katie Rainey is laid – in which, as we see on our visit to the cemeteries in first Morgana, then MacLain, so many people of these communities with whom we have concerned ourselves – or of whom we have only heard – are laid. In Morgana (among a host of others) lie Mr Sissum, on whom Miss Eckhart was sweet; Mrs Morrison (Cassie's and Loch's mother, who so unexpectedly killed herself); Maideen Sumrall (with the other Sojourners); Virgie's brother, Victor. In MacLain lie MacLains, the forebears of King and the twins; and Eugene, who came back from San Francisco to Mississippi after all, completely forsaking his wife, Emma, to die of tuberculosis. It is just outside the latter cemetery that we leave Virgie, with the smell of earth – appropriately – in her nostrils, and the rain falling down, the rain that in so many mythologies is the symbol of creativity, related in the primitive mind to the sperm, to the continuation of life, even where – earth to earth – there is death. And the rain is falling not just over MacLain, but over the whole South. For all the sadness and uncertainty, there is a profound comfort to be had here.

The elements of water and earth permeate this story. In other respects it is an *omnium gatherum* of the community, and the account of how one person can and does leave it, in a spirit of true freedom. But both what we learn about the many characters of this book and what we learn about Virgie, who proves to be of stronger, finer stuff than the others, must be taken as part of a shapely whole, to whose complex meaning the elements richly contribute.

Katie Rainey's life underwent a change after her stroke, which occurred 'while separating my cows and calves'; she grew fearful of departure from any routine, and perhaps obsessively reliant on Virgie maintaining hers. Too kindly to be tyrannical, and too genuinely attached to Virgie, Katie did nevertheless hold her daughter close unto herself. Not that Virgie did not have something of a life of her own, but always under the shadow of her home life, where she scrupulously and feelingly discharged all her duties . We learn that she did go away to New York City, and that she came back, when she was still only seventeen, to join her mother, who had now lost both her husband and her son, and to help her with the dairying and the smallholding. Her job never fulfilled Virgie; her pianist fingers had to become a typist's, and she had to put music behind her, and the men who pursued her (as they did) were mostly a dull, unsatisfactory lot, no real compensation for the heady Bucky ('Kewpie') Moffitt, the sailor, from whom she had to part: 'And if, as she dreamed one winter night, a new piano she had had turned, after the one pristine moment, into a calling cow, it was by her own desire.'[51]

Outwardly, perhaps, she is no different then from Cassie Morrison, seemingly at ease with her spinster's life, cheery, full of somewhat platitudinous good spirits, dispensing comfort at such times as this funeral for Virgie's mother, growing her own Mama's Name in spring flowers, relaying her brother Loch's letters from New York. The other girls we met have settled into matrimony, if not matronhood; Nina Carmichael is Mrs Junior Nesbitt, Jinny Love has patched up her marriage to Ran, though there are hints that even their conjugal love is tempestuous (at any rate, it is strong). Ran has renounced his earlier wildness – indeed, he has succeeded Drewsie Carmichael as Mayor (though the aura of old misdeeds and Maideen's death hangs over him, drawing people to him rather than the reverse, as Eudora Welty brilliantly and truthfully makes clear). The children this couple have produced, little Jinny and little King, do not stand for any synthesis or harmony; they are wild, imaginative, amoral – though these may, it is inferred, be the qualities of childhood rather than those they will take with them into adult life.

But perhaps the most astonishing development is the return to the community of King MacLain himself. Miss Snowdie, who is revealed as perhaps the most completely virtuous of all the people (her albino whiteness signifying perhaps her purity of soul), kind and considerate to all with whom she has to do (as evidenced in the laying out of Miss Katie's body), has her old age complicated by the man who deserted her in her youth and middle age:

'I don't know what to do with him,' Miss Snowdie said, in a murmur as quiet as the world around them now. She did not know she had spoken. When her flyaway husband had come home a few years ago, at the age of sixty-odd, and stayed, they said she

---

51. C.S. p. 453.

had never gotten over it – first his running away, then his coming back to her.[52]

If a major theme of *The Golden Apples* is the passing of time, nothing brings this irrevocable truth home to us with sadder, more irrefutable clarity than the degeneration of this Jovian wanderer into a muddle-headed, thwarted captive of the domesticity that has always bored him. All he has are his reminiscences, and who knows how accurate these are (though surely he is telling us a truth when he speaks of an understanding between himself and the late Katie Rainey). He is the human counterpart of his former new house, just across the road from the Raineys' – now a ruin, with even the chinaberry tree cut down (though its stumps, in natural obstinacy, fountain forth leaves).

Yet King still has a valuable truth to impart to us, one that casts a backward light over the whole work:

Every now and then Mr King, his tender-looking old head cocked sidewise, his heels lifted, his right hand pricking the air, tiptoed down the hall to the table to pick at the ham – all as if nobody could see him. While Mamie C. Loomis, a child in peach, sang 'O Love That Will Not let Me Go,' Mr King sucked a little marrow bone and lifted his wobbly head and looked arrogantly at Virgie through the two open doors of her mother's bedroom. Even Weaver Loomis and Little Sister Spights, holding hands on the back row, were crying by now, listening to music, but Mr King pushed out his stained lip. Then he made a hideous face at Virgie, like a silent yell. It was a yell at everything – including death, not leaving it out – and he did not mind taking his present animosity out on Virgie Rainey; indeed he chose her. Then he cracked the little bone in his teeth. She felt refreshed all of a sudden at that tiny but sharp sound.[53]

And in the very last paragraph of the story – of the entire book – we read: '[Virgie] smiled once, seeing before her, screenlike, the hideous and delectable face Mr King MacLain had made at the funeral,

52. C.S. p. 438.
53. C.S. p. 446.

and when they all knew he was next – even he.'[54] There is a deep and deliberate doubleness here, summed up in the imaginative paradox 'hideous and delectable'.

In Freudian terminology, Eros and Thanatos stand in a perpetual relationship of tension, and here King is seen as able to maintain, even in the confused old age of his misspent life, a near-heroic disdain and resentment of the latter. This is not the only way to confront death, of course, and perhaps other ways may be both more attractive and more satisfying – Miss Katie's and Miss Snowdie's attitudes to ageing are certainly a lot more dignified, and theirs, maybe, are the more desirable to emulate. But that does not detract from the validity of King's own – whatever else one thinks about it, it is authentic. It has a long precedent, too: gods do not so easily lie down and die.

In one of my earliest conversations with her, Eudora Welty called 'The Wanderers' the 'story in which practically everybody turns out to be a son or daughter of old King MacLain'. Certainly, as we have already seen, in addition to his legitimate progeny, Ran and the dead Eugene, both the departing Virgie and the already absent Loch may well be his. There is evidence for thinking this in Cassie's valedictory words to Virgie:

> Virgie lifted her hand, and the girls waved.
> 'You'll go away like Loch,' Cassie called from the steps. 'A life of your own, away – I'm so glad for people like you and Loch. I am really.'[55]

But it must be clear that actual flesh-and-blood relationship is not the real issue at stake. Eudora Welty intends King to stand – ambivalently, teasingly, but none the less insistently – for something that will not be satisfied with the quotidian round which swallows up almost everybody else, for some overreaching or romantic principle, often morally dubious, but constituting a fact of existence that cannot be gainsaid; for even those who are not his children can feel – and occasionally act upon – that disquiet of the soul (and of the flesh in which the soul is cased) which for him is an article of faith.

---

54. C.S. p. 461.
55. C.S. p. 457.

Whether or not she is a real daughter of his, Virgie is one in spirit –
yet she is also his superior, even in her young womanhood; for she has
assimilated what to him was compulsion into a mature but non-
submissive realization of the nature of existence:

> Virgie never saw it differently, never doubted that all the
> opposites on earth were close together, love close to hate, living
> to dying; but of them all, hope and despair were the closest blood
> – unrecognizable one from the other sometimes, making
> moments double on themselves, and in the doubling double
> again, amending but never taking back.[56]

In the long journey of the book Virgie alone combines those twins
of hope and despair, acceptance and resistance. She accepts a great deal
– having to play the piano in the cinema, receiving the advances of only
tedious men, having to comply with her mother's increasingly nervous
and insistent demands. But she never gives in or goes under, pretends
that she is what she is not. Her duty to her mother lovingly and
responsibly discharged, she can now go forth into an ampler, less
fettered life, with the strength that comes from both endurance and the
preservation of ideals.

III

The very last pages of 'The Wanderers' resemble the coda of a
symphony: gathering material from what has gone before, they
transform it into something that binds up and unifies our earlier
experiences, and endows them with a latent but new-seeming quality
that will remain in our minds as the very essence of the work.

Virgie, seated outside in MacLain 'on a stile, bereaved, hatless,
unhidden now, in the rain', feels herself reconciled at last with Miss
Eckhart, object of both her love and her hatred; consequently, one of
the old teacher's 'pictures from Europe' comes back to her, the one that
depicted Perseus with the head of the Gorgon Medusa ('"The same
thing as [the Germanic] Siegfried and the Dragon."'):

---

56. C.S. p. 452.

The vaunting was what she remembered, that lifted arm.

Cutting off the Medusa's head was the heroic act, perhaps, that made visible a horror in life, that was at once the horror in love, Virgie thought – the separateness. She might have seen heroism prophetically when she was young and afraid of Miss Eckhart. She might be able to see it now prophetically, but she was never a prophet. Because Virgie saw things in their time, like hearing them – and perhaps because she must believe in the Medusa equally with Perseus – she saw the stroke of the sword in three moments, not one. In the three was the damnation – no, only the secret, unhurting because not caring in itself – beyond the beauty and the sword's stroke and the terror lay their existence in time – far out and endless, a constellation which the heart could read over many a night.

Miss Eckhart, whom Virgie had not, after all, hated – had come near to loving, for she had taken Miss Eckhart's hate, and then her love, extracted them, the thorn and then the overflow – had hung the picture on the wall for herself. She had absorbed the hero and the victim and then, stoutly, could sit down to the piano with all Beethoven ahead of her. With her hate, with her love, and with the small gnawing feelings that ate them, she offered Virgie her Beethoven. She offered, offered, offered – and when Virgie was young, in the strange wisdom of youth that is accepting of more than is given, she had accepted *the* Beethoven, as with the dragon's blood. That was the gift she had touched with her fingers that had drifted and left her.

In Virgie's reach of memory a melody softly lifted, lifted of itself. Every time Perseus struck off the Medusa's head, there was the beat of time, and the melody. Endless the Medusa, and Perseus endless.[57]

As in 'A Still Moment', we are reminded here of the mystery of love and separateness, the unanswerable problem of which came first – the element of love, in the need for which we all of us move; or the element of single identity, which propels us to make contact, to reach

---

57. C.S. p. 460.

out for assurance. It is the latter that is responsible for the heroic in life. Frustrated, lonely Miss Eckhart knew the heroic through the medium of Beethoven, and was able to transmit her knowledge – though Virgie is one who, however little she would seem to have to show for it, belongs to the element of love.

The Medusa, the Gorgon, we have already – in 'June Recital' – associated with Miss Eckhart, especially through understanding Loch's paternity, and therefore associating him with Perseus. Alone of the three Gorgons the original Medusa was mortal, and had at one time been a beautiful woman. She had an affair with the sea god Poseidon, and as punishment she was changed by Athena into the form by which we know her: snaky-locked, and with eyes that turned people into stone.

Miss Eckhart may well have been beautiful, at any rate in her soul (hence her playing, and her passion for ceremony); but exile, wandering, feelings of alienation ruined her. As we meet her, she is (as we have noted), monstrous, in the popular sense of the word. Perhaps it can indeed be put down to a liaison with Poseidon, brother to Zeus himself (King MacLain), who stands in qualities halfway between the father, air, and the mother, earth, the tempestuous ambisexual world of emotion, most fittingly represented by music (Virgie, Easter, Scooter MacLain, the Spaniard).

Throughout life, says *The Golden Apples*, with its terrible transience, with the war it declares on all living beings through its instrument of Time, we have to make the permanent choice of surrender to custom, or ceaseless resistance.

Just as repeatedly in the sequence we have been given that vaunting, that raised arm (Loch Morrison, the orphan Easter, the Spaniard as he stands on a 'numbered avenue, not far . . . from the ocean', dying Miss Katie), just as over and over again there have been details of gold (the West in the opening story, Easter and dead little Fan's hair, the sunset-soaked ocean in San Francisco), so those apples of Yeats's quest feature recurrently. But not as something from lore, from men's heads, but as real fruit, the only kind we can know in our lives, though we can translate what we learn from them into eternal and mythic terms. Perhaps no passage goes deeper than the one which transcribes the thoughts of the generally unremarkable Nina Carmichael. It is another proof of the literary democracy that is Eudora Welty's fictional world that this passage, which contains so quintessential a part of the book's philosophy, should belong to this ordinary small-town middle-class Girl Guide, on a routine enough woodland camp at Moon Lake:

> For a moment, with her powerful hands, Nina held the boat back. Again she thought of a pear – not the everyday gritty kind that hung on the tree in the backyard, but the fine kind sold on trains and at high prices, each pear with a paper cone wrapping it alone – beautiful, symmetrical, clean pears with thin skins, with snow-white flesh so juicy and tender that to eat one baptized the whole face, and so delicate that while you urgently ate the first half, the second half was already beginning to turn brown. To all fruits, and especially to those fine pears, something happened – the process was so swift, you were never in time for them. It's not the flowers that are fleeting, Nina thought, it's the fruits – it's the time when things are ready that they don't stay. She even went through the rhyme, 'Pear tree by the garden gate, How much longer must I wait?' – thinking it was the pears that asked it, not the picker.[58]

With this wonderful passage we are in the realm of the great vatic modernist poets; and I reminded Eudora Welty of Sonnet XIII in Rilke's *Sonnets to Orpheus* (first suite):

> Voller Apfel, Birne und Banane,
> Stachelbeere. . . . Alles dieses spricht
> Tod und Leben in den Mund. . . . Ich ahne. . . .
> Lest es einem Kind vom Angesicht,
>
> wenn es sie erschmeckt. Dies kommt von weit.
> Wird euch langsam namelos im Munde?
> Wo sonst Worte waren, fliessen Funde,
> aus dem Fruchtfleisch überrascht befreit.
>
> Wagt zu sagen, was ihr Apfel nennt.
> Diese Süsse, die sich erst verdichtet,
> um, im Schmecken liese aufgerichtet.

---

58. C.S. p. 355.

klar zu werden, wach und transparent,
doppeldeutig, sonnig, erdig, hiesig –:
O Ehrfahrung, Fühlung, Freude – riesig.

(Banana, rounded apple, russet pear,
gooseberry. . . . Does not all this convey
life and death into your mouth? . . . It's there! . . .
Read it on a child's face any day,

when it tastes them. What infinity!
Can't you feel inside your mouth a growing
mysteriousness, and, where words were, a flowing
of suddenly released discovery?

Dare to say what 'apple' has implied!
Sweetness, concentrated, self-repressing,
slowly yielding to the tongue's caressing,

growing awake, transparent, clarified,
double-meaning'd, sunshine-full, terrestrial: –
O experience, feeling, joy, – celestial!)[59]

I have mentioned the similarity between the end of 'The Hitch-Hikers' and the work of another modernist poet, García Lorca – the end of 'El Rey de Harlem', the black child ushering in the new kingdom. He is in our thoughts as we read of Virgie sitting in the rain being joined by an 'old wrapped-up Negro woman'. The woman lighting out and an old woman indelibly of the place, clutching a red hen – they provide a fitting juxtaposition for the close. And the rain coming down over everywhere brings to mind the snow falling at the end of James Joyce's 'The Dead' (indeed, it is a part-conscious echo).

Rilke, Lorca, Joyce – I repeat again: this is Eudora Welty's rightful company here. And none of them has surpassed, for majesty and subtlety, the beauty of the two sentences that bring the whole book to its close:

---

59. Rainer Marie Rilke, *Sonnets to Orpheus* (Sonette an Orpheus, 1923), English transl. J.N. Leishman, Hogarth (1957), pp. 58–9.

Then she and the old beggar woman, the old black thief, were there alone and together in the shelter of the big public tree, listening to the magical percussion, the world beating in their ears. They heard through falling rain the running of the horse and bear, the stroke of the leopard, the dragon's crusty slither, and the glimmer and trumpet of the swan.[60]

A NOTE

The resemblances between William Golding's *The Pyramid* (1967) and *The Golden Apples* have never, to my knowledge, been commented on; to me they seem very striking.

Both are linked sequences of interrelated stories: the magic seven in Eudora's case, the magic three in Golding's. At the centre of both books is a small town, and Golding's – rather heavy-handedly named Stillbourne, but palpably part of its countryside (Wiltshire) – is no less stifling to the free spirit than Morgana. Both books, too, show time at work on the community and on the physical place which contains it; Golding's spans the 1920s to the 1960s (roughly the same length of time as Eudora Welty's). Evie, a promiscuous girl, gives her favours to several young men, paralleling King MacLain's generous dealing out of himself to the girls and women of Morgana/MacLain.

But there is a more remarkable similarity still than any on this list (which could indeed be extended). Dominant in the long third story is a music mistress (piano teacher), a thwarted unmarried woman known as Bounce, whose impact on all who know her is strongly akin to Miss Eckhart's: domineering, unlovable, impressive. Furthermore, she has a violent crush on an uneducated man, the mechanic (later garage proprietor) Henry Williams – like Miss Eckhart's with Mr Sissum. Like Miss Eckhart, too, Bounce goes off her head, and her crazed behaviour, as in Eudora Welty's story, is symbolic of the kind of unhappiness small-town living can make for: too much denial in life. When the narrator, Oliver, returns to Stillbourne and sees her memorial stone:

CLARA CECILIA DAWLISH 1890–1960
Heaven is Music

---

60. C.S. p. 461.

he thinks: 'I was afraid of you, and so I hated you. It is as simple as that. When I heard you were dead I was glad.' This is astonishingly reminiscent of Virgie Rainey's state of mind at Miss Eckhart's grave.

What should we make of all this? I do not know. Golding was the most honourable of writers; he may have read Eudora Welty's book, for he was a well-read man – or he may not have done, but merely heard it discussed, or read reviews. I certainly cannot believe that the resemblance is coincidental. After *The Lord of the Flies*, I have long thought *The Pyramid* the best novel of Golding's first phase, warmer and wider-ranging in its sympathies than its fellows, and so I like to number it among the more prominent examples of Eudora Welty's benign and creative influence.

6

THE BRIDE OF THE INNISFALLEN, 'WHY I LIVE AT THE P.O.' AND THE PONDER HEART

I

THE STORIES on which Eudora Welty worked after those that constitute *The Golden Apples* are deliberate departures from both the subjects and methods with which she was now associated; 'Circe' – inspired, perhaps, by her research for *The Golden Apples* – is a direct first-person-narration excursion into the world of Greek mythology, and quite different from anything she had written before; as is 'The Burning', her only fictional visit to the Civil War South. 'The Bride of the Innisfallen' takes the reader on a journey from London to Cork; it is something of what Henry James called an *amour de voyage*, and it is not only its Irish people and scenery which make us think of Eudora Welty's friend, Elizabeth Bowen. 'No Place for You, My Love' also partakes of this genre, Southern though its scene is – but the South of New Orleans and beyond, rather than of Jackson and Mississippi. It carries on from its direct predecessor in its refusal to name its principal characters, but in this story, the characters – there are only two – enjoy a strange suspension of identity which their adventures serve to undermine and to enhance in simultaneous and equal measure. 'Kin' certainly takes us back to Mississippi but (uniquely in Eudora's *œuvre*) through the eyes of someone who has lived away from it for by far the greater portion of her life – in fact, since she was eight years old.

The next story, *The Ponder Heart*, a novella in terms of length and substance, has become one of Eudora Welty's best-known and best-loved productions. Published in the *New Yorker* in 1953, it appeared in book form (with delightful drawings by Joe Krush) in 1954. The other short stories were collected in one volume the following year. Together with 'Ladies in Spring' and 'Going to Naples', they make up *The Bride of the Innisfallen* (1955).

'Circe' is a monologue spoken by Homer's enchantress, which not only tells of the sojourn on her island of Odysseus and his crew (the metamorphosis of all but the herb-protected Odysseus into pigs, and back again) from her point of view, but presents her as a subject of sympathy – lonely even in her power, heartsick with unfulfilled desire and love. Comparing her own lot as daughter of the Sun with that of the humans on whom she has exercised her powers, she says:

> There exists a mortal mystery, that, if I knew where it was, I could crush like an island grape. Only frailty, it seems, can divine it – and I was not endowed with that property. They live by frailty! By the moment! I tell myself that it is only a mystery, and mystery is only uncertainty. There is no mystery in magic! Men are swine; let it be said, and no sooner said than done. Yet mortal alone can divine where it lies in each other, can find it and prick it in all its peril, with an instrument made of air. I swear that only to possess that one, trifling secret, I would willingly turn myself into a harmonious dove for the rest of eternity![1]

It is hard not to take this as a covert justification of Eudora Welty's creative decision to stay with the ordinary mortals of her own Mississippi rather than, as a sophisticated writer honoured by literary critics, to deal with the predicament and consciousnesses of more rarefied beings – a temptation to which many authors succumb once they are famous. For magic one can read 'artistry', the extraordinary alchemy of what Eudora Welty calls in an essay 'Words into Fiction', of which she had already proved herself such an unusual and blessed mistress. Nevertheless, in all the stories in *The Bride of the Innisfallen* one has a sense, as one has nowhere else in the corpus of her work, of

---

1. C.S. p. 533.

Eudora Welty wrestling with herself: over both the subjects appropriate to her art, and the methods by which she, who had gained such uncanny control over her medium, should present them.

'The Burning' is a story which she has as good as rejected (unusually; for – this story apart – though she is diffident about giving her own assessment of individual works, of only 'The Purple Hat' and 'At The Landing' does she speak dismissively). She tried to dissuade the distinguished Southern historian and novelist Shelby Foote from including it in an anthology of Civil War stories by writing to him: 'I hate for you to use it; I think it is the worst story I ever wrote.' Shelby Foote replied: 'I think it is a good story, and I'm a Civil War expert; you're not.'

Perhaps Eudora Welty's animus against this story is that here she for once defied (at least on one level) her hatred of the Civil War, and did what every Southern writer (virtually) feels obliged to do – look with her own eyes at that terrible time and find an episode that represents both the Southern defeat and the writer's vision of things. Her Jackson has already burned twice on the orders of General Sherman, by the time the story opens, though the Federalists' work is not yet complete there. In 'The Burning', further fires are lit. The story's very real intensity doubtless gains from the author's – to adapt Allen Tate's lines from 'Ode to the Confederate Dead' – lifting her eyes from Jackson 'to the immoderate past', and finding there a horror that makes the present seem temporarily uncertain and vulnerable. Rereading this story at a time when reports from the former Yugoslavia have shaken us all, I have to say that 'The Burning' seems able to meet these tragic times of ours as few other works of fiction do; *mutatis mutandis*, its horrifying events were repeated in Bosnia and Croatia throughout 1992–3, right down to circumstantial details of the human capacity for gratuitous infliction of humiliations and cruelties that we would all greatly prefer to forget. Nor does the story's elaborate elliptical technique diminish their effect.

'The Burning' is presented for the most part through the baffled, fearful eyes of Delilah, black slave to a Jackson household reduced by the ravages of the War to two sisters, Miss Theo and Miss Myra, and a mysterious child, Phinny – certainly a bastard, very possibly part-black, and most probably fathered by the dead brother, Benton.

During the course of the story we learn of Miss Myra's rape by a Union soldier, of Phinny being burned alive until he becomes a mere heap of charred bones, of Miss Theo hanging her sister before trying – with less than total success – to hang herself. (Instead, she twists 'in the grass like a dead snake till the sun went down'.) The needless destruction of the whole antebellum world is epitomized in a drummer-boy's wanton wringing of the necks of the sisters' peacocks. Later, all the burning over, Delilah, the sole survivor of this Old South household, receives hallucinated visions of past, present and future from the glass of an elaborately framed mirror that has fallen into the grass:

> She put her arms over her head and waited, for they would all be coming again, gathering under her and above her, bees saddled like horses out of the air, butterflies harnessed to one another, bats with masks on, birds together, all with their weapons bared. She listened for the blows, and dreaded that whole army of wings – of flies, birds, serpents, their glowing enemy faces and bright kings' dresses, that banner of colors forked out, all this world that was flying, striking, falling, gilded or blackened, mortally splitting and falling apart, proud turbans unwinding, turning like the spotted dying leaves of fall, spiraling down to bottomless ash; she dreaded the fury of all the butterflies and dragonflies in the world riding, blades unconcealed and at point – descending, and rising again from the waters below, down under, one whale made of his own grave, opening his mouth to swallow Jonah one more time.[2]

This is a powerful evocation of an unsophisticated mind almost at breaking point, beset by images it can neither comprehend nor control. At the same time these images are perhaps too obscure, derive too much from a private world incompletely filtered into the objective one. We can note the authorial obsession (in the words concerning Jonah and the whale) with the perpetual recurrence of mythological happening: like Perseus and Medusa in 'The Wanderers'; like Odysseus and the Cyclops in Circe's mind in the previous story, without feeling that

2. C.S. p. 493.

we have been made properly privy to the idea. Maybe here, for once, Circe has turned in on her own magic.

'The Bride of the Innisfallen' is a very different matter, fully in the here and now. Both it and 'Going to Naples' are of the same type. By the Jamesian term of *amour de voyage* I mean fiction in which travel itself is the essential subject; its theme will therefore be the change of perception, even the change in moral perspective, brought about by change of place, the unfamiliar and demanding being substituted for the familiar and protective. In the first story an American girl has decided to leave her husband and board the train that departs from Paddington, London, at four o'clock for Fishguard and the boat to Cork. In the second a rather younger Italo-American girl is on board the *Pomona* from New York to Naples. Both seem correlatives for Eudora Welty's temporary need to abandon her own, so deeply known territory.

During this abandonment, for the first and only time in her career, the influence of another writer is everywhere apparent. She never succumbed to the power of her co-Mississippian author Faulkner, but I think, when she left Mississippi, that she did yield somewhat to Elizabeth Bowen (1899–1973), a lesser writer than herself, albeit a considerable one.

Elizabeth Bowen, born in Ireland into a family of the Anglo-Irish 'ascendancy', despite spending most of her life in England, retained certain fundamental attributes of her Irish origins: a poetic apprehension of the visible world, in which invisible forces seem not only immanent but susceptible to probing; a robust humour and courage which go individualistically hand in hand with artistic delicacy and spiritual strength. Her most successful novels, *The House in Paris* (1935) and *The Death of the Heart* (1938), carry on Henry James's preoccupation with the confrontation of experience by innocence to the former's disparagement, the demonstration showing up the corruption and spiritual nullity of contemporary civilization. These novels and others – though, like Eudora Welty's, they spring from the moment of vision that is more usually the short story's – operate by their dramatic enmeshing of the innocent; this makes them very unlike anything in Eudora Welty's fiction, where innocence, experience and the reaction against experience are successive stages of individuation (it does, however, give them a strong family resemblance to certain other British novels of their period – those of Rosamond Lehmann, L.P. Hartley and Graham Greene). Nevertheless, their sense of place, their complex atmosphere – revealing the author's near-hallucinatory awareness of interiors, times of day, the weather – certainly suggest a kinship with Eudora Welty.

In her short stories Elizabeth Bowen comes much nearer to greatness than she does in her novels. Her heightened sensory awareness, which transfixes a moment in time, a spot in space, is more suited to the shorter length; in the longer it can be at odds with thematic development. And during the Second World War this extraordinary awareness was responsible for some of the most powerful evocations of wartime England (particularly London) that we have been given – such stories as 'Mysterious Kor' and 'Those Happy Autumn Fields', which disturbingly and movingly relate inner and outer worlds, imposing the inner on the shattered outer one and then bringing it back to the mind transformed. In these wartime stories (collected in *The Demon Lover* [1945]) Elizabeth Bowen stands very close to Eudora Welty – and it was in the 1940s that their friendship began, and it continued until Elizabeth Bowen's death. Eudora went to stay at Bowenscourt, the house Elizabeth Bowen inherited in County Cork, and took photographs which show the magical effect of the soft Irish light on house and countryside. In addition to other bonds, the two women felt that there was a deep similarity between Ireland and the South: a passionate people, a pressing past, a diminished present, an ubiquitous religion that had bestowed even on unbelievers a spiritual sense; a beautiful, often sad landscape – and the Anglo-Irish 'ascendancy' connects easily to the white Southerner landholders, whose legacy perforce includes guilt and resentment. Elizabeth Bowen cared for angels (in her own phrase) and believed in ghosts; Eudora Welty has a preternatural sense of past lives, especially in her beloved River Country.

I met Elizabeth Bowen at the house of some friends when I was twenty; I found her charming, friendly and, even in that short time, fascinating (she described to me the genesis of *The House in Paris* –

how she had seen, in her mind's eye, the room in which the two children of the novel encounter each other – and told me of the shattering effect on her of having had to sell Bowenscourt). Tall, distinguished-looking, with a surprisingly massive head, and a stammer that curiously intensified her conversation, she has remained strong in my memory – and I do not think it is only hindsight that enables me sharply to distinguish these two friends. Although she was very kind to a young man, Elizabeth Bowen's manner was essentially patrician, just as her writing surely is; she extends sympathies to, but never identifies significantly with, those beyond herself and her peers. Indeed, her sensibility often seems affronted by those less sensitive than herself; this gives an odd edge of irritable intolerance to such scenes as Portia's stay with the rather 'common' Heccombs in *The Death of the Heart*. Eudora Welty, in both her manner and her writing, is generously inclusive; to say that this makes her the more democratic writer is almost absurdly unnecessary, for democracy is one of the conditions of her art, as aristocratic refinement was of Elizabeth Bowen's.

Elizabeth Bowen and her family house would have been Eudora Welty's own destination when she travelled from London to Cork, so perhaps it was inevitable that the older, Irish writer would cast her shadow on the title story of a volume that is dedicated to her. Certain sentences seem to have Elizabeth Bowen's very accent (and that accent was quite idiosyncratic):

> She was big-boned and taller than the man who followed her inside bringing the suitcase – he came up round and with a doll's smile, his black suit wet; she turned a look on him; this was farewell. The train to Fishguard to catch the Cork boat was leaving in fifteen minutes – at a black four o'clock in the afternoon of that spring that refused to flower. She, so clearly, was the one going.[3]

Of the Cork-bound travellers, one (the principal one) is an American girl who has temporarily walked out on her life; at the end of the story

---

3. C.S. p. 495.

this journey, this scene shift, will give her her life back (as she has intended, hoped) in a beautiful double epiphany (that Irish-originated term seems, for once, the only one to use). First, a bride is on board the crossing steamer, and casts something of her own joy on all who see her; then, as the American girl walks around Cork, rain falls, restoring her to herself (she is able to use 'I' again) and making her close cousin to Virgie Rainey:

> For a moment someone – she thought it was a woman – came and stood at the window, then hurled a cigarette with its live coal down into the extinguishing garden. But it was not the impatient tenant, it was the window itself that could tell her all she had come here to know – or all she could bear this evening to know, and that was light and rain, light and rain, dark, light, and rain.[4]

Eudora Welty has become herself again. Earlier, the Elizabeth Bowen-influenced combination of humour and sense of mystery does not, I think, succeed with the train passengers, whose conversation is too prolix. (And there are little inaccuracies, too: no Briton would need to ask, as the Welshman does, whether Ireland is a Catholic country; and the word 'car' is not one the British apply to any railway carriage but the restaurant one.)

'Going to Naples', though also a little prolix, is the better of the two stories partly, I think, because the journey is given a real human dimension in the flirtation of the fat Italo-American girl, Gabriella, with the enigmatic Aldo, a flirtation that is touching, significant and comic. As someone who has known many English-speaking Italians (from both the United States and the United Kingdom) I can vouch-safe for the accuracy of the dialogue here, though Mr Ugone has his own vital individuality:

> For one thing, is in Genoa most beautiful cemetery in world. . . . You have never seen? No one? Ah, the statues – you could find nowhere in *Italia* more beautiful, more sad, more real. Envision with me now, I will take you there gladly. Ah! See here – a mama, how she hold high the little daughter to kiss a picture of Papa

---

4. C.S. p. 518.

– all lifesize. See here! You see angel flying out the tomb – life-size! See here! You see family of ten, eleven, twelve, all kneeling lifesize at deathbed. You would marvel how splendid Genoa is with the physical.'[5]

The story abounds in humour and keen observation – La Zingara, the celebrity aboard the ship, is particularly amusingly done – but does not build up sufficiently to a whole.

The travellers at the centre of 'No Place for You, My Love', however – whose journey has about it something of the accidental, the arbitrary – define an existential predicament which makes this story not merely the best of those in *The Bride of the Innisfallen*, but one of Eudora Welty's most interesting, subtle and complex productions. The value that she attaches to it herself is perhaps evidenced in her choosing it for discussion (as illuminating her own creative processes) in her essay 'Writing and Analyzing a Story'.

A man and a woman, both Northerners, meet at a lunch party in New Orleans (actually, at Galatoire's, one of the most famous restaurants in that gastronomically rich city). He senses in her an emotional unhappiness, presumes her (surely correctly) to be caught in a hopeless relationship with a married man. He invites her to go on a drive with him, asking: '"Have you ever driven down south of here?"' and getting the reply that is to reverberate throughout the story: '"South of New Orleans? I didn't know there was any south to *here*. Does it just go on and on?"' Immediately the direction south – or rather, south from South – acquires a metaphoric quality, becomes some ultimate of the spirit as well as of physical geography – and the hot, invincibly hot, sun-dominated land into which the two strangers journey in the man's 'faded-red Ford convertible' becomes metaphoric also, shimmering, primitive, and eventually amphibious, a meeting of earth and water which defies all sophisticated approaches to time and space.

The two people are not so much brought together by the region into which they have driven as made to receive from it a sense of the humanity they deeply share, which can even be said to distinguish them from the local inhabitants, so very much formed by a place apart.

5. C.S. p. 581.

There is contact, both physical and psychological, between them: they dance together at the Shrimp Dance at Bab's Place, he puts a silencing hand on her when she attempts to ask him about his private life; he sees the bruise at her temple (the scar, presumably, of a passionate quarrel); they kiss when he stops the car on the long, dark way back. But this is not the beginning of a new relationship; it was never envisaged as such by either person; instead it is an experience deeper than that word can normally encompass, a drive into the southern land that is a drive into deep recesses of being, where neither joy nor sorrow, neither desire nor need, can be separated. Fairly early in their ride the couple take a small ferry, see an alligator, the captive of some boys:

> He thought, Well they had to catch one sometime. It's Sunday afternoon. So they have him on board now, riding him across the Mississippi River. . . . The playfulness of it beset everybody on the ferry. The hoarseness of the boat whistle, commenting briefly, seemed part of the general appreciation.
>
> 'Who want to rassle him? Who want to, eh?' two boys cried, looking up. A boy with shrimp-colored arms capered from side to side, pretending to have been bitten.
>
> What was there so hilarious about jaws that could bite? And what danger was there once in this repulsiveness – so that the last worldly evidence of some old heroic horror of the dragon had to be paraded in capture before the eyes of country clowns?[6]

There is no passage more important to the story than this: the alligator is, above everything else, an alligator; to call him a symbol is to reduce, to impoverish, his appearance here. Rather, he contains in his ugly, primeval form secrets of life which all the humiliations imposed on him by humans cannot altogether disguise, and which parallel the secrets of the land itself, and those hidden deep in the (fittingly unnamed) man and woman, as they prepare for further travel.

Originally, says Eudora Welty, the story concerned the young woman (at this stage from the South itself) locked in a hopeless relationship. A drive with an acquaintance 'south from South' ('that once-submerged strange land') interposed itself between her and her story,

---

6. C.S. p. 470.

profoundly changing it. The woman, like her acquaintance, became not a Southerner but someone from Toledo, Ohio, which was to compound her sense of both foreignness and discovery. And the country itself:

> . . . which had so stamped itself upon my imagination put in an unmistakable claim now as the very image of the story's predicament. It pointed out to me at the same time where the real point of view belonged. Once I'd escaped those characters' minds, I saw it was outside them – suspended, hung in the air between two people, fished alive from the surrounding scene. As I wrote further into the story, something more real, more essential, than the characters were on their own was revealing itself. In effect, though the characters numbered only two, there had come to be a sort of third character along on the ride – the presence of a relationship between the two. It was what grew up between them meeting as strangers, went on the excursion with them, nodded back and forth from one to the other – listening, watching, persuading or denying them, enlarging or diminishing them, forgetful sometimes of who they were or what they were doing here – in its domain – and helping or betraying them along.[7]

This observation, so germane to the mystery established with such intellectual concentration in the story itself, applies also, obviously, to the relationship of writers themselves with (and to) their subjects. Theirs is the constant, transforming presence, at once visible and morally exigent. As throughout this volume of stories, Eudora Welty is concerned here with the baffling business of the writer's vision: the conflicts between the internal and the external, between the felt and the assessed, between the known and the apprehended, the certain and the uncertain, the single and the shared, the concluded and the ever-in-flux.

The remaining two stories in the collection, 'Kin' and 'Ladies in Spring' take us to Mississippi again. 'Kin' is a first-person account of the return to her State of a not-so-young-woman; 'Ladies in Spring' is a story of country life, featuring a walk under a large umbrella down a

---

7. Eye pp. 111–12.

village street, reminiscent of the river-dragging expedition in 'The Wide Net'. 'Kin', trying to see the Mississippi landscape through distanced, if sympathetic, eyes, also tries to focus on 'good country people' and their inability to shake off the past. For the second time in this volume the Civil War asserts itself; old Uncle Felix, his mind wandering, believes himself once more to be the drummer-boy he was then: '"Hide,"gasped the old man . . . "and I'll go in. Kill 'em all. I'm old enough I swear you, Bob."' And he mistakes Dicey, the woman narrator, for a boyhood sweetheart (Daisy). The story thus develops the volume's overriding concern with perceptions and assessments of reality. Dicey can almost believe that she is Daisy. A significant moment comes when she finds an old eye-contraption known as the stereopticon, in which, she feels, just by holding it up to the eyes, she can 'dissolve [my] sight, all our sights'.

'Ladies in Spring', if less ambitious, is more successful than 'Kin'; Miss Hattie's production of rain in a hot dry summer spell is a comic counterpart of Miss Eckhart's – or Circe's – lonely dedication to knowledge, a humane pursuit; and is delightfully exhibited through the consciousness of an errant father and son, both playing truant, fishing by a creek in the woods.

II

Eudora Welty's investigation of different methods of presentation, of various levels of subjectivity and objectivity, gave her the courage to use the extended first person for her longest single work of fiction between *Delta Wedding* and *Losing Battles*, the novella *The Ponder Heart* – and to create a narrator wholly different in personality and position from herself. But in fact she had made a comparable excursion into an assumption of another's voice, another's mind, in one of her most popular and admired early stories. I refer, of course, to 'Why I Live at the P.O.' from *A Curtain of Green*. 'Would you be able to give us any of it?' the English programme-maker and interviewer Patchey Wheatley asked her in 1986. 'I should be able to,' she replied. Within less than a minute her face and voice had undergone a real transformation, and she became the woman she had created in rural Mississippi back in 1941, as she delivered those now famous lines:

I was getting along fine with Mama, Papa-Daddy and Uncle Rondo until my sister Stella-Rondo just separated from her husband and came back home again. Mr Whittaker! Of course I went with Mr Whittaker first, when he appeared here in China Grove, taking 'Pose Your Own' photos, and Stella-Rondo broke us up. Told him I was one-sided. Bigger on one side than the other, which is a deliberate, calculated falsehood: I'm the same. Stella-Rondo is exactly twelve months to the day younger than I am, and for that reason she's spoiled.[8]

Already the author has let us know all we really need to know to make sense of what follows. The woman addressing us is obsessively jealous of a younger sister, who is better-looking and more personable than herself, and will distort any picture of life to suit her willed dark vision of her sibling rival. Don't we know even from those few sentences that there never really was anything between the narrator and Mr Whittaker, and that Stella-Rondo's marriage to him was done entirely fairly?

In *A Curtain of Green*, Eudora Welty moved among her subjects like a photographer. 'Why I Live at the P.O.', all voice as it is, might seem to have little appeal to the visual imagination – though the author did see a post office with an ironing-board in the back, on her travels, such as appears at the story's conclusion. Nevertheless, the story is a reminder of her photographs, especially those in which the subjects turned to the camera, or rather to its holder. The postmistress thrusts her whole face into the lens, as it were, insisting that she and only she will be the object of interest. Her voice drowns all other possible voices, all other possible interpretations of things. The comedy of 'Why I Live at the P.O.' is the comedy of personality, of rampant egotism.

In her introduction to *A Curtain of Green* Katherine Anne Porter draws attention to this story, and calls the heroine 'a terrifying case of *dementia praecox*'. Surely she is wrong to do so, and Eudora Welty has distanced herself from this description. The postmistress of China Grove, if more extreme in her behaviour – at any rate during that Fourth of July and its aftermath ('five solid days and nights') – is no more seriously deranged than the rest of us. We all have her inside us,

---

8. C.S. p. 46.

and at times she lets rip from even the most composed member of society – self-willed, self-justifying, self-centred, spiteful. And I believe there could even come a time when she abandons the position she has landed herself in by flouncing out of her home, and even laughs at herself. (Eudora Welty has confessed that in adolescence she herself was a maker of scenes, a packer of suitcases.) The heroine is a woman of quick wits, ready invention, her malice driving her to sharp comments and retorts to just about everybody.

She is incurably stubborn; once she gets an idea in her head, she will not dislodge it. She has said that her sister has not adopted Shirley-T, as she claims, but gave birth to her, and so her sister's own child she must stay, despite all the evidence to the contrary. Similarly, her overweening jealousy makes her insist that Mr Whittaker left Stella-Rondo, and not the other way round, as is the actual case. Readers can judge the truth of things by the rise and fall of the postmistress's wonderfully caught voice; when it soars, and approaches the hysterical highest register, then she is probably not sticking too closely to the truth. . . . Eudora Welty has said that the story derives from the small-town habit of dramatizing everything. The dullness, the circumscription of life, demanded that; the South's storytelling tradition could accommodate such dramatizations.

The Ponder Heart continues where 'Why I Live at the P.O.' broke off; our car has broken down, we have had to call at the Beulah, the only goodish hotel in the whole town of Clay, Mississippi; and the proprietress, Miss Edna Earle Ponder, confronts us. The name Edna Earle may sound familiar. It was heard before, in a fragment of conversation in 'The Wide Net', in the passage which, in its illumination of human diversity, made the teenage Anne Tyler want to become a novelist herself:

> 'She's a lot smarter than her cousins in Beulah,' said Virgil. 'And especially Edna Earle, that never did get to be what you'd call a heavy thinker. Edna Earle could sit and ponder all day on how the little tail of the C got through the L in a Coca-Cola sign.'[9]

But this may not be the same Edna Earle; the name had become extremely popular all over the South because of *St Elmo*, a romantic

9. C.S. p. 171.

Victorian novel, by Augusta Jane Evans Wilson in which a virtuous heroine, author of pious 'improving' novels, reforms a roué. But in her introduction to the British edition of *The Ponder Heart* Helen McNeil rightly points out that the words 'Beulah' and 'ponder' both occur in this passage.

Edna Earle is not going to give us any time to avoid listening; she will hold us to her story which, with all its apparent digressions (in fact, of course, most artistically designed), rises to a very dramatic climax – in addition to accounting for the situation we will find at the hotel. Any moment now the story's central figure, Uncle Daniel Ponder, will be coming down to see us. Indeed, Edna Earle ends her tale by hollering for him: 'I'd like to warn you again, he may try to give you something – may think he's got something to give. If he does, do me a favor. Make out like you accept it. Tell him thank you.'[10]

Giving is at the core of *The Ponder Heart*. Daniel, simple-minded youngest son of Grandpa Ponder – and not only uncle to Edna Earle but her older contemporary and childhood companion – loves, above everything else, to give. Even internment in an institution in Jackson does nothing to cure him of his compulsive generosity; and after Grandpa's death, he is, by small-town standards, a rich man. A sociable, affectionate individual, he marries twice: once, before his father's death, to a widow, Miss Teacake Magee; the second time (well, it is only a trial marriage) to Bonny Dee, a lively but delicate girl not yet out of her teens, from the vast poor-white Peacock clan.

It is scarcely surprising that Bonnie Dee, after a time, 'lights out' from her life; for one thing, Uncle Daniel, though still excessively generous, never gives her any *money*, this being a commodity he has never learned to handle. Edna Earle has to resort to putting a notice (in the form of a poem) in the local paper to entice Bonnie Dee back. Quoting it is not to be resisted; its clumsy lines, with their jejune mixture of poetic diction and business jargon, illuminate both the writer's own mind and that of her small town:

Bonnie Dee Ponder, come back to Clay.
Many are tired of you being away.

---

10. P.H. p. 132.

O listen to me, Bonnie Dee Ponder,
Come back to Clay, or husband will wonder.
Please to no more wander.
As of even date, all is forgiven.
Also, retroactive allowance will be given.
House from top to bottom now spick and span,
Come back to Clay the minute you can.
Signed, Edna Earle Ponder.
P.S. Do not try to write a letter,
Just come, the sooner the better.[11]

Clearly it is the 'retroactive allowance' that gets to Bonnie Dee; come back she does, but she insists that Uncle Daniel move out of the Ponder house just outside the town, back to the Beulah Hotel with his niece. However, Edna Earle is up to dealing with the situation; she cuts off Bonnie Dee's money supply; as a result, Bonnie Dee asks Uncle Daniel to come up to the house 'before it storms'. Uncle Daniel asks Edna Earle to accompany him, to witness the reconciliation: 'Well, to make a long story short, Bonnie Dee sent him word Monday after dinner and was dead as a doornail Monday before supper. Tuesday she was in her grave. Nobody more surprised than the Ponders.'[12]

This startling revelation occurs halfway through the story; probably through practice, Edna Earle shows herself a real mistress of the art of suspense. As she tells us of the burial ('"Look, Uncle Daniel. It looks right cool, down yonder in the ground. Here *we* are standing up on top in the burning heat. Let her go"') and of Uncle Daniel's arrest for murder 'the minute the funeral was over good', doubts assail us. Are we in for an account of a terrible deed? After all, it is not hard to seek a motive. And why this wilful lack of openness about what happened that Monday? Edna Earle moves us now to the Courthouse and Uncle Daniel's trial, and despite the incompetence and the prejudice, and the interruptions, and the day's insufferable heat, which affects everybody, we learn the truth – *not* from the witness stand (Edna Earle won't let the real story be spoken, and it is Uncle Daniel's

---

11. P.H. p. 53.
12. P.H. p. 67.

generosity with money that saves the day for him) but in a burst of confidence to us listeners from Edna Earle herself.

On their arrival at the Ponder house Bonnie Dee had been recalcitrant, for all the kindness and delight in her on Uncle Daniel's face. Then the storm came nearer; curled up on the sofa, Bonnie Dee became frightened (and with reason – electric storms are no small matter in Mississippi). To comfort her, Uncle Daniel started tickling her. The diversion worked:

> When the storm got right over the house, he went right to the top with 'creep-mousie', up between those bony little shoulder blades to the nape of her neck and her ear – with the sweetest, most forbearing smile on his face, a forgetful smile. Like he forgot everything that she ever did to him, how changeable she'd been.
>
> But you can't make a real tickler stop unless you play dead. The youngest of all knows that.
>
> And that's what I thought she did. Her hands fluttered and stopped, then her whole little length slipped out from under his fingers, and rolled down to the floor, just as easy as nod, and stayed there – with her dress up to her knees and her hair down over her face. I thought she'd done it on purpose.[13]

Not at all! She has died – Uncle Daniel has literally killed her with kindness.

In my experience *The Ponder Heart* is a novel that changes, like fermenting wine, in one's mind, and each return to it is to a subtly different book. This is because of the intentional – indeed, marvellously evoked – discrepancy between the telling and the tale. Edna Earle, with her breezy confidence and her unassailable prejudices and conviction that both right and good sense can be nowhere but on her side, is not an imaginative or a sensitive person; she, to a perhaps more damaging extent than many of us, can see only a *part* of a situation. This makes her strange story of a simpleton's passion and altruism the more moving, but we have to detach it from the presentation for ourselves. Nothing in her *œuvre* suggests better Eudora Welty's

---

13. P.H. p. 119.

Shakespearian quality; a farcical chain of events related by an egotistic vulgarian (Edna Earle is undoubtedly kin to that postmistress of China Grove, albeit considerably more amiable) is also a (skilfully worked) paradigm of human longings, needs and abilities to rise to the occasion above all limitations.

There are two moments in particular in *The Ponder Heart* for which the word 'Shakespearian' seems especially appropriate, when the whole convention of the work is called into question and transcended, without being broken. First there is the parenthesis which Edna Earle suddenly inflicts on us, after she has told us the truth about the death of Bonnie Dee Ponder: '(And I don't give a whoop for your approval! You don't think I betrayed him by not letting him betray himself, do you?)'[14] The second comes right at the end, and seems (temporarily) to overturn so much:

> And you know, Bonnie Dee Peacock, ordinary as she was and trial as she was to put up with – she's the kind of person you do miss. I don't know why – deliver me from giving you the *reason*. You could look and find her like anywhere. Though I'm sure Bonnie Dee and Uncle Daniel were as happy together as most married people.[15]

So – we haven't heard from her all there was to hear about Bonnie Dee. How could we have! Our own minds have got to get work again – and once more the whole story shifts, as if shaken in a kaleidoscope.

The Ponder Heart has been dramatized twice: by Joseph Fields and Jerome Chodorov for Broadway (1956; it enjoyed a successful, if somewhat modest, run) and then by the author's friend Frank Hains for the New Stage Theater in Jackson, where another old friend, Jane Reid Petty, played the role of Edna Earle herself. But of course, as Eudora Welty (who enjoyed these plays very much) has commented, dramatization undoes the deliberate form of the book. It inevitably transfers attention on to Uncle Daniel (it must be said that the Jackson production, a 'labour of love', was faithful to the original aim). Truly he is a most poetic and moving creation; I very much like

---

14. P.H. p. 125.
15. P.H. p. 132.

Helen McNeil's linking of him to Faulkner's 'idiot' Benjy, the con-sciousness of the first part of *The Sound and the Fury*. But for the kind of appreciation of his virtues I have intimated, we must have him refracted through a more conventional – not to say commonplace – mind than either his own or the omniscient author's; we also need to be interested in Edna Earle herself, in what she says and in what she doesn't say; and having her as buttonholing storyteller seems to me inseparable from knowing her in the way Eudora Welty intends. As we have noted, she can rise to a moving superiority to her mundane self. A bigoted person – in many ways the very pattern of what critics of the small-town Deep South would turn on – she has, of course, depths and beauties of which she is largely unaware. To have made *us* aware of them – and of their existence in countless similar unremarkable-seeming people – is not the least of Eudora Welty's triumphs here.

The Ponder Heart, which makes a work of art out of the rhythms and idioms of ordinary Southern speech, clearly turned Eudora Welty's mind to the whole Southern oral tradition. Out of it she was to make the novel which is, in my view, her supreme achievement: *Losing Battles*.

The Ponder Heart was published in book form in 1954, *The Bride of the Innisfallen* in 1955, *Losing Battles* in 1970. In the great gulf between the first two books and the large-scale novel Eudora Welty knew much personal difficulty and sorrow, and the Southern situation underwent a terrible worsening before the overdue reforms could be allowed to take place. Events that shocked the whole world occurred, becoming paradigms for the kind of stubborn attachment to the priv-ileges of the past that does not baulk at cruelty – indeed, perforce has to resort to it in its blind-alley hysteria. One thinks of the Mississippi lynching of the fourteen-year-old black girl Emmett Till in 1955.

But in retrospect, 1955 was a watershed year; in December the now famous bus boycott began in Montgomery, Alabama; it lasted for a year. It began as a result of a black woman, Mrs Rosa Parkes, being arrested for sitting down in a 'white' bus seat (segregated buses were one of the most glaring and ubiquitous of the racist obscenities of Southern life). The attention the boycott attracted all over the

United States did the cause of racial equality untold good. It also saw the appearance on the public political stage of Martin Luther King, who emerged after his triumphant bus-seat-taking in December 1956 as the cause's most eloquent and gifted leader. In the subsequent years – in which King went to prison sixteen times – he was a source of strength and inspiration, a pivotal figure indeed. First the Kennedys, both Jack and his brother Bobby, and then Lyndon Johnson were to recognize the stature of King, as the Republicans, Eisenhower and Nixon, had not been able to.

At the very beginning of this study we appreciated the appalling crescendo of 1963–4, in which Mississippi was perhaps the worst theatre of them all; the murder of Medgar Evers was only one of many dreadful racist killings. Like all white Mississippians of principle and conscience, Eudora Welty was outraged by the atrocities, and full of sympathy – and more – on behalf of the victims, and of the black community as a whole to which each individual brutal act was offered. As a result, many black Jacksonians speak of her with affection.

The Gandhian non-violence with which Martin Luther King and his followers opposed both the Southern status quo and the violence exercised on its behalf against their sit-ins and other peaceful protests must have found an accord in Eudora Welty with her general peaceful philosophy. In these years she distanced herself from any cultural attempt to falsify the South's past. She declared, for instance, that she was not the least interested in preserving the house of Jefferson Davis (the Confederacy's first and only president) – knowing, of course, how the Confederate flag has been used to taunt the black population of the South. On a panel led by William F. Buckley in 1972 she stated: 'I am interested in human beings who are alive. I mean, I respect history for what it is, but I am speaking as a worker, somebody who likes to write. What I want to do is find out what people alive today [feel].'[16] In a very real sense, I believe, we can see her fiction, with its insistence on complex human entities and non-judgemental dealings between people, as Tolstoyan, Gandhian, fitting contemporary productions with the powerful wave of anti-violent movements.

However, in her writing and in conversation Eudora Welty has

16. C.E.W. p. 104.

insisted that creative writers have no need to propagandize directly on behalf of what they support. They have to go their own way, the way that their deepest imagination and artistic abilities dictate. This is the substance of her famous essay of 1965, 'Must the Novelist Crusade?'

Propagandizing, if the cause is honourable, is itself an honourable enough activity, but it is a journalist's, and it inevitably has limitations. Provided we see these, we can by all means salute it, practise it; but it must not be confused with the purpose – if one can use so utilitarian a term – of imaginative writing, which is to show human life in its mystery, and to point a way beyond simplifying judgements or solutions.

Not that that should incur any blurring of moral perception. Eudora Welty says sharply and strongly enough:

> It can be said at once, I should think, that we are all agreed upon the most important point: that morality as shown through human relationships is the whole heart of fiction, and the serious writer has never lived who ever dealt with anything else.[17]

There is no ambivalence here, nor – as the essay makes plain enough – is there any concerning the issues that promoted its writing: the issues of the divided South. What, though, is a source of ambivalence, and thus also of fruitful creative strength, is the mysterious coexistence of qualities. Those white Southerners whom Eudora Welty knew so well at first hand, while they subscribed to a morally detestable and destructive code, knew love, fear, tenderness, feeling for nature, passion for justice – indeed, even community with others (including black people). She was not going to deny these people her knowledge, her attention founded on years of scrutiny and understanding. In her work she was laying the foundations of a new South born of the realization of these other qualities, which the outside world was denying, of a South where the emotions she had drawn up from often hidden depths could emerge, and make for more harmonious living. She states emphatically:

17. Eye p. 148.

People are not Right and Wrong, Good and Bad, Black and White personified; flesh and blood and the sense of comedy object. Fiction writers cannot be tempted to make the mistake of looking at people in the generality – that is to say, of seeing people as not at all like us. If human beings are to be comprehended as real, then they have to be treated as real, with minds, hearts, memories, habits, hopes, with passions and capacities like ours. This is why novelists begin the study of people from within.[18]

The essay was written in anguish at a time of anguish, with horrific recent events fresh in Eudora Welty's mind (indeed, she alludes to them); she is aware of the opprobrium in which the whole of the South (irrespective of the complexity of its make-up) was being held at that time, and appreciates why. She does not try the mental convenience and pretence of distancing herself from her society; on the contrary, the troubles compel her to an unusually close identification with it, in the hope that humanity and kindness may prevail. 'For some of us have shown bad hearts,' she admits courageously and large-heartedly, for she and her associates have never been of their number. Still, she does not find the first person plural inappropriate, for what she is exhorting her readers towards – Southern and non-Southern alike – is inclusiveness, perhaps the novelist's most essential article of faith.

In the hard times in which she was writing there was the temptation to be exclusive, but she resisted it:

There have already been giant events, some of them wrenchingly painful and humiliating. And now there is added the atmosphere of hate. We in the South are a hated people these days; we were hated first for actual and particular reasons, and now we may be hated still more in some vast unparticularized way. I believe there must be such a thing as sentimental hate. Our people hate back.

I think the worst of it is we are getting stuck in it. We are like trapped flies with our feet not in honey but in venom. It's not love that is the gluey emotion; it's hate. As far as writing goes,

---

18. Eye p. 150.

which is as far as living goes, this is a devastating emotion. It could kill us.[19]

The way out is to continue to revere and serve what is creative in everybody, the task of all serious fiction. Honesty, says Eudora Welty, can never be faked; rather than follow some predetermined programme, the novelist must write out of personal vision, personal emotion, personal observation – synthesized by the impersonal laws of art. The result – whether tragic or comic, or a strange mixture of both – will be an affirmation of the plenitude and ultimate meaning-fulness of life, of which aberrations – such as cruel racism and the ensuing violence – are such denials. A good novel will always be restorative of values and sanity.

19. Eye p. 155.

7

LOSING BATTLES

I

THE TRAMP with the guitar in 'The Hitch-Hikers' told Tom
Harris: "'I came down from the hills. . . . We had us owls
for chickens and fox for yard dogs but we sung true.'"[1] This is
an instance of vernacular speech, attentively reproduced, taken
to poetic heights of which the speakers themselves are only partly
aware. Only in a culture with a strong tradition of both oral narrative
and aural receptivity, of a deep and intimate relation between teller and
audience, could it occur. The great Irish dramatist J.M. Synge provides
many similar utterances, raising to the degree of poetry both the
speakers' perceptions of the life around them and that life itself.
Christy, the eponymous playboy of the western world, for example,
defying Pegeen, who has accused him of flattering her with a compli-
ment he has used before, says to her:

> 'I've said it nowhere till this night, I'm telling you; for I've seen
> none the like of you the eleven long years I am walking the world,
> looking over a low ditch or a high ditch on my north or south,
> into stony, scattered fields, or scribes of bog, where you'd see
> young, limber girls, and fine, prancing women making laughter
> with the men.'[2]

---

1. C.S. p. 64.
2. J.M. Synge: *Playboy of the Western World*, 1907.

Such remarks are not only revelations of the person delivering them, they are marvellous testimonies to the culture that has nurtured such a way of speaking, testimonies in which the very rhythm of the words has a vital part to play. In *Losing Battles* Eudora Welty returns to those Mississippi hills from which the tramp and Troy Flavin, the overseer of *Delta Wedding*, came, and in which the protagonist of her very first story, 'Death of a Traveling Salesman', got lost and died. Appropriately, this novel is her largest-scale tribute to the richness of Southern vernacular (and thus, by extension, to the vernaculars of unsophisticated communities all over the world); a great democratic statement of the eloquence latent in and potentially available to everybody. Every now and again, like a sudden flowering into melody, the conversation at the reunion that fills *Losing Battles* bursts into such verbally perfect yet spontaneous and organic statements as the tramp's to Harris. Brother Bethune, more at ease with a gun than with a sermon, says of himself: "'I may not have very many earthly descendants; if you want to come right down to it, I ain't got a one. Now I *have* killed me a fairly large number of snakes.'"[3] Gloria, looking at the grave of the man who might possibly have been her father, says sadly: "'He'd be old like the rest of 'em now. Even if he was just the baby brother, if he hadn't died, he'd be old, and expecting to be asked to tell everything he knew.'"[4]

This sums up admirably an axiom of the society of *Losing Battles*; its members are *expected* to talk. Conversation is not just a great social pleasure (indeed, the greatest one) but a hallowed way of transmitting experience, knowledge (your own, other people's) – a form of culture in itself. What it imparts can assist listeners with their lives – nothing better exists for this wholly serious purpose. It will present key information about the people they are likely to encounter and form relationships with, and the stories presenting those people can give the audience ways of coping with just about everything that will beset them from birth through to death.

The importance of oral storytelling in Southern life has been more frequently and emphatically insisted on in discussions of the

---

3. L.B. p. 213.
4. L.B. p. 427.

phenomenon of Southern literature than any of its other features, not least by Eudora Welty herself. Indeed, among the Southern writers mentioned here, only Walker Percy dissents from according talk the highest place. In my own travels round the South, time and again the writers I interviewed returned to the subject; some of the younger ones, Reynolds Price and Anne Tyler, are its most ardent proponents. In the South (so the insistence goes) conversation is always person-centred (and therefore grist to any novelist's mill); it starts with the unique individual, who may or may not be known to the assembled company, and who is discussed from this angle and from that. It is not analytical or intellectual, though it may go over the same territory, and the greatest importance is attached to the telling itself, which has a kind of unstated traditional ritual to it. In this respect conversation is very much part of a rural way of life, of a society not unduly literate or reliant on literary communication, and aware of itself as bound together by occupations, concern, and therefore standards – as well as blood. Storytelling is thus both a way of cementing the group (everyone's interest is aroused by a particular story) and in itself an expression of solidarity, of shared principles, affections and kin.

Eudora Welty's love of listening, and her ability to render the spoken, the verbally dramatized, was the bedrock of *The Ponder Heart*; in *Losing Battles* we are involved not with individuals like Edna Earle dramatizing their lives, but with a more general pooling of stories, with a group using stories to prove the essentially harmonious nature of its make-up: all this is associated in the popular mind (on the whole rightly) with images of Southerners sitting on porches and talking away the seemingly timeless, if not measureless, hot hours of the day. But that is not all they are doing – indeed, that is its smallest part. They are also talking themselves in, singly and collectively.

When Scott Haller, in *The Saturday Review* (April 1981), asked Eudora Welty: 'Do you believe that the South perhaps has a monopoly on the best stories and the conversation to overhear?', she answered:

> Yes, I do. I don't think there's any doubt that you grow up being aware of being amused and delighted and impressed by things that are told. And also I think – this is probably no longer true in the South or anywhere – in the days when no one moved around

very much and you and everybody else in town lived in the same place for a long time, you followed the generations. You had a wonderful sense of the continuity of life. And I think that's terribly important. It gives you a narrative sense without knowing it. Cause and effect. And the surprises of life and the unpredictability of life. I do think that's important.[5]

This echoes many of Eudora Welty's earlier words on the subject, even if a certain cautious elegiac note has now crept in. Southerners still tend to stay in their native region in a way other Americans do not, and even if they do so somewhat less than they did, she thinks that an awareness of continuity is still very much a Southern characteristic: 'I believe it will always be in our roots, as Southerners, don't you? A sense of the place. Even if you move around, you know where you have your base.'[6] Storytelling and sense of place are thus viewed as inextricable from each other as far as Southerners are concerned.

And certainly Faulkner's roots in oral lore are of the profoundest kind (consider, for example, the way 'A Rose for Emily' unfolds). His Jefferson is a community of stories as much as a community of people. Stories both weld it together and drive rifts through it. And the educated lawyer-interpreter Gavin Stevens is as fully a repository of them as any illiterate poor white or black. Peter Taylor's stories very often take the form of pieces of gossip; while Flannery O'Connor's (for all their theological content and significance) can be read as presentations of strange histories in a given community.

But *Losing Battles* is the very apotheosis of Southern storytelling; indeed, a *ne plus ultra* as far as the novel form is concerned. Reunited for the ninetieth birthday of Granny Vaughn, her descendants, their kin and associates spend the anniversary day principally in talk, and in that talk is principally the novel – a very long one, 436 pages in the original edition. Nor is this, for the most part, talk of the kind usually meant by the term 'dialogue', speech which furthers action, or is the instrument by which actions, changes in relationships, are made known, as in the novels of Ivy Compton-Burnett or Eudora

5. C.E.W. pp. 311–12.
6. C.E.W. p. 180.

Welty's admired Henry Green (for example, *Nothing*). In *Losing Battles*, Jack Renfro comes back from the state penitentiary (Parchman, 'the pen') just in time for the celebrations. As it really might have been in a large extended family on a summer's day in the remotest part of Mississippi, the talk is mostly concerned with reactions to his return, or generally retrospective. And the action of the book as such is, paradoxically – for this really is a most extraordinary novel – of the very kind with which novelists in their dialogue (or, indeed, discursive prose) rarely concern themselves: the very practical business of how to get a stranded car out of the ditch into which it has fallen. (It is, however, very much the appropriate material for a – usually male – 'tall story'.)

Although the talk may sound inconsequential, it is orchestrated with near-inaudible artistry by the author, and each part of the novel, though directly sequential to what has gone before, is distinguishable in its preoccupations and texture, and marks a stage in our knowledge of matters (as it may or may not do in that of the characters themselves). And as I said of the function of talk in a traditionalist community, it encompasses as near everything as seems possible in a novel. As Beechams and Renfros exchange anecdotes and parry remarks, we hear of births, deaths, tragic accidents, partings, dedications to and derelictions of duty; of joys and difficulties at work, and in love; of castration, fear of dying, delight in animals, hopes, despairs, and resignations. If no work of Eudora Welty's has a more astoundingly and audaciously simple structure, no work is more complex, or explores so many facets of existence.

II

The preparations for *Losing Battles* may have started between fifteen and ten years before the novel was completed; undoubtedly it was eight years in the writing; this, if often intensely enjoyable, was also exceptionally demanding (even by Eudora Welty's exacting standards).

The years at which she was at work on this novel were difficult, indeed exceedingly sad ones for her. Her mother suffered a long, grave illness, and died in 1966; she had to be nursed at home, which meant that Eudora Welty undertook fewer commissions that took her away from Jackson, Mississippi than she would otherwise have done. A good part of *Losing Battles* was written while there were nurses in attendance in the Weltys' Pinehurst Street house. To ease the financial burden this incurred, she took a job at Millsaps College, teaching a group of students, and she found this very satisfying.

But her mother's death was not the only one she sustained in this period. Both her younger brothers, Edward and Walter, died while still only in their fifties, leaving families behind them. *Losing Battles* is dedicated to them – as *The Optimist's Daughter* was to be to Chestina Andrews Welty. These losses – in complex ways – stand behind both novels, giving them not just their darknesses but their overall depth, their immensity of understanding. There are qualities of the heart in *Losing Battles* that were not even present in *The Golden Apples*.

To these personal tragedies must be added the civic unrest, the national and international upheavals of the 1960s – the bloodstained, hate-ridden, forced emergence of the South into a society that accepted desegregation, the long, death-dealing, bitterly resented US involvement in Vietnam, the death of President John Kennedy, the tortured presidencies of Johnson and Nixon, the widespread cynicism and rebellion all over the country (as elsewhere in the Western world) – see 'The Demonstrators' – with youth seeking alternative cultures in protest against the limitations and cruelties of orthodoxy and the Establishment. The (now almost mythical) America of Watts, Kent State, Mayor Daly in Chicago, Bobby Kennedy's assassination and the reluctant acceptance of My Lai, was the country in which *Losing Battles* was composed – while its own country-within-a-country, the South, was in a state of turbulence unequalled since the Civil War, with conflict and agonies in communities the whole region over – from, say, Governor Wallace's obstinacy in Montgomery and Martin Luther King's Birmingham march in April 1963 to King's assassination in Memphis, Tennessee, almost exactly five years later, with his haunting last words – spoken to Mississippian Jesse Jackson – 'Be sure to sing "Precious Lord" tonight, and sing it well.' This was the period when Eudora Welty, like most Southern writers, would receive midnight calls; and when outside anger was turned against white Southerners, only intensifying their beleaguered position.

233

The writing of *Losing Battles* was difficult for intrinsic reasons, too, though it is surely legitimate to think that with so much that was demanding pressing on any sensitive and thinking person, externals may well have imposed themselves on and even partially shaped the former. Eudora Welty has said:

> I first thought of it as a story of the return of a boy from the pen, and I was going to end it when he got home. My idea was to show the difference between how people thought of him and what he was. It was to be just a pure talk story. Well, the moment he arrived, it became a novel. Because he was somebody. And the story was his. I realized the scope of the thing was a good deal larger than I had counted on. But I was still interested in trying to work something out in the technique I started with, altogether by talk and action, trying to show everything and not as an author enter the character's mind and say, 'He was thinking so-and-so' . . .[7]

As if all this did not present problems enough, there was the question of the novel's setting in place and time, and its significance to the book's overall meaning. Eudora Welty returned to the red-clay hill country of north-east Mississippi because she wanted to write about those people who, among those she had encountered and entered into some kind of imaginative dialogue with, had nothing, never could have anything much, and for whom keeping going was a mighty as well as an uncertain business. And the time should be that which showed this life at its most exigent: clearly the Depression (in fact an unidentifiable year in it), the period when Eudora herself first journeyed into Tishomingo County, finding there the landscape of 'Death of a Traveling Salesman'. It was surely necessary, anyway, to set a book with the theme of *Losing Battles* (I say this advisedly, because the title did not come to Eudora Welty as right for her work until she had finished it) at a fair distance from the writer but in the recent past – so that in imaginatively ranging over the subsequent lives of her people she could, to her own satisfaction, know just how 'lost' they had been and become.

---

7. C.E.W. p. 46.

Each of these ambitions made its own demands, uniting to make it impossible that the short-story length, even the long short story so dear to her (*The Robber Bridegroom* or *The Ponder Heart*), could contain all that was forcing itself on her mind. But it is interesting and revealing to note that this work of such amplitude, massive detail and deliberately, demandingly slow pace originated in the 'moment of vision' peculiar to the short-story form, and to a very real extent operates as something akin to this, offering, in addition to all its manifold riches, a dazzling singleness of illumination.

III

Knowing that she would be unable to resist exploring Jack's return from the pen, Eudora Welty had to make other changes of plan for the novel (as well as having to rework that entire opening section in the light of the whole to come). Her reliance on conversation as the means of presentation – and on the conversation of a specific occasion – meant she had to structure the novel round the clock time of its duration.

At first this seemed to point to the novel taking place in a single day, Granny Vaughn's ninetieth birthday. But difficulties arose. In the interview with Charles T. Bunting already quoted from, Eudora Welty said:

> I had originally planned *Losing Battles* to happen in one day, but you see it goes over the night into the next morning. That is probably a flaw, but I couldn't resolve it, mainly because the day was a Sunday. I had to have Monday morning. I realized it while I was working because I kept making notes, putting them in another folder saying 'Next A.M.' and then I realized that that was a whole section. I realized that I could not incorporate everything into the one day, so I had to have Monday. But everything does have to be compressed, of course, in any work of fiction. It has to have bounds. You can't begin without staking something off in time and place.[8]

Eudora Welty is perhaps too conscious of the disappointment she felt (one conjectures) on appreciating that the obstinacy of her material

---

8. ibid.

was going to make that single day an impossibility. The time-scale is as vital to the success, to the imaginative effect, of *Losing Battles* as it is to those other comparable modernist masterpieces *Ulysses*, *Mrs Dalloway* or *Berlin Alexanderplatz* – or *The Sound and the Fury* and *Absalom, Absalom*. The continuation of the novel on to Monday morning which logic and contingency demanded, far from being a flaw, gives it its curiously moving and satisfying shape. For one thing, a day cannot be seen as an entity until it is over – and that does not just mean the descent of darkness ("'Nightfall!' said Aunt Birdie. "When did that happen?'"); it means the following morning when the wholeness, the peculiar form and texture of the previous day, finally asserts itself.

Eudora Welty brings the long, hot, talkative Sunday to its true (rather than literal) end with two wonderfully imaginative strokes. Without warning she abandons her eschewal of the analysis of character, and suddenly takes us inside one member of the huge cast whose voice has scarcely been heard (though the keen-eared will have found the remarks he has made worthy of study): Vaughn, Jack's twelve-year-old brother. Vaughn, fond though he is of Jack, feels as younger brothers are wont to do: that there are other ways of viewing the elder boy than with the admiration he has inspired in almost everyone. Vaughn's comparative clarity of vision helps us to achieve it for ourselves; new perspectives on people and their fortunes begin to open for us. . . . 'Had today been all brave show, and had Jack all in secret fallen down – taking the whole day to fall, but falling, like that star he saw now, going out of sight like the scut of a rabbit?'[9] Vaughn proceeds to rescue the stranded school bus that he has driven for the past year and a half in lieu of Jack ('"Without Jack, nothing would be no trouble at all." Vaughn spoke it out'). The obviousness of the symbolism does not make it any the less effective – or affecting. Vaughn, perhaps inheriting qualities from his great-grandfather, the Baptist preacher after whom he has been named, is obviously going to have a different future from Jack – or, for that matter, anyone else in the novel: one in which learning and serious religion may play a part, though we cannot doubt that he too, in his way, will fall, will lose or lose out.

---

9. L.B. p. 363.

With her portrait of this boy falling asleep while saying his prayers, Eudora Welty has changed the entire book. (Those who on first reading, have felt jolted by what seems like the intrusion of a different style into a loving, carefully worked unity will, I believe, feel otherwise on rereading.) In the brief section that follows, bringing to a close the penultimate 'Part', another shift takes place: a storm breaks, the rain comes down: 'Then the new roof resounded with all the noise of battle. With the noise and the smell as sudden as from water being poured into a smoking skillet, in the black dark it began to rain.'[10] Thus the metaphor of the 'battle' is given a fresh development. The day of the anniversary, indissoluble from the languorous heat which promoted all its long storytelling, is well and truly over now; the different weather puts it thoroughly into the past. The rain-washed world, marvellously, sensuously evoked, brings new demands, new duties. The Judge's Buick cannot remain stranded any longer but must get back on the road again; Aycock Comfort, Jack's chum who has spent twenty-four hours locked up in it, must be liberated; and Miss Julia Mortimer, schoolteacher and stern tutelary spirit of just about everybody, whose death took place on Sunday, must on Monday, *this* day, be buried.

Conversation, Eudora Welty has emphasized in discussing *Losing Battles*, meant the comedy mode, and in her opinion the comedy mode makes for a greater inclusiveness than the tragic; it can include the dark, but can also penetrate it, and thus point the way to conditions in which it can be accepted, even transcended. She has said that she prefers Faulkner's comedies even to his great tragic masterpieces because 'they have *everything*'. Yet even bearing these observations in mind, the comedy in *Losing Battles* can surprise even admirers of 'Why I Live at the P.O.', 'The Wide Net' and *The Ponder Heart*. In these works the comedy comes essentially from character; in *Losing Battles*, though knowledge of the character enhances the comedy, much of the humour derives from circumstance – or, better, happenstance. We are, I think, in the (very American) territory opened up by Mark Twain in such stories as 'The Celebrated Jumping Frog of Calaveras County', which seems to the English mind strongly

---

10. L.B. p. 368.

237

connected to the frontier/pioneering experience of America, and a very long way indeed from the comedy of manners of Jane Austen and her progeny. In his percipient and very favourable review of the novel, Reynolds Price remarked of its comedy:

> Its faith is clearly that the world is ordered, that life – even a Renfro's – unfolds to messages contained in its seed and that any man's efforts to misread the commands, even decipher them, must only end in laughter. And if only God laughs – well then, only He was watching.[11]

Even where one would least expect it, farce, the comic stuff of 'tall stories', pertains.

Jack Jordan Renfro, we learn right at the beginning, has been sent to the pen – Parchman – for 'aggravated battery'. The very name 'Parchman' would obviously have a resonance for a Mississippian – indeed, for a Southerner – that it cannot have for others, but its infamy has, quite literally, not gone unsung; wonderful blues singers were interned there: Dobie Red, Bama, Jimpson, who called the institution 'The Murder's Home'. Alan Lomax, who over many years recorded the music of the inmates, described Parchman vividly in *The Land Where the Blues Began*:

> Only a few strands of barbed wire marked the boundary between the Parchman State Penitentiary and the so-called free world. Like the plantation on the other side of the fence, the state pen was a vast checkerboard of cotton fields cut by wide drainage ditches and graveled roads, sprawling interminably under a hot sky . . . the sharecropper loaded with debts he could never pay, or the mule-skinner escaping from Mister Chobby, might not care too much which side of the barbed wire he found himself on. . . . But the pen soon taught him how wrong he was. It was a Marine boot camp where you were never made private; boot camp that ran as long as a man's sentence, and that could mean the rest of his life.[12]

It was a place of savage deprivations, punishments and deaths, and this

---

11. Reynolds Price, *A Common Room: Essays 1954–1987*, p. 72.
12. Alan Lomax, *The Land Where the Blues Began*, Methuen (1993), p. 256.

is implicit, if not explicit, in the novel. But what is the crime, the aggravated battery that has earned Jack his place in such a hell?

A fight – one that would not disgrace a Buster Keaton film – with his contemporary and lifelong associate Curly Stovall, keeper of the Banner Stores. Curly, preventing Jack's younger sister from taking the wineballs she likes to suck in school hours but perhaps doesn't always pay for, seizes her ring (a loved family heirloom) and Jack, outraged, flies at his pal and rival, and ties him down in a coffin that is standing rather invitingly in the shop.

Yet we do not disbelieve that he would be imprisoned for his part in this mayhem. The farce acts as a kind of guarantee of innocence (in the non-legal sense), and though we cannot be sure that Jack did not in some way succumb to either depression or depravity in Parchman, we can see from his behaviour in these antics that he has enough strength, enough natural virtue, to be carried through the evils of prison, and well beyond. And so it goes on. Jack and his buddy, Aycock Comfort, who was sent to the pen with him, leave Parchman a day earlier than they officially should have done in order to be back for Granny Vaughn's birthday. For the last stage of the journey back, they ride on the tyres of a Buick that is headed in the right direction – until it encounters Willy Trimble's ditch. And who is the driver of that car but Judge Moody, the very judge who sentenced the two boys to the penitentiary?

Misadventures now come with a Chaucerian plenty. Jack, received into the enthusiastic bosom of his large and loving family, is nevertheless taken to task for having done nothing to avenge himself on his enemy. In the company of Gloria, his wife, and his baby, Lady May, he goes back up to Banner Top to arrange to ambush the Judge, who will be passing that way soon. But in an ensuing accident, the Judge's foresight saves Gloria and the baby, so Jack is beholden to him. This time, however, the Buick truly *is* stuck – and by a physical mishap again reminiscent of the silent cinema – Aycock, Jack's buddy, is marooned in it, with his old guitar for company. Jack, out of gratitude to the Judge, feels obliged to invite him and his wife to the reunion meal. So much for his plans for revenge!

Here Jack's good nature and instinctive code of honour thwart his less sensible plans, and the laws of causality and contingency seem – temporarily – to be on their side.

For a last example of the control of the comic spirit in this novel, one turns to the character who stands in an extreme contrapuntal relation to Jack Renfro, the newly dead schoolteacher Julia Mortimer – female, elderly, educated, sagacious, influential; all things that Jack most definitely is not. Her will is read out by Judge Moody, and her ageing whims seem to have aligned themselves with the physical laws of farce. Of her funeral she has written:

'The mourners will keep good order among themselves and wait till I reach the schoolhouse. Good behavior is requested and advised on the part of one and all as I am lowered into my grave . . . already to have been dug beneath the mountain stone which constitutes the doorstep of Banner School. The stone is to be replaced at once after the grave is filled, so the children will be presented with no excuse for staying home from school.'[13]

This does not lessen the pathos of the spartan old woman's fear of death and reluctance to die; rather, it accentuates them from another angle, that of the perpetual comedy of humankind's inability to exert complete control, however vigorous its intentions of doing so.

And so to Jack, who compelled the restructuring and rewriting of the book.

Jack is really the reason I went on and made a novel out of this. Because when I first began it, it was a short story which was to end when Jack came home. The story was about why he happened to go to the pen. All that crazy story about the fight. And he was to come home and wonder why they thought anything was wrong. You know: 'What's happened?' Well, as soon as he walks in the door, I think, 'No, I want to go on with him.' I had to start all over and write a novel. . . . Jack is really a good person, even though he is all the other things. . . . Yes, I really like Jack.[14]

That liking, that love, that goodness are evident not only in the portrait of himself but in the delineations of the reactions of all with whom he comes into contact (even his critical brother, Vaughn). While it is

---

13. L.B. p. 291.
14. C.E.W. p. 306.

immediately obvious that Eudora Welty departed from her first intentions, and that the scene of his return is a lot more complex than the original scheme could have allowed for, an element of it has persisted. This relates to Jack's abundant innocence. He is impetuous, ingenuous, the willing victim of his own excitable and infectious optimism. Parchman could force him to behave cautiously, no more than common sense, yet he is no asocial figure; he is needed by a community, just as patently as he is needed by his large clan of relations for the success of the reunion. As Reynolds Price says in his review of *Losing Battles*, 'Frightening Gifts', he is a 'golden boy'.

He is very beautifully presented, in a double sense, for there is truly something beautiful – indeed, radiant – about Jack, rough, unselfconscious unsophisticate as he is, and Eudora Welty establishes, conveys that beauty by a multiplicity of cumulative details. Physically he is clear (and eminently credible) to our eye and ear, which makes the attributes of his spirit the easier to accept. After he has leaped on to the front gallery 'riding a wave of dogs', Eudora Welty presents him to the reader:

> He might never have been under a roof from the day he left home until this minute. His open, blunt-featured face in its morning beard had burned to a red even deeper than the home clay. He was breathing hard, his chest going up and down fast, his mouth was open, and he was pouring sweat. With his eyes flared wide, his face smileless as a child's, he stood and waited, with his arms open like a gate.[15]

How much that tells us about Jack, and how important it all is to the book's meaning. Face expressively and arms literally 'open', he naturally belongs to the spaces of the land, for his are rural values (the colour of his complexion derives, of course, from the heavy outdoor labour he must have been ordered to perform day in, day out at Parchman – it even rivals the red of the clay of the hill country which has and always will define him; he has the seriousness of a child (throughout he is quite innocent of irony; boyish badinage is more his métier), and there is an urgency about him. While he often proves

---

15. L.B. p. 71.

himself strong in the fields of loyalty and intimacy, he wants – is prepared – to enjoy amiable relations with the whole world. When he looks at you, Eudora Welty writes later, he fixes you with a clear blue intent gaze; almost from this alone one can build up the sort of person he is, at once strong and vulnerable.

He is stubborn, a source of good as well as of the more unfortunate things – yet his amiability often leads him into actions whose consequences would have been better avoided. It is clear that the wishes of the whole family tribe will prevail over the fervently expressed wishes of his wife Gloria (whom he dearly and sincerely loves); they will not go and live by themselves; his whole life long – and if he were alive he would, at the time of writing, be eighty now – he will be surrounded by his family, with their ceaseless comments, interference, claims, assumptions, affections. Any search for independence would be a 'losing battle' indeed.

Headstrong and proud, he is also, as are many people of his physical type, unfeignedly tender-hearted. He has a deep affection for his old horse, and has to prevent himself from crying when informed that he has been sold (and has therefore almost certainly gone to the knacker's); Jack's joy at the very end of the novel in finding Dan still alive, and his acceptance that the old horse really does now belong more to his rival Curly than to himself, reveal much about his generosity of spirit. Towards his truck – and towards other mechanical things – he entertains an emotion little short of passion. His delight in Lady May, his infant daughter, is exuberant, and he is constantly affectionate towards Gloria ('Possum' is his principal term of endearment for her), an affection that springs from depths of feeling of which desire is a harmonious component; even so, he will never be one of those lovers who seek the true realities of self and existence in a relationship by being half of a couple (Ran MacLain in *The Golden Apples* perhaps belongs in this category).

The last dialogue of the whole day, between Gloria and Jack, reveals the really important thing about Jack and his relationship with the world. (The beginning of the quotation refers to the clan's attempt to prove that Gloria's unknown father was Jack's uncle, Sam Dale, with whom Granny Vaughn confuses her great-grandson.):

'They tried making me your cousin, and almost did.'

'Be my cousin,' he begged. 'I want you for my cousin. My wife, and my children's mother and my cousin and everything.'

'Jack, I'll be your wife with all my heart, and that's enough for anybody, even you. I'm here to be nobody but myself, Mrs Gloria Renfro, and have nothing, and have nothing to do with the old dead past. And don't ever try to change me,' she cautioned him.

'I know this much; I don't aim to get lonesome no more. Once you do, it's too easy to stay that way,' said Jack.

'I'll keep you from it,' she vowed.

'And you'd better.'

'Jack, the way I love you, I have to hate everybody else.'

'Possum!' he said. 'I ain't asking you to deprive others.'

'I want to!'

'Spare 'em a little bit of something else,' he pleaded.

'Maybe I'll learn after a long time to pity 'em instead.'

'They'll take it a good deal harder!' he cried.

She drew still closer to him.

'Don't pity anybody you could love,' whispered Jack.

'I can think of one I can safely pity . . . Miss Julia.'

'I know she hated to breathe her last,' he said slowly. 'As much as you and me would.' He took her hand.

'Are you trying to say you could do better than pity her?' Gloria asked him. 'You never laid eyes on her.'

'I reckon I even love her,' said Jack. 'I heard her story.'[16]

Jack Renfro, whose radiance penetrates every corner of the novel, makes by implication two important distinctions here: between the love that would exclude and the love for which any kind of exclusion is anathema; and between pity (of which condescension can so easily be a concomitant) and love which goes out to and identifies with its object. That he identifies with Miss Julia just from hearing her story – one which, in its intellectual and moral dedication is a long way from his own – is the final demonstration of his own spiritual status. Miss

---

16. L.B. p. 361.

Julia (far more than Gloria, her protégée and Jack's own wife), forms with him a kind of axis for the novel: she belonging to the past (by the time we hear of her she has been received into it), he to the present and future; she caring deeply, insatiably, for books, he, we are told, never having cared unduly for pen or paper; she formidable, shy of love, he, easy-going in many respects, and giving; she female, he male – but both of them caring people, who are concerned about others and consequently mean a lot to many.

It is essential to any true appreciation of the novel to stress Jack's maleness; his energy, optimism, his strengths and his vulnerability are all of an extremely masculine kind. As a male reader I am pleased, grateful, moved that this tribute to the beneficent aspects of maleness, one of the fullest and most satisfyingly realized in modern literature, is paid by a woman. Maleness is seen here as a creative, life-enhancing force; its special merits and its special limitations, flourishing in correct balance with the female, are utterly essential to wholeness.

Different though they may in many respects have been (both were college graduates), I feel that Jack's radiance derives its force from Eudora Welty's deep feelings for her brothers, Edward and Walter.

IV

It is through Miss Julia that the idea of 'losing battles' is received. If the story of Jack fills us with an almost vitalist happiness, seems to express all we hopefully believe about some life force, then Miss Julia's (conveyed to us through the reminiscences of the company) inspires sorrow, a near-unassuageable sense of the sadness and destruction inherent in existence. When she was a young woman, new to the community, she announced to her class:

> 'Children of Banner School! It's the first day for both of us. I'm your teacher, Miss Julia Mortimer. Nothing in this world can measure up to the joy you'll bring me if you allow me to teach you something.'[17]

---

17. L.B. p. 273.

And to an important degree she remained true to her vision; teaching *was* her joy, and she served her calling faithfully. But the strict methods she started importing in order to carry out her intentions alienated many before long; the difficulties of education in a poor State were expressed in a speedy reduction of her salary (not very generous in the first place). Anyway, what did education really matter to these people of north-east Mississippi, all engaged in coaxing a living out of the land? How many of all those assembled for Granny Vaughn's birthday, though they all remember her vividly enough, have retained anything much of all she tried so hard to inculcate in them? For the most part they are quite indifferent to any kind of learning.

Miss Julia was retired against her wishes, and resented this bitterly, as she was to resent the infirmities of old age, illness, and impending death. She was never reconciled to her lot, and felt that she received little support even from her protégée, Gloria, for her struggle against it. Her last and hardest losing battle is one that awaits us all; her fight is distinguished only by its openness, its fierceness and pride, and it makes almost unbearably moving reading:

'She wanted the school bell!' said Miss Lexie.

'Why, that's a heavy old thing,' said Uncle Curtis. 'Solid brass and a long handle –'

'She couldn't have raised it. Never at all. Never again in her life. And I told her so. "And no matter if you could," I reminded her, "you haven't got the school bell. Banner School's got it! It doesn't belong to you," I said, "Banner School's got the bell and you've been put out to pasture – they're through with you." I thought that would finish the subject. But "Give me back my bell," she'd say. And look at me, with living dread in her face.'[18]

What can be done in the face of the unbeatables, decay and death? Does all Jack's optimism and trust in love mean anything when one is confronting them? *Losing Battles* does not let the one cancel out the realities of the other. Just as in *The Golden Apples* Eudora Welty declared, through the mind of Virgie Rainey: 'Endless the Medusa, and Perseus

---

18. L.B. pp. 279–80.

endless,' so here she could pronounce 'Endless Jack's high spirits and kindness, and endless Julia's disappointment and decrepitude'. But the difference is that in the first instance there was direct opposition – indeed, direct deathly conflict – in the second Jack has to broadcast his statement of a love which can reach out and contain the other, the darker, so that the unfortunate and inevitable condition is, in a very real sense, transcended – even if it is not in the tormented mind of the sufferer.

In life Miss Julia was a far more influential and important person than Jack Renfro ever could be (and her benevolence was both thoroughly practical and far-reaching) but in her sad death she has need, so to speak, for the loving acceptance of such as him, who, in an impressively direct and unabashed manner, can show others ways of assimilating tragic inevitability into their experience.

Between the poles of Jack and Miss Julia stand the whole assortment of relatives and neighbours who make up the reunion – whose lives are filled in by the range of the talk, like the slow movement of a search-light which sooner or later picks out everyone, living or dead. If there are the usual anniversary activities of eating, singing, children's games and music-making (Uncle Noah Webster's banjo, Uncle Nathan's cornet); if there is, thanks to Jack's reappearance, genuine rejoicing at the way things have turned out, this is by no means to say that what that searchlight finds is not often extremely disquieting. Yet somehow the comedy mood, which is such close kin to love, can hold it all.

Uncle Nathan, the man devoted to God, turns out to have killed Dearman, the one man who might have married Miss Julia Mortimer and rescued her from her doomed life of overintensity. Nor is killing the end of it. In Uncle Nathan's own tormented words to Jack:

'Son, there's not but one bad thing either you or I or anybody else can do. And I already done it. That's kill a man. I killed Mr Dearman with a stone to his head, and let 'em hang a sawmill nigger for it. After that, Jesus had to hold my hand.'[19]

Then there is the sad story of Gloria's putative parents: Rachel Sojourner, who was almost certainly her mother, and who died so

19. L.B. p. 344.

young: and Jack's uncle, Sam Dale. But just as we are beginning to accept this story, which so many seem so eager to believe, a troubled memory of Jack's mother comes to the surface: of when she was minding the infant Sam Dale, and he suffered an intimate injury with coals. And there is also Sam Dale's own premature death ('Far from home. Under Georgia skies').

Nor are all the currents that pass through the company harmonious or desirable. One moment threatens the comedy mood altogether, violently and disturbingly. Gloria, who has been living with her parents-in-law during Jack's imprisonment, has always held herself a little distant from the family; the knowledge that she might be a blood-member of it, a Beecham through Sam Dale, perturbs her. The other women resent what they think of as her overfastidiousness. Breaking out into a terrifying viciousness, they turn on Gloria, using the ubiquitous watermelon as an instrument of punishment:

> They were all laughing. 'Say Beecham!' they ordered her, close to her ear. They rolled her by her shoulders, pinned her flat, then buried her face under the flesh of the melon with its blood heat, its smell of evening flowers. Ribbons of juice crawled on her neck and circled it, as hands robbed of sex spread her jaws open.
>
> 'Can't you say Beecham? What's wrong with being Beecham?'
> . . .
> 'Come on, sisters, help feed her! Let's cram it down her little red lane! Let's make her say Beecham! We did!' came the women's voices.[20]

The farce that has reigned in the novel is showing its other side now, constituting an explosion of sheer gratuitous cruelty, that is there in wait for us all internally, externally, a constant shadow-guest at the feast. But again, while Jack is making love to Gloria that night, he is able – if not exactly to dispel the incident – to reduce its power until it is assimilable.

In the same way, a terrible accident such as the one in which Granny Vaughn's daughter and son-in-law, Jack's grandparents, died, the bridge giving way and the couple being drowned in the river, is the

---

20. L.B. p. 269.

obverse of – yet closely related to – such farce as the one involving the Buick and Jack's truck. It underlines the precariousness of our existence, how we are at the mercy of non-human as well as human forces, and insists that any sane view – and comedy always speaks on sanity's behalf – must accommodate this.

The words of the title, as Eudora Welty herself points out, can be taken two ways: 'losing' can be read either as an adjective agreeing with 'battles', as in the common expression 'Oh, that's a losing battle!' or as part of a verb with 'battles' as its object. The second reading is subtly expressive of a more optimistic point of view than the first. Undoubtedly life for the Beecham/Renfros must be a battle: against the elements, against poverty – the realities of these are brought home repeatedly in details about the house, the work on the farm, the food, the clothes; no question, for instance, but that in Jack's absence his truck and his favourite horse had to go, and when he arrives home, he has to keep on the same pair of ragged trousers that he put on in the pen. But perhaps to use the word 'battle' is to stress unduly the combative, the aggressive, the disharmonious forces of life. Acceptance of hardship and pain is a wiser, a more rewarding course, even in the face of adversity, and so perhaps to lose the battle is to find a way to that acceptance, in which love and (if only qualified, limited) contentment can flourish. For, as the first and more obvious reading of the phrase tells us, there was no real chance of winning those battles anyway. In this family's life getting a living, making ends meet, will always be exhaustingly difficult – and then, as Miss Julia Mortimer's instance shows, every living being is programmed to run down and die.

V

Both Tolstoy and D.H. Lawrence insisted that any major creative work demands its own form; indeed, form, which certainly has its own laws, its own compelling structure, comes into being to meet the specific needs of the writer, exploring new territory, doing what has not been done before. Tolstoy proved his own point right at the outset of his career; *Childhood, Boyhood and Youth* is formally as unlike anything that had gone before as *War and Peace* itself was to be. Similarly, *The Rainbow* and *Women in Love* structurally express their author's revolutionary vision, which could not accommodate itself to conventional fictional modes. So it is with *Losing Battles* – indeed, the originality of form here is a double tribute: to the author's mind, and to the culture on which she is drawing. Out of a dominant feature of Southern life, its talk, she has created a wholly independent work of art that sustains and illuminates that tradition, and also manages to convey her personal vision of love and decay in life.

As well as constituting something of an apotheosis of Southern ways, *Losing Battles* also seems an extraordinarily American novel – in what constitutes the good in it, freedom and individual responsibility; in its zest for the use of personal gifts in difficult situations, even in its paeans to the car, the schoolteacher, the land. And that very freshness of form is American too; indeed, a dominant characteristic of American literature is how often a form is reinvented – think of the fictive liberties of *Moby-Dick* or *Winesburg, Ohio* or *My Ántonia* – and very often the freshness comes from reaching across from the literary given to the vernacular. This, and its omnipresent humour, make us think of *Huckleberry Finn* as *Losing Battles'* rightful peer.

It is indeed a quite gigantic achievement. Paradoxically, this novel in which Eudora Welty loses herself almost as thoroughly as any author could, with virtually no authorial comment, and only the similes and metaphors of linking paragraphs to indicate the cast of her mind, also constitutes the most complete and *sui generis* expression of her experience and contemplation of life.

On 15 March 1969 the *New Yorker* was pleased to devote a whole half-issue to a long (30,000 words) short story by Eudora Welty, 'The Optimist's Daughter'. This was the first story she had published since 'The Demonstrators', and it was obviously far more substantial in both its scale and its scope. With it she broke a silence of fifteen years. But she did not let this new work stay as she had released it; the long book which had absorbed her for well over a decade had to come out first, and Eudora Welty went on not just to revise but to add another 10,000 words to *The Optimist's Daughter*, making it a true novel.

8

THE OPTIMIST'S DAUGHTER
AND BEYOND

I

The climax of *The Optimist's Daughter* occurs when its central character, Laurel McKelva Hand, enters her dead parents' bedroom into which a bird, a chimney swift, has just flown. Outside the house, a storm has got up:

> Windows and doors alike were singing, buffeted by the storm. The bird touched, tapped, brushed itself against the walls and closed doors, never resting. Laurel thought with longing of the telephone just outside the door in the upstairs hall.
>
> What am I in danger of here? she wondered, her heart pounding.
>
> Even if you have kept silent for the sake of the dead, you cannot rest in silence, as the dead rest. She listened to the wind, the rain, the blundering, frantic bird, and wanted to cry out as the nurse cried out to her, 'Abuse, abuse!'[1]

Laurel stands here trapped by realities: the storm is real; neither enjoyment (her dead mother's girlhood response to storms) nor fear can do anything to change its course, while the bird, though it may eventually be coaxed or driven out, has its own unique individual life. Nothing Laurel can do or think can bring either of her parents

---

1. O.D. p. 130.

back to life. All her protest, all her horror, are to no avail. The nurse she is remembering, who had tended her dying father back in New Orleans, and exclaimed at her young stepmother Fay's treatment of him, had not been able to change events one whit: Judge McKelva had died notwithstanding her indignation. If Laurel had been able to have access to that telephone, how would it have helped her to combat the difficulties within and without? There is a limit to any aid we can call in. As Laurel appreciates here, we are in danger throughout our lives, whether there is rational cause to acknowledge it or not. And throughout our lives too – though as a rule more commonly after their middle point – we have to live alongside the cancellations of those we have known and loved – indeed, still love; whose being (however defined) now belongs irretrievably to death. Of all Eudora's works of fiction, *The Optimist's Daughter* confronts existence at its most ungovernable, its laws at their most cruel.

This confrontation – like Laurel's, in that room with the bird – is made without props, or the comfort of a simplifying philosophy. There is indeed an exposure, a nakedness, here which – because of the absence of any fictionalizing, any distortion for the sake of either artistic effect or comfort – makes one almost disinclined to use the word 'novel' about *The Optimist's Daughter*. The word 'falsifying' is the book's major term of condemnation. Yet paradoxically, this is Eudora Welty's most consummate work of art, the one which, in its classical perfection, belongs to the tradition of art-novel as developed in English by Henry James and Edith Wharton from their immersion in Russian (Turgenev) and French (Flaubert and Maupassant) mentors. If *Losing Battles* is a very American act of artistic freedom which makes us reach for *Huckleberry Finn* for comparison, *The Optimist's Daughter* needs as points of reference Turgenev's *Nest of Gentlefolk*, Flaubert's *Un coeur simple*, Henry James's *Washington Square* and *The Europeans*, Edith Wharton's *Ethan Frome*, Willa Cather's *A Lost Lady* and *The Professor's House*, Scott Fitzgerald's *The Great Gatsby*.

At the same time, by another paradox, *The Optimist's Daughter*, of all Eudora Welty's works, is the most infused by particular situations from her own life, by aspects (aspects only, one must stress) of people inextricably dear to her, by her own difficulties and anguish. She has permitted readers to realize just how deep its roots are in her personal, familial life – not only through interviews she gave at the time of publication, but through the central section of her marvellous auto-biography, twelve years later: *One Writer's Beginnings* (1984). One avoids the word 'autobiographical' in connection with *The Optimist's Daughter* because the author withdraws from it herself; clearly, Laurel McKelva Hand's personality and position are quite different from those of her creator. Nevertheless, behind Laurel's relationship to her mother stands Eudora Welty's to her own.

Chestina Andrews Welty, a teacher – responsible, perhaps, for the high predominance of teachers among the characters of her daughter's fiction – a 'mountaineer' with a free, passionately independent spirit, passed on to her daughter many of her best and most robust qualities. She was a great reader – as a young woman she had rescued her copies of Dickens from a burning house – and continued to read novels (a genre Eudora Welty's father had taken no interest in, because they were not 'true') for as long as she was able to, having a particular attachment to Thomas Mann's tetralogy *Joseph and His Brothers*. She was hospitable; John Woodburn told Eudora Welty that he knew everything would be all right in their mutual dealings the moment he had tasted her mother's waffles – and the Pinehurst Street house became quite a centre of informal cultural activity (though Chestina put her foot down when it came to Henry Miller's possible visit to the house: she thought he was a pornographer).

Mother and daughter worked in the garden together, one of their keenest interests. This explains not only the many loving references to flowers in Eudora Welty's fiction, but the shared interest in them that distinguishes Laurel's relationship to her mother, Miss Becky, in *The Optimist's Daughter*. Not that relations between two such strong and interesting people could not be difficult. Eudora Welty many years later summarized this aspect of their relationship in *One Writer's Beginnings*:

[Independence] was my chief inheritance from my mother who was braver. Yet, while she knew that independent spirit so well, it was what she so agonizingly tried to protect me from, in effect to warn me against. It was what we shared, it made the strongest bond between us and the strongest tension.[2]

Eudora Welty thinks that her mother never got over her failure to save her husband in that desperate attempt at blood transfusion, though she was to suffer other great blows, including ill health and near-blindness in later life. She was not free from morbidity, yet her spiritedness and her free intelligence contributed inestimably to the work of the daughter she so greatly encouraged.

In an interview with her old friend Charlotte Capers, Eudora Welty does confess that Laurel's mother, Becky, bears a deep and intimate relationship to her own mother, only recently dead when she began on the story. And that relationship affects – indeed, determines and nourishes – every aspect of the novel, and is absolutely crucial to its climactic scene.

> *Capers*: . . . I think it would be extremely hard . . . so close to you that it was painful.
> *Welty*: I don't know. It was very painful; but also, it helped me to understand and so I don't know whether you'd call that auto-biographical or not. The situation is made up, characters are made up.
> *Capers*: Did it not help you to work through your own emotions after the death of your mother?
> *Welty*: I think it did; although I did not undertake it for any thera-peutic reasons, because I don't believe in that kind of thing. I be-lieve in really trying to comprehend something. Comprehension is more important to me than healing . . . [3]

This novel shows that comprehension is itself a *form* of healing – a form only, one must say; our pains and griefs can never be wholly assuaged, and perhaps they should not be, otherwise we would be guilty of 'falsifying'. The one attitude towards the complexity of life that leads to disaster is to deceive ourselves that it is not complex.

---

2. O.W.B. p. 60.
3. C.E.W. p. 116.

II

Every sentence of *The Optimist's Daughter* has its own work to do, like a bar of music in a symphony (and, like a symphony, this is a work in four movements, intricately related to one another but distinct, the fourth gathering up the material of the previous three and attempting their resolution). And appropriately the very opening of the novel tells us a very great deal, establishes themes and images, as well as the immediate area of interest:

> A nurse held the door open for them. Judge McKelva going first, then his daughter Laurel, then his wife Fay, they walked into the windowless room where the doctor would make his examination. Judge McKelva was a tall, heavy man of seventy-one who customarily wore his glasses on a ribbon. Holding them in his hand now, he sat on the raised, thronelike chair above the doctor's stool, flanked by Laurel on one side and Fay on the other.[4]

The windowless room, the position of the Judge's glasses, introduce the subject of sightlessness, which, on both a literal and a metaphoric level, is so dominant in the novel. (*Sore Eyes* was a first title for it.) Judge McKelva has come to the doctor's consulting-rooms because of grave disturbance in his right eye (in fact his retina has slipped), although he also has a cataract in his so-called 'good' eye. But as we readers will very soon be shown, his vision has been deficient of late in another respect too: he has married an insensitive – indeed, vicious – much younger woman, Fay; to see him flanked by daughter and by recent wife (they are virtual contemporaries, both in their forties) is to put him between his wiser, happier, sighted past and his blind, bungled present. Furthermore, the juxtaposition of thronelike chair and doctor's stool epitomizes the decline of this distinguished ageing professional man; once known for his seat on a throne, the Judge's chair, he is now at the mercy of medicine if he is to continue to function as an ordinary human being. Everything in the novel grows out of what is given us here, in the very first paragraph.

Part One presents the deterioration and death of Judge McKelva.

---

4. O.D. p. 3.

From an early point we absorb the seriousness of Laurel's concern for her father (she takes leave from her designer's job in Chicago to be with him), a seriousness which in part derives (we realize) from what had befallen her mother. ("'It's like Mother's,'" she says of the Judge's cataract. "'This was the way she started'".) And simultaneously, we take in Fay's childish selfish refusal to accept her husband's problems for what they are; she insists that his eye has been hurt through a trivial external scratch from a rose-briar, and that a lot of fuss is being made over nothing. She resents Laurel's presence, and the way it has turned the Judge's mind back to his first wife, Becky. Of Becky we learn principally that she loved and tended flowers and gardens – there is a rose called Miss Becky's Climber; so the images of Laurel's mother with which we start our journey through these intertwined lives are connected with creativity and peace, in contrast with Fay's petulant rasping vulgarity.

The surgeon does a beautiful job, but the Judge needs complete stillness and day-and-night surveillance if the operation is to approach success. It is arranged that Fay and Laurel will take turns in watching over him at the hospital; they put up at adjacent rooms at the Hibiscus Hotel, but – an index of things to come – have nothing to say to each other, though Laurel does elicit from Fay that she has no family ("'None of 'em living'"). Despite all the attention and the good prognostications, the Judge, 'optimist' though he declaredly is, sinks into an increasingly impenetrable gloom; it is hard to get any responses out of him, and those he does give are less than whole. Almost enviable seems his fellow-patient, an old man from Mississippi, who has lost his mind but has a lively, caring family waiting for him. Fay grows ever more resentful of the situation; after all, it's Mardi Gras out in New Orleans, and the Judge had promised its festivities as a treat for her. Things come to a head as Mardi Gras itself increases its pace: 'the atmospheric oppression of a Carnival night' makes Laurel uneasy as, with difficulty, she gets a taxi to take her from the Hibiscus to the hospital. Her foreboding heightens her reaction even to the now familiar institution itself: 'Laurel had never noticed the design in the tiling before, like some clue she would need to follow to get to the right place.'[5] This feeling is to be vindicated:

---

5. O.D. p. 31.

An intense tight-little voice from inside there said at that moment in a high pitch, 'I tell you enough is enough!'

Laurel was halted. A thousand packthreads seemed to cross and crisscross her skin, binding her there.

The voice said, even higher, 'This is my birthday!'

Laurel saw Mrs Martello go running from the nurse's station into the room. Then Mrs Martello reappeared, struggling her way backwards. She was pulling Fay, holding her bodily. A scream shot out and ricocheted from walls and ceiling. Fay broke free from the nurse, whirled, and with high-raised knees and white face came running down the corridor. Fists drumming against her temples, she knocked against Laurel as if Laurel wasn't there. Her high heels let off a fusillade of sounds as she passed and hurled herself into the waiting-room with voice rising, like a child looking for its mother.

Mrs Martello came panting up to Laurel, heavy on her rubber heels.

'She laid hands on him! She said if he didn't snap out of it, she'd –' The veneer of nurse slipped from Mrs Martello – she pushed up at Laurel the red, shocked face of a Mississippi country-woman, as her voice rose to a clear singsong. 'She taken hold of him. She was abusing him.'[6]

This appalling scene (revisited by Laurel at the very climax of the novel) has to be borne in mind throughout a reading of *The Optimist's Daughter*. Eudora Welty has said that Fay is evil (and she does not use such terms lightly); asked why she lacked the obsession, said to be such a characteristic of Southern fiction, with evil embodied in human form (as in Faulkner's *Light in August*), she pointed to Fay. In my experience it is easy to do as Laurel's Mount Salus friends and their mothers do: to view Fay in the light of her social origins, and the values of that world – easy but mistaken, for Fay has a maleficent being all her own. She has a stubborn child's ability to reject other people's feelings, to assert always, regardless of circumstance, her own immediate wants, that day's wishes, that moment's impulses. Her birthday and Mardi Gras are filling her mind now, the pleasures these occasions should

6. O.D. p. 32.

bring her; and, dramatizing her self-pity, she launches herself on acts of deliberate cruelty. These surely relate to a sexual wantonness that has been part of her allure to the Judge.

Judge McKelva dies shortly after – within minutes of – Fay's onslaught on him, though it can never be unequivocally stated that Fay in effect killed him (though Laurel is to be haunted by this notion). Part One ends with the train journey from New Orleans to the little southern Mississippi town of Mount Salus, for the two women and for the coffin containing the dead Judge. Laurel is returning to Mount Salus both as daughter and as outsider, for she has spent half her life in Chicago.

Part Two concerns the preparations for the Judge's funeral and the funeral itself, and Laurel's reception back into the mutually supportive families of Mount Salus, with the gossip of the older women and of Laurel's own contemporaries, the 'bridesmaids', filling out our picture of both Judge McKelva's life, now completed, and Laurel's, which, unexpectedly, has come to a kind of crossroads. Into this Mount Salus reunion, however, comes a sudden troupe of *real* strangers, clamorous, unstoppable – the Chisholms, Fay's family (she is Wanda Fay to them), the family she has denied. Though originally Mississippians, they now come from Madrid, Texas; and if they are somewhat grating in their ways, they are far from cold-hearted, and their clumsily good hearts are not to be underestimated. A good heart is not an attribute that has been passed on to Fay.

Indeed, one of them, a small boy 'wearing cowboy suit and hat and double pistol holsters', makes a peculiarly strong impression on Laurel which is to come back to her during a later confrontation with Fay:

> Wendell began to cry. Laurel wanted at that moment to reach out for him, put her arms around him – to guard him. He was like a young, undriven, unfalsifying, unvindictive Fay. So Fay might have appeared, just at the beginning, to her aging father, with his slipping eyesight.[7]

---

7. O.D. p. 76.

Now through the inquisitive Chisholms, we learn more about Laurel herself – her widowhood, its length (since the Pacific War), and (by implication) its permanence.

After the funeral – at which Fay stages a little hysterical exhibition ("'. . . why was he so *bad*?'" she asks about the dead Judge, who had loved her too much for too long. "'Why did he do me so *bad*?'") – there is a fresh awareness of loss. Fay decides, on the spur of the moment, to go back to Madrid, Texas, with her family, to see the brother who did not come to the funeral, and with whom she feels most at ease ("'He speaks my language, . . . I've got a heap of things to tell DeWitt'"), while Laurel will spend a few days alone in Mount Salus for, she knows, the last time in her life – the house now belongs to Fay.

With the opening of the third part, the rhythm changes: becomes more throbbing, more urgent, yet all the real movement is within. Laurel, as Eudora Welty herself has said, grows before us, turns from a quiet passive victim of events into a woman of impressive stature, of mental action; at once an individual and an example to us all.

Through the Mount Salus chitchat Laurel comes to understand the old man's whim, born of loneliness and unquenched desire, that made the Judge plump for Fay; the picture gossip paints contrasts sadly with the distinguished public man presented at the funeral obsequies, whom Laurel meets again (in spirit) in the quiet dignity of his library: "'Sunday after Sunday we saw 'em through the dirty plate-glass window,'" said Miss Tennyson. "Billing and cooing. No tablecloth."'[8] And even among the law books and the touching evidences of his honourable career as lawyer and Mayor, there are reminders of the destructive intrusion that has been Fay. Laurel finds vermilion drops of nail varnish on the old desk, and her mother's letters (written every day of any absence) have vanished. We can already hear, in Laurel's reactions, the accents of heartbreak. And her feelings of desolation perhaps separate her from her friends, the bridesmaids, whom she meets the next day; they have, she thinks, already started to imprison her newly dead father, so complex but so large-spirited a man, in the humour of their endless anecdotes. She even accuses them

---

8. O.D. p. 108.

of this; there are hurt feelings on both sides. When she returns 'home' she is perhaps (though consciously) in a frame of mind in which she can admit to herself the immeasurable extent of her losses, of what loss signifies. A storm is brewing; a bird gets into the house, and even finds its way into her parents' room.

Once inside the room Laura begins a near-involuntary confrontation of all the truths that are hemming her in, beating against her being like the bird's wings against the wall. She can no longer deny the wall that divides all dead from all living; she can no longer pretend that Fay is not an indefatigably malign woman, whose malignity was shown once and for all in that fatal scene at the hospital – whose malignity is *real*:

> And I can't stop realizing it, she thought. I saw Fay come out into the open. Why, it would stand up in court! Laurel thought, as she heard the bird beating against the door, and felt the house itself shake in the rainy wind. Fay betrayed herself: I'm released! she thought, shivering; one deep feeling called by its right name names others. But to be released is to tell, unburden it.
>
> But who could there be that she wanted to tell? Her mother. Her dead mother only. Laurel must have deeply known it from the start. She stopped at the armchair and leaned on it. She had the proof, the damnable evidence ready for her mother, and was in anguish because she could not give it to her, and so be herself consoled. The longing to tell her mother was brought about-face, and she saw the horror.[9]

There then follow the most beautiful and profound pages in all the novel – perhaps in all Eudora Welty's *œuvre* – where Laurel, unable to confide in her mother in any literal sense, explores – not so much in memory as in re-visioning – the older woman's life, her childhood in West Virginia (essentially that of Chestina Andrews Welty), her marriage and her terrible, senseless, unjust last years of blindness, mental disturbance and bedridden illness. To these pages we shall be returning; these it was that Eudora Welty found so painful and yet so helpful to write. And they have a coda of, if anything, a more

---

9. O.D. p. 131.

harrowing nature still. Back in her father's study, Laurel had looked up at the one surviving wedding photograph of herself and her husband, Phil Hand, and thought of the 'ease' of their brief life together. Now, after her dead mother, her longer-dead husband presents himself to her:

> A flood of feeling descended on Laurel. She let the papers slide from her hand and the books from her knees, and put her head down on the open lid of the desk and wept in grief for love and for the dead. She lay there with all that was adamant in her yielding to this night, yielding at last. Now all she had found had found her. The deepest spring in her heart had uncovered itself, and it began to flow again.
> *If Phil could have lived –*
> But Phil was lost. Nothing of their life together remained except in her own memory; love was sealed away into its perfection and had remained there.
> *If Phil had lived –*
> She had gone on living with the old perfection undisturbed and undisturbing. Now, by her own hands, the past had been raised up, and *he* looked at her, Phil himself – here waiting, all the time, Lazarus. He looked at her out of eyes wild with the craving for his unlived life, with mouth open like a funnel's.
> What would have been their end, then? Suppose their marriage had ended like her father and mother's? Or like her mother's father and mother's? Like –
> 'Laurel! Laurel! Laurel!' Phil's voice cried.
> She wept for what happened to life.
> 'I wanted it!' Phil cried. His voice rose with the wind in the night and went around the house and around the house. It became a roar. 'I wanted it!'[10]

No passage in contemporary prose is starker, braver, more powerful than this. The starkness – due to that absence of any patina, intellectual or aesthetic, over the outward gaze – is, of course, responsible for

---

10. O.D. p. 154.

its power, and without bravery it would not be sustainable. But sustain that gaze Laurel does. Taken in its context, that single sentence 'She wept for what happened to life' has for me the simplicity and force of Shakespearean tragic utterances: Macbeth's 'She should have died hereafter' or Cleopatra's 'I dreamed there was an Emperor Antony'.

One is tempted to call Laurel's confrontations with her dead cathartic, yet perhaps that term is too definite. Likewise Eudora Welty suggests the limitations of our common belief that release can be found in calling a deep feeling by its right name. Life cannot be tied up in that kind of way, either by literature or by such systems as psychoanalysis. It is better to say that we all move towards our unknown destinations, yet there are hidden paths for us to follow. Laurel has reached the stage where it is possible for her to open out her mind beyond her present predicament and, taking heed of external phenomena – indeed, finding help in them – in storm, bird, solitude in a familiar place turned strange – she finds herself able to do so. One cannot know what further distress is in store for her, but one can say that after this night it will never manifest itself in this form again.

A reason for believing this comes from Laurel's dream with which Part Four opens, which marks the beginning of the gathering up and resolution of themes that is to continue through this 'movement' until its very close. She dreams that she is a passenger on a train with her husband, Phil, and on waking realizes that she has projected herself back into 'something that really had happened'. She now re-creates in her mind a moment on that long train journey down from Chicago to Mount Salus (where she and Phil were to be married):

> When they were climbing the long approach to a bridge after leaving Cairo, rising slowly higher until they rode above the tops of bare trees, she looked down and saw the pale light widening and the river bottoms opening out, and then the water appearing, reflecting the low, early sun. There were two rivers. Here was where they came together. This was the confluence of the waters, the Ohio and the Mississippi.
>
> They were looking down from a great elevation and all they saw was at the point of coming together, the bare trees marching

in from the horizon, the rivers moving into one, and as he touched her arm, she looked up with him and saw the long, ragged, pencil-faint line of birds within the crystal of the zenith, flying in a V of their own, following the same course down. All they could see was sky, water, birds, light and confluence. It was the whole morning world.

And they themselves were part of the confluence. Their own joint act of faith had brought them here at the very moment and matched its occurrence, and proceeded as it proceeded. Direction itself was made beautiful, momentous. They were riding as one with it, right up front. It's our turn! she'd thought exultantly. And we're going to live forever. Left bodiless and graveless of a death made of water and fire in a year long gone, Phil could still tell her of her life. For/her life, any life, she had to believe, was nothing but the continuity of its love.

She believed it just as she believed that the confluence of the waters was still happening at Cairo. It would be there the same as it ever was when she went flying over it today on her way back – out of sight for her, this time, thousands of feet below, but with nothing in between except thin air.[11]

The moment again – the moment which, in Ellen Fairchild's words, tells you 'the great things', which is 'enough for you to know the greatest thing'. The belief in perpetual confluence is something to which Eudora Welty returns at the end of One Writer's Beginnings, when she quotes the whole of this passage. She observes:

It is our inward journey that leads us through time – forward or back, seldom in a straight line, most often spiraling. Each of us is moving, changing, with respect to others. As we discover, we remember: remembering, we discover; and most intensely do we experience this when our separate journeys converge. Our living experience at those meeting points is one of the charged dramatic fields of fiction.

I'm prepared now to use the wonderful word confluence, which of itself exists as a reality and a symbol in one. It is the only kind

---

11. O.D. pp. 159–60.

kind of symbol that for me as a writer has any weight, testifying to the pattern, one of the chief patterns, of human experience.[12]

So this remembered still moment has brought Laurel a sense of pattern, a pattern not discernible as such, only apprehendable.

And with this awareness she is able to achieve the eviction of the bird, which flies off as 'nothing but a pair of wings – she saw no body any more, no tail, just a tilting crescent being drawn back into the sky'; her inner leave-taking of Mount Salus; and finally, a direct confrontation with Fay, who, unobserved by anyone, has returned to the house – *her* house, as it must now be considered. What communication can be possible with this malignity, this wilful yet total indifference to others! Laurel has found a breadboard, dear to her, but – '"yet another object!"' – desecrated by Fay:

'Do you want to know why this breadboard is such a beautiful piece of work? I can tell you. It's because my husband made it.'
'*Made* it? What for?'
'Do you know what a labor of love is? My husband made it for my mother, so she'd have a good one. Phil had the gift – the gift of his hands. And he planed – fitted – glued – clamped – it's made on the true, look and see, it's still as straight as his T-square. Tongued and grooved – tight-fitted, every edge –.'
'I couldn't care less,' said Fay.[13]

The struggle between the two women ends in Fay saying – more by way of underlining her contempt for Laurel than anything else – '"Take it! It'll give me one thing less to get rid of."' But the quiet, subtly victorious close of the whole work has now been reached:

'Never mind,' said Laurel, laying the breadboard down on the table where it belonged. 'I think I can get along without that too.' Memory lived not in initial possession but in freed hands, pardoned and freed, and in the heart that can empty but fill again, in the patterns restored by dreams.[14]

---

12. O.W.B. p. 102.
13. O.D. pp. 175–6.
14. O.D. p. 179.

III

And what of the pain that Laurel's remembrances of her mother brought her? What of Becky's own pain, which she endured for so long, without relief, without comprehension? We would know from the very tone of Laurel's memories, I think, that this part of the book, its radiant heart, came from the very deepest storehouse in the author's mind, even if we did not have *One Writer's Beginnings* to set beside it. But we do have it, and can see where the power of these pages of *The Optimist's Daughter* comes from, as we read of Chessy's family and early life, of her time as a country schoolmistress, her courtship by a fellow-teacher (as he then was), Christian Webb Welty, the young man from the Ohio countryside who had come to work for the summer in the office of a nearby lumber company; as we receive pictures from her life as a wife and parent, and of her terrible last years, aged, ill, almost blind, possessed of unbearable longings for her past, especially her past in the mountains of West Virginia. She once asked her daughter to play on the piano a song from her native State, and later, from her wheel-chair, picked it out herself:

'O the West Virginia hills,
How my heart with rapture thrills . . .
O the hills! Beautiful hills!'[15]

Becky, of course, comes to us through Laurel's love for her, and through her own feelings about what she had glimpsed or seen of her mother's pre-married life, just as Eudora Welty's mother's past is trans-figured by her daughter's legacy of feeling, as well as of memory. The West Virginia mountain on top of which lived Grandma (Becky's and Chessy's mother both) is illuminated by a small girl's gratitude for being taken into a different but cherishing world, one that relates her to her kin, to lines of antecedents (in a general as well as a literal sense). Everything acquires a special, charged significance for her, and so, surrounding her, it all defines the mother more brightly, more clearly: the grass, the bird dogs, the boat on the river, the pigeons, the hermit

---

15. O.W.B. p. 61.

as neighbour, the woodland tasks, and the 'boys' – Mother's adored brothers, youthful embodiments of country living:

> Bird dogs went streaking the upslanted pasture through the sweet long grass that swept them as high as their noses. While it was still day on top of the mountain, the light still warm on the cheek, the valley was dyed blue under them. While one of 'the boys' was coming up, his white shirt would shine for a long time almost without moving in her sight, like Venus in the sky of Mount Salus, while grandmother, mother and little girl sat, outlasting the light, waiting for him to climb home. (*The Optimist's Daughter*)[16]

> Mother's brothers were called 'the boys'. Their long-necked banjos hung on pegs along the wide hall, as casually as hats and coats. Coming in from outdoors, Carl and Mose lifted their banjos off the wall and sat down side by side and struck in. . . . They played together like soulmates. . . . That effortless, drum-like rhythm, heard in double, too, would have put a claim on any child. They had a repertoire of ballads and country songs and rousing hymns. My mother would tell her brothers, plead with them, to stop – I didn't want to go to bed. 'Aw, Sister, let Girlie have her one more song,' and one song could keep going without loss of a beat into still one more. (*One Writer's Beginnings*)[17]

A life such as this, if it had keen joys, also had very keen hardships. Both Becky and Chessy had to make raft journeys with their sick fathers down to Baltimore, where, on arrival at the hospital, the older men said, 'If you let them tie me down, I'll die.' – and did die. The girls had to travel back home on the same train as their fathers' coffins.

Both Laurel and Eudora Welty believe that they have inherited much that is vital (perhaps what is most vital) to their being from their mountaineer-mothers: independence, a certain ultimate faith in their

---

16. O.D. p. 139.
17. O.W.B. p. 52.

own judgement. To a non-American reader a cultural as well as a personal force appears to be honoured in these pages. Behind the novel's civilized foreground of scrutiny of character, motive, conscience, stands the invigorating, demanding, austere, but finally beneficent background of American pioneer life – at once practical and charged with a kind of quotidian romanticism born of strength of will and closeness to Nature, hard-working, essentially virtuous, profoundly Protestant in every sense of the word. Becky, like Chestina Andrews, is that pioneer Protestantism's vessel; from her, and from the pages containing her, light emanates to make every part of the book meaningful. I can only think of one novel comparably structured and irradiated: Willa Cather's supreme masterpiece, *The Professor's House*, which Eudora Welty reveres (though we are dealing with kinship here, not influence), where the young Tom Outland's experiences in the abandoned pueblo in the New Mexico mesa, told in an inset story, casts redemptive light over the main part of the novel – which is about claustrophobic family life in a middle-class Chicago suburb.

The pain has meaning, then? That question is as unanswerable in the book as in life. It has to be asked, to be lived with. Becky going blind and witless, accusing her daughter, during her endless-seeming unmerited infirmity, of having failed to save her mother's life, coexists now in memory with the fearless, intelligent young woman of the West Virginia mountains, relishing 'the boys' and their banjos, the height and freedom of 'up home'; that is all one can say. As Eudora Welty puts it, referring back to that episode of Becky's girlhood which had belonged to her mother's: 'Baltimore was as far a place as could go with those you loved, and it was where they left you.'[18] For the rest, there is only the courage to realize, with William Blake: 'Joy and Woe are woven fine . . . '

The title, as ever in Eudora Welty's work, speaks for the novel. Judge McKelva was a declared optimist (as, we understand from *One Writer's Beginnings*, was Eudora Welty's own father, with his unshakeable belief in progress); as an honourable man he was an honourable optimist, and is not to be blamed for his wife turning away from him in sickness as she does. But the novel shows that the Judge's faith is

18. O.D. p. 151.

inadequate – it cannot quite cope with the reality of his wife's sufferings, and after her death it leaves him a little empty, and so all too vulnerable – ready to receive the lubricious idiocies and seductions of Fay.

Nevertheless, optimism, in its trust in humanity, in life, is not to be disparaged. Laurel is the optimist's *daughter*; that is, on one level she is her father's child, with something of his energy and talent (transferred from law to design, as Eudora Welty must have inherited energies and talents from *her* father, transferred to the domain of writing). But she also marks another stage from his way of looking at things. She is something else, something more rewarding than an optimist. It is the daughter rather than the father who will remain with us, as guide.

Of the three classical works of fiction, *The Optimist's Daughter* seems to me at once the most artistically perfect and, particularly in its last quarter, the most profound in its explorations. Nevertheless, the novel has a vitiating flaw, oddly at variance with its artistic and thematic purity of concentration: the character of Fay. My perceptions of her have, I will concede, changed on my many readings of the novel, and I do not now see her, as I once did, as inextricable from the values she represents, which are (roughly) those of Faulkner's Snopes clan: poor-white, cultureless, go-getting, envious, vengeful, amoral. I can feel now, instead, that she has her unique being, which is set – for a reason beyond the powers of ordinary analysis – in a permanent quest for destruction.

Her portrait, however, still does not wholly satisfy me. The fact that in her speech – and in some of her attitudes too – she *does* represent a certain social class cannot be subtracted from her as she is given to us; and against the fundamentally honorific, if also ironic and detached, portrayal of the Old South characters – Miss Adele, Miss Tennyson, and others – it is hard at times not to see this aspect of her as part of her malignity, as demonstrating the rootless, parasitic lifestyle of the one social group against the rooted and responsible one of the other (the established small-town gentry and professional class). Perhaps Fay should have been offset by another character from outside. In a way, of course, she is – by Laurel's husband, Phil (hence the force of the struggle over the breadboard), a country boy from Ohio who won the hearts and admiration of the family into which he married. But Phil, being so long dead, cannot exert enough pressure on present-day people to counterbalance Fay adequately.

Fay works best when she is seen as the temperamental foil to Laurel – hard, spoilt, stupid, even detestable, but carrying no real metaphysical or cultural burden. The last scene between the two women, with the breadboard between them, is superb; it lingers in the mind because it is completely *humanly* realized.

Fay, however, is but one skein of this rich, astonishingly dense novel, which makes a fitting culmination to Eudora Welty's corpus of imaginative work, one constituting a heroic journey from the objective studies of *A Curtain of Green*, with the author as photographer meeting her subjects with curiosity, goodwill, and sometimes love, to this artefact of great sophistication which nevertheless courageously releases passionate secrets from her own and her parents' lives. *The Optimist's Daughter* is also of great significance in that its portrait of Laurel is Eudora Welty's strongest vindication of the independent woman.

Eudora Welty's initial reception of the Women's Movement would appear to be somewhat diffident, judging by her answers to a questionnaire submitted to her in autumn 1970. Her dislike of public aggression or confrontation perhaps caused her to edge away from its more ideological pronouncements, and she repeatedly removed herself from the articulations of any generic attack on the male sex. All the same, reading through interviews she has given and articles she has written, I believe she has a deep affinity with feminism and a firm place in it, too, for her work – like her life – is distinguished by an intense valuation of what she as a woman sees, feels, thinks, perceives, finding wisdom and truth in herself and other women, refusing any precepts imposed by the male hegemony.

Comparisons between works of such stature as *The Golden Apples*, *Losing Battles* and *The Optimist's Daughter* are tempting, but perhaps pointless. At the Jackson conference in April 1984, Reynolds Price said that generally speaking, *The Golden Apples* is regarded as her finest achievement, and Eudora Welty, tying this with that universally admired story 'A Still Moment', would seem to agree. I would say that for originality and amplitude *Losing Battles* seems the most remarkable; for visionary intensity and intellectual complexity *The Golden*

Apples; while *The Optimist's Daughter* is the most beautifully wrought, and reaches furthest into the springs of love and sorrow. But each book shares the attributes I have chosen for the other two, and who knows what perspectives – on themselves, and on life beyond their pages – one's next readings of them will bring forth? So if I say that, as I write, *Losing Battles* is for me her greatest achievement, that is not to deny that I may well tilt the balance in favour of another work in the future. The final success of her *œuvre* lies in the fact that in every work, but most spectacularly in the three classic books, she gives herself unsparingly, working every seam intensely.

In each case the structure of the book is in complete accord with – indeed, inextricable from – the thematic intention; this is as true of the relatively conventional *Delta Wedding* as it is of *sui generis* productions such as *The Golden Apples* or *Losing Battles*. There is a complete harmony, of a very rare kind, in her writing between the intellectual, the imaginative and the emotional: a story like 'June Recital' is interpenetrated by all three elements in equal measure. In the same way Eudora Welty attains a balance of the senses, so that a book which depends on the ear, like *Losing Battles*, also involves vision, and even a story which eschews dialogue, like 'A Still Moment', is distinguished aurally by its rendering of the rhythms of thought inside the three characters' heads.

IV

Although Eudora Welty has *written* stories – some of them relating to the 1960s in the South, which as yet she has reserved from the public – she has published no purely imaginative work since *The Optimist's Daughter*, but in 1978 she collected many of her best occasional pieces in *The Eye of the Story*. They include rich childhood reminiscences, portraits (among them one of the black midwife she'd photographed with such love, Ida McToy) essays on literature, and studies of individual writers – Chekhov, Willa Cather, Katherine Anne Porter – with whom she has an affinity, or matters that have engaged her during her long working life, such as 'Place in Fiction', 'Writing and Analyzing a Story'. She claims she is reviewer rather than critic. If this is true, it must also be said that the concentration she brings to each of these essays gives them a seriousness, a sharpness of intellectual focus, which elevates them way above the level of 'an occasional piece'. They seem worthy chips from her workshop; her praise for a book (for example, Willa Cather's *The Professor's House* or Henry Green's *Concluding*) often serves to illuminate her own practice. Two general literary essays, drawn on in this study, are surely outstanding: 'Place in Fiction' and 'Must the Novelist Crusade?'

In 1980 her *Collected Stories* came out, and the acclaim this volume received changed Eudora Welty's status as an American and an international writer, both commercially and in the breadth of her reputation. Consequently, it does not seem surprising that her beautiful autobiography, *One Writer's Beginnings*, should have enjoyed a long stay on the American bestseller lists. This work, with much honesty and not a little humour, offers unusually objective insights into a writer's development. She describes her education through the ear (listening not only *to* stories, but *for* stories, for the entities that people, seemingly artlessly, made out of the flux of life); her education through the eye, and finally her appreciation of the 'confluence' of the inner life and the external world, that confluence that is responsible for all true works of art. *One Writer's Beginnings* is also remarkable for its portrait of Eudora Welty's parents, a wonderful extended act of empathic charity – and perhaps the last literary act that she will choose to make public.

This autobiography is the only place where Eudora Welty writes about her father. Her picture of him and his Ohio farm origins is deeply memorable because it is so deeply felt, not least because of the shadow across it of his (comparatively) early death. His own mother, we read here, died when he was seven years old, writing to him on the very day of her death: 'My dearest Webbie: I want you to be a good boy and to meet me in heaven. Your loving Mother'; while the local doctor wrote prognostically in his keepsake book: 'May your life, though short, be pleasant/As a warm and melting day'. Such sentences, culled from real experiences, have the haunting beauty of similar moments in Eudora Welty's own art.

With whose work shall we rank Eudora Welty's rich and complex productions? The question has to be asked; no writer can be viewed in a vacuum.

Some critics – for example, Ruth M. Vande Kieft, whose 1962 study established so many areas of Eudora Welty's excellence – feel that the work of Elizabeth Bowen provides the appropriate context. There is a strong kinship between the two as I have shown, and Eudora Welty declared that she did not want the enormous critical attention given to Virginia Woolf (especially after Quentin Bell's 1972 biography) to obscure the achievements of Elizabeth Bowen, whom she considered no less remarkable and worthy of admiration. I feel that Virginia Woolf is, for stature, a more appropriate point of reference, though the two women's temperaments and consequent preoccupations are less similar than they might appear at first. Less innovative, less preoccupied with theory, Eudora Welty is more deeply rooted; her people and places spring from the kind of knowledge the English writer could not, for social and psychological reasons, possess. For me this gives Eudora Welty's work an enormous advantage; its command of the normal proves a far stronger base for the journeys into the depths of the mind – and beyond, to the sphere of the numinous. But one has to acknowledge that *To the Lighthouse* and *Between the Acts* are works which made Eudora Welty's more easily possible.

When, in the 1930s, Eudora Welty was still sending her stories out, she received a letter from Ford Maddox Ford, novelist, editor and indefatigable helper of young authors. He asked to see her stories and offered to assist her. (Before his death in 1939, Ford – who had heard about Eudora Welty from Katherine Anne Porter – tried them out on a number of British publishers, but without success.) Ford's pared and probing art, seen at its most perfect in *The Good Soldier* (1915), was perhaps an exemplar for the Eudora Welty who created *The Optimist's Daughter*. It must be said, however, that their emotional worlds are very different.

Another British writer who admired her work was E.M. Forster who, in the 1950s, invited her to lunch. (She accepted, of course, and the waiter turned out to be drunk, which eased the occasion socially.) Forster is a constant reference point for Eudora Welty in both her essays and her conversation. She likes what she calls the 'sylvan' element in his work, his sense of the numinous which serves to show up the motions of the conventional world. Forster's short stories, even the posthumously published homosexual ones, are, I think, nearer to

Eudora Welty's work in spirit than the novels. With their all-pervasive use of the authorial voice, commenting on the characters and their action, these are distant in form from Eudora Welty's modernist empathic work, however kindred the humanist spirit behind them.

Eudora Welty's friend V.S. Pritchett suggests himself as another point of comparison. His great work has been in the domain of the short story – and coming as he did from the precarious meeting point of the working class and the lower middle class, he has a far wider social franchise than most British writers. This, combined with a dedication to and fascination with the striving of art, gives him a distinct relation to Eudora Welty: indeed, if you had to search for an English story to put alongside 'Why I Live at the P.O.', you could not do better than choose such jewels as 'The Saint', 'When My Girl Comes Home' and 'The Key to My Heart'. Pritchett, however, does not have that power which unites disparate elements that Eudora Welty evidences so considerably, nor has he her insights into what inspirits life, human and non-human alike.

If one *has* to find a British writer with whom to compare Eudora, the Henry Green she admires so much suggests himself more satisfactorily, I believe; he shares her formal adventurousness and capacity for invention, her great social curiosity and range – from the Birmingham factory workers of *Living* (1929) to the doomed upper-class socialites of *Party Going* (1939) – her blend of person of the world with modernist visionary. As with Eudora Welty, each of Green's novels is a world in itself, deriving imaginative power from the psychically resonant images round which it centres; like hers, too, his work encompasses both fiction which relies on the visual approach (*Concluding*) and fiction dependent (like *Losing Battles*) on dialogue (*Nothing*, *Doting*). Henry Green, however, has not enjoyed the solid reputation, has not elicited the gratitude from his fellow-countrymen, that Eudora Welty has from hers, despite such distinguished advocacies as those of Angus Wilson and Paul Bailey (both admirers of Eudora Welty too). This, perhaps, says as much about British society versus American as it does about the writers. Britain it seems, lacks generosity here, as in many other spheres of life.

Among American writers, there is Willa Cather. There is a real affinity in the clarity of the two writers' art and mystery of vision. As for Southerners, Eudora Welty has taken a great interest in the work of Walker Percy (1916–90) and Peter Taylor (born 1917), – colleagues, friends, admirers. Walker Percy's intellectually searing novels – at best given a human warmth by the depth of his charity – have nothing but their literary merit in common with Eudora Welty's work. Even the South itself presents a different aspect. Two of his novels, *The Moviegoer* (1961) and *The Last Gentleman* (1966), deserve permanent classic status. *The Moviegoer*, the story of a youngish man's redemption from anomie by his love for his mentally disturbed cousin and his almost involuntary return to the Catholic Church, is a wonderful evocation of New Orleans (the city of its residents and workers, not that of the tourists). *The Last Gentleman* is far nearer to being a work of Catholic apologetics, but its picaresque structure contains an intense picture of the South as it strikes someone returning to it – and a moving portrait of perhaps a specifically Southern familial tragedy. Allen Tate said in conversation with me that perhaps Walker was a French-style *philosophe* rather than a novelist as conventionally understood. This remark, not intended as adverse criticism, points to the absence in his fiction of amplitude, personal or social, of the kind that Eudora Welty possesses.

Peter Taylor's marvellous short stories – gossip raised to the level of high art – explore a wide range of feeling and human relationships. He is also an intriguing instance of a writer who, while remaining faithful to his own idiosyncratic methods and subjects, has grown both finer and stronger as he has gone on, so that his last volume, *The Oracle at Stoneleigh Court* (1993), produced in old age, contains possibly his finest work of all, 'The Witch of Owl Mountain Springs'.

There are those who would introduce Flannery O'Connor (1925–64) here. She is, as E.M. Forster said of Scott in 'Aspects of the Novel', a 'writer over whom we shall divide'. Her deft fictions – brilliant short stories, two superb novels – marry presentations of extreme Fundamentalist Southern country folk to a Jansenist vision of a damned world from which salvation can come only through the operations of God's grace. Although I appreciate and – to some extent – admire Flannery O'Connor's artistry, my repulsion at the vindictive

273

cruelty of both her vision and her fictional realization of it completely vitiates my reception of her work. Eudora Welty speaks favourably of it, of certain stories in particular; though I note that she distances herself from the beliefs that animate it. I have to say that I find even the artistry suspect, since it has been honed for such essentially sadistic and untenable purposes.

Finally, one has to go to the other Mississippian, William Faulkner (interestingly, Henry Green's favourite novelist) to find Eudora Welty's true peer. The greatness of Faulkner's art is to be found in the style with which he explores – more, plumbs – fathomless regions of human experience, so that *The Sound and the Fury* and *Light in August* are, in the true sense of the word, great *creations*, every sentence of which is a living organism.

V

She chose to entertain friends for her seventy-fifth birthday dinner not at some grand restaurant but at Bill's, a favourite diner on the outskirts of town, run by a dark, exuberant, enterprising Greek (Bill) whose most frequent exclamation was: 'God Bless America'. Bill's wife and daughters had made her a cake shaped like a book, its iced top reproducing the cover-design for the then bestselling *One Writer's Beginnings*. After all the lectures and discussion sessions of the conference – to which Eudora Welty had paid the closest, most interested attention – the atmosphere was relaxed. She was surrounded by Jackson friends dear to her for many years of her long life: Charlotte Capers and Patti Carr Black, successive directors of the Mississippi Archives; Jane Reid Petty, Director of the New Stage Theatre, in which Eudora Welty has taken so consistent an interest; Paul Hardin from Millsaps College.

Writers and critics were there too, reminding me of the extent to which Southern writers have looked to Eudora Welty in gratitude as an inspiration. At Bill's Diner was Reynolds Price. Handsome, with liquid, very dark eyes, and a deep voice, firm but gentle, Reynolds Price has – ever since the publication of his remarkable novel *A Long and Happy Life* at the age of twenty-nine – testified to the importance of Eudora Welty's example for him, its opening up of the mundane lives of the ordinary (and extraordinary) people of his own society as proper territory for the writer. She had encouraged him right from the first, bestowing on his first novel public praise of a kind that was of real assistance to him, and she has keenly followed his every work since. Perhaps he, more than any other writer, can be said to be her heir, and he has written on her with great penetration, observing that in her preoccupation with pattern she is, metaphysically, a writer of comedy:

> All patterns are comic – snow crystal or galaxy in Andromeda or family history – because the universe is patterned, therefore ordered and ruled, therefore incapable of ultimate tragedy. . . . God's vision is comic, Alpha and Omega.[19]

Comedy in the accepted sense of the word was certainly dominant in their reminiscences that evening about a Southern reading tour. An assignment had ended far later than they had expected, and after driving some distance, they had put up at a crumby motel deep in the Alabama countryside. As they surveyed their caravan quarters, its atmosphere bespeaking so many lost or misspent nights, Eudora Welty said to Reynolds Price: 'If this sofa could talk, we'd have to *burn* it.'

Reynolds Price and Eudora Welty had also shared a mutual fascination with the contents of the *National Inquirer*, a fascination that was to become mine during my time in Jackson. (I used to pick up copies of this popular and idiosyncratic paper at the local Jitney Jungle supermarket, staggered by its ceaseless and inventive preoccupation with the odder vagaries of coupling and birth.) 'But could it be true?' someone remarked. 'I've always *assumed* it was all fiction,' Eudora Welty said, in her wry, somewhat husky voice; 'maybe I was wrong to do so.' Her favourite among the many stories she had noted was one in which a girl, having had the Devil's baby – photographed complete with horns and a forked tail – vowed to bring her offspring up 'as a normal human being'. 'I guess she could do nothing less,' said Eudora Welty, 'but it would be hard work, wouldn't it?' One heard here the author of 'Why I Live at the P.O.' and *The Ponder Heart*.

One measure of a writer is the meaning for younger practitioners of

---

19. Reynolds Price, *A Common Room: Essays 1954–1987*, p. 67.

their art. Eudora Welty's meaning for Reynolds Price has been made clear; it has been an invaluable source of inspiration for a novelist of a very different imaginative hue, Ellen Douglas (Jo Haxton, born 1921), a valued friend. Ellen Douglas's imagination is indeed galvanized by social conflict, political upheaval, though like Eudora Welty she prefers (on the whole) to confine her theatre to domestic life. The novel she was working on when I lived in Jackson seems to me her very strongest: *Can't Quit You, Baby* (1987), about the long, difficult, yet close relationship between two women, one white, one black. It is a most powerful and illuminating work.

Stronger still has been Eudora Welty's effect on Anne Tyler (born 1941) and on (Jackson-born) Richard Ford (born 1944), writers whose fame has been independent of their Southern origins. Richard Ford's *The Sportswriter* was on Eudora Welty's books table when I was living in Jackson; she spoke of it with great admiration. If there is an influence of any Southern writer here, I think it is more that of Walker Percy, with his existentialist examination of life and his discursive analysis; Eudora Welty's example is more evident in his delicately wrought, emotionally compelling novella of adolescent discovery, *Wildlife* (1990). As for Anne Tyler, author of so many generous-spirited, humane and life-enhancing novels, I cannot do better than quote her letter to me:

> I can't think of a better subject [for a book than Eudora].
>
> As I've probably told everyone in the western hemisphere by now, she has been an enormous influence on me since I read *The Wide Net*, at age fourteen. . . . As for Eudora Welty the person, she remains for me the model for how all writers (and all human beings) ought to be; she is gracious, modest, and kind-hearted, and very much in touch with the non-writerly rest of the world. I have never heard her utter an 'arty' sentence in my life.[20]

After the meal in Bill's Diner, Reynolds Price and I, a little exhausted by all the day's activities, went back to our hotel, and had a nightcap before retiring. Reynolds Price said to me: 'It really is all completely *true*, all the good things they're saying about Eudora. She really is as

---

20. Letter to the author.

good as she's said to be, and I've known her for long enough.' His words echoed those of Allen Tate, whom I had visited back in 1978, when he was confined to bed with the emphysema that was to kill him later that year. I shall never forget his refined face and bright eyes as he spoke of his own work, and of Eudora Welty (whom I had not yet met), whose writings and personality he admired without reservation – adding (and he was a great and, at times, lightly malicious gossip) that he had never heard anyone speak other than warmly and admiringly of her. (She herself speaks warmly of Allen Tate and his first wife, Caroline Gordon. She used to stay with them when they lived in Tennessee – something she greatly enjoyed, though she added that a weekend with them turned into 'one long drink'.)

On one line of my vision of my life, I shall be, I am sure, always in Jackson, living in the quiet woody neighbourhood called Belhaven, on a street which, only a matter of yards from the small white timber house I rented, intersected with Eudora Welty's own Pinehurst. I shall be shopping at the same Jitney Jungle that she patronized, where she was a familiar, friendly, fondly regarded figure; I shall be stopping at Primo's (where I might run into other friends) for a hearty Southern-style breakfast, before walking on to Millsaps College (where Eudora Welty had herself taught, and where she gave that first Jackson address before a mixed black-and-white audience) to lecture or give classes. I shall be admiring the magnolia and dogwood which come into bloom in March, and going out to the luxuriant countryside of the Trace. I shall walk with my dog (towards whom Eudora Welty was always solicitous) round the grounds of Belhaven, from the open window of which the author long ago now, heard drifting Beethoven's 'Für Elise' which inspired her to write 'June Recital'. I shall be – to use her now rather famous words to Katherine Anne Porter – 'underfoot locally' in the neighbourhood.

Of course Eudora Welty has not been able to avoid celebratory status, despite her intense privacy; schools and colleges are proud of her, citizens bathe in the reflection her reputation bestows on Jackson, a city whose image had badly needed redemption after the brutalities of its resistance to civil rights. While I was there, the Eudora Welty Public Library was opened: a splendid institution, a great contrast to the one-woman affair Eudora Welty remembers so amusingly and so gratefully in her accounts of her childhood. She has been widely honoured, from the White House to many universities and colleges all over the United States and beyond. But she goes about her daily life as she always has done, as the daughter of her parents and the graduate of Jackson schools would have done whether she was a writer or not, whether she was famous or not – caring for her friends, interested in the welfare of her city and her State, following the news (she is exceedingly well informed about current affairs) and generally being a conscientious citizen. She has welcomed the Bill Clinton administration particularly its health and social programme. Eudora reads a great deal – indeed, a very great deal, and wide-rangingly (she lent me detective novels by her great friend Ross Macdonald, whose fictions show an artistry and a deep sense of kinships comparable to hers; and by an older, lighter writer, Elizabeth Daly).

Two of my most cherished memories of her connect her with great writers of the past. I entitled one of the courses I decided to teach at Millsaps 'Three Generations of Poets: the Spanish Generation of 1927', centring on Federico García Lorca (on whom I had just published a study), the American (indeed, Southern) Fugitives, and the British Auden Generation. Although Eudora Welty knew Allen Tate and Robert Penn Warren, who featured in the second group, and is a friend of Stephen Spender, who was prominent in the third, it was the Spanish Generation who prompted me to invite her to one of the lectures. Hearing her talking with great warmth of feeling about the Cotton Club and its Harlem venue Small's Paradise, which she frequented during her time in New York (1929–30), I suddenly realized that not only had she and the Spanish poet been in New York at the same time, it was completely possible that they had both been in Small's Paradise together:

In one cabaret – Small's Paradise – [wrote Lorca] I saw a naked dancer shaking convulsively under an invisible rain of fire. But while everyone shouted as though believing her possessed by the rhythm, I was able, for a second, to catch remoteness in her eyes – remoteness, reserve, the conviction that she was far away from the admiring audience of foreigners and Americans. All Harlem was like her.[21]

'Ay Harlem! Ay Harlem! Ay Harlem!' Lorca uttered the traditional Andalusian cry of pain at the reduced rank of the Negroes in America, believing that they were its ultimate saviours from the curse of materialism. Listening to the great jazz musicians of the Harlem Revival in Small's Paradise drove him to write his great odes 'El Rey de Harlem' and 'Oda a Walt Whitman', with their apocalyptic visions of American society redeemed through the upsurge of the atavistic. These were the poems I was studying with my class when Eudora Welty came to visit us.

She conveyed to the students most vividly, in her quiet, intent voice, the atmosphere of Harlem in those now remote days, the magic of its singers and instrumentalists. She made notes on the poems we were looking at that day, having read them carefully beforehand, and this seemed to me to be a demonstration of the humility of a truly distinguished mind, as well as of good manners.

And yet Eudora Welty had from the first personally assisted towards the arrival of Lorca's kingdom, with such stories as 'Keela, the Outcast Indian Maiden' and 'A Worn Path'. Her work, like Lorca's to Spain, belongs to her own society – the South, America; but, like his, it has a revolutionary quality, in a non-political sense. She may respect conventions, but she is never conventional.

The other memory comes from the visit Eudora Welty made to London in spring 1990. She had come to a city she loves to see such old friends as V.S. Pritchett and his wife, and her publishers, Virago. By this time her arthritis was making her less mobile than she liked; I suggested that a friend and I take her for a drive and, finding that she had never seen Jane Austen's house at Chawton (near Winchester, Hampshire), decided on that destination.

It was a cold, if sunny, day; daffodils, narcissi, apple and pear blossom were out, but harassed by the wind which pinched the streams

---

21. Federico García Lorca, *Deep Song and Other Prose*, transl. Christopher Maurer, p. 96.

and ponds in the Hampshire countryside. In contrast, the mellowed red brick of the seventeenth- and eighteenth-century buildings of Chawton, especially the Austens' house, glowed as touched by a latent, different, fuller sunshine. Eudora Welty walked round the surprisingly small house, attentive to its every exhibit, its every detail. No one knows Jane Austen's novels better than she, as her essay 'The Radiance of Jane Austen' shows. There she praises what I have never seen praised before: the noise of Jane Austen's books – their chatter, the sound of dances beginning, of high spirits and conversation – which pulls the reader to the pressing lives of those who, if they had really existed, would have been dead for almost two hundred years. It is that noise which allows Jane Austen to articulate her moral authority. We need the books to bring that noise back; the house – a museum now, if a convincingly domestic one – cannot do so. In the same way Eudora Welty's books bring the beating of the hearts of her Mississippian people to her readers. Somehow, it seemed only appropriate that as we stepped back out of the cold spring wind into the car, Eudora Welty was talking about the other visitors to Jane Austen's house – who they were, where they had come from, what they had been feeling, how they had reacted to what they'd seen. And conversely, the books – Jane Austen's and Eudora Welty's alike – can bring us the still moment of profound comprehension.

For me this has been perhaps the greatest gift her *œuvre* has bestowed – one, I believe, that is inseparable from Eudora Welty's gender. By temperament – though of course I am attached to my country and to individuals (people, animals) – I am far closer to the 'wanderers' of *The Golden Apples* than to most other characters in fiction; I feel that I am a member of the restless band of King and Scooter MacLain, of Virgie Rainey and Miss Eckhart. Eudora Welty has made me understand this in myself better; she has accepted it, assimilated it. Male, not a Southerner, not an American, I have been enriched, assisted, supported by this woman writer from Jackson more than by any author alive. Nor is my case unique, I believe; among non-American English-language writers, Stephen Spender, Angus Wilson, William Cooper, Seamus Heaney, Paul Bailey, Jonathan Raban, Christopher Hope, Salman Rushdie, Desmond Hogan have all expressed heartfelt admiration for Eudora Welty's work.

Already, I think, the cluster of Eudora Welty's books – as much as any of our century and language, as much as the complete works of Willa Cather or William Faulkner, E.M. Forster or D.H. Lawrence or Virginia Woolf – are acquiring what she brilliantly ascribes to the body of Jane Austen's novels in that moving last paragraph of her essay:

> No, Jane Austen cannot follow readers into any other time. She cannot go into the far future, and she never came to us. She is there forever where she wrote, immovable to the very degree of her magnitude. The readers of the future will have to do the same as we ourselves have done, and with the best equipment they can manage, make the move themselves. The reader is not the only traveler. It is not her world or her time, but her art, that is approachable, today or tomorrow. The novels in their radiance are a destination.[22]

What an appropriate final statement on Eudora Welty's own work! And behind the novels, we should add, there is the inclusive spirit of the writer herself. When the white heron in 'A Still Moment' was resting in the evening grasses, it seemed, 'its motion calm', as if it were offering to the whole waiting world the proposition 'Take my flight'. That, I think, is what, poised for the most adventurous of journeys, Eudora Welty's writings – from 'Death of a Traveling Salesman' to *One Writer's Beginnings* – say to us; and we should accept it with gratitude.

---

22. Eye p. 13.

SELECT BIBLIOGRAPHY

Primary Works
Eudora Welty

A Curtain of Green and Other Stories, Doubleday Doran, New York (1941).

The Robber Bridegroom, Doubleday Doran, New York (1942)/Virago Press, London (1982).

The Wide Net and Other Stories, Harcourt, Brace and Co., New York (1943).

Delta Wedding, Harcourt, Brace and Co., New York (1946)/Virago Press, London (1982).

The Golden Apples, Harcourt, Brace and Co., New York (1949).

The Ponder Heart (first published in *New Yorker*, 5 December 1953) Harcourt, Brace and Co., New York (1954)/Virago Press, London (1983).

The Bride of the Innisfallen and Other Stories, Harcourt, Brace and Co., New York (1955).

Losing Battles, Random House, New York (1970)/Virago Press, London (1982).

One Time, One Place: Mississippi in the Depression: A Snapshot Album, Random House, New York (1971).

The Optimist's Daughter (first published in *New Yorker*, 15 March

1969) Random House, New York (1972)/Virago Press, London (1984).

The Eye of the Story (Selected Essays and Reviews), Random House, New York (1978)/Virago Press, London (1987).

Collected Stories (all above collections plus 'Where is the Voice Coming From?' and 'The Demonstrators'), Harcourt, Brace, Jovanovitch, New York (1980).

One Writer's Beginnings, Harvard University Press, Cambridge, MA (1984).

Photographs, University Press of Mississippi, Jackson (1989).

Secondary Works
On Eudora Welty

Ruth M. Vande Kieft: *Eudora Welty*, Twayne Publishers, (1962).

Michael Krayling: *Eudora Welty's Achievement of Order*, Louisiana State University Press, Baton Rouge (1980).

Albert J. Devlin: *Eudora Welty's Chronicle* (A Story of Mississippi Life), University Press of Mississippi, Jackson (1983).

Peggy Whitman Prenshaw (editor): *Conversations with Eudora Welty*, University Press of Mississippi, (1984).

Suzanne Marrs: *The Welty Collection*, Mississippi Department of Archives and History (1988).

Louis R. Rubin Jr: *Writers of the Modern South*, University of Washington Press (1963).

Richard Gray: *The Literature of Memory* (Modern Writers of the American South), Johns Hopkins University Press (1977).

Richard Gray: *Writing the South* (Ideas of an American Region), Cambridge University Press (1986).

Paul Binding: *Separate Country*, Paddington Press, London and New York (1979); revised edition University Press of Mississippi, Jackson (1988).

INDEX

Individual titles by Eudora Welty appear as separate entries in **bold type**; the articles 'A/An' and 'The' are ignored in the alphabetization. Page numbers in bold indicate extended discussion of a text.

285